## About the author

Denise Leith has a PhD in international relations from Macquarie University. After initially working in stockbroking, she has taught politics and international relations at university with special interests in US foreign policy and the Middle East.

Her first book, *The Politics of Power: Freeport in Suharto's Indonesia*, examined the operations and political relationship between the American transnational mining company, Freeport McMoRan, the Suharto government, the Indonesian military, and the traditional landowners around the company's mining concession in West Papua.

Denise is currently writing full time, is an Honorary Associate of Macquarie University and is on the management committee of International PEN (Sydney).

# BEARING WITNESS

## The Lives of War Correspondents and Photojournalists

### DENISE LEITH

RANDOM HOUSE AUSTRALIA

Random House Australia Pty Ltd
20 Alfred Street, Milsons Point, NSW 2061
http://www.randomhouse.com.au

Sydney   New York   Toronto
London   Auckland   Johannesburg

First published by Random House Australia 2004

Copyright © Denise Leith 2004

All rights reserved. No part of this publication may be reproduced, stored in a retrieval system, or transmitted in any form or by any means, electronic, mechanical, photocopying, recording or otherwise, without the prior written permission of the publisher.

National Library of Australia
Cataloguing-in-Publication Entry

   Leith, Denise.
   Bearing witness: the lives of war correspondents and photojournalists.

   ISBN 1 74051 260 X.

   1. War correspondents - Australia.  2. News photographers - Australia.  3. War - Press coverage.  4. Disasters - Press coverage.  5. War in mass media.  I. Title.

070.4333092

Cover photograph © Juda Ngwenya/Reuters/Picture Media
Cover design by Ankya Clarke
'The Unjust' reprinted with permission of John Gaps III
Internal design and typesetting by
Midland Typesetters, Maryborough, Victoria
Printed and bound by Griffin Press, Netley, South Australia

10 9 8 7 6 5 4 3 2 1

Alex and Matt

*Such a perfect day*
*I'm glad I spent it with you*

# CONTENTS

*Preface*     xi
*Introduction*     xv

1. Eddie Adams     1
2. Peter Arnett     15
3. Monica Attard     34
4. David Brill     52
5. Peter Charley     72
6. Marie Colvin     92
7. Robert Fisk     113
8. Suzanne Goldenberg     135
9. Roy Gutman     155
10. Ron Haviv     178
11. Ahmed Jadallah     199
12. Donatella Lorch     213
13. Susan Meiselas     234
14. Glenn Middleton     255
15. Christopher Morris     273
16. David Rieff     290
17. Sorious Samura     308
18. Max Stahl     331
19. Penny Tweedie     350

*Bearing Witness to War*     371
*Afterword*     393
*Acknowledgments*     397

**The Unjust**

Close your eyes and remember
my fingers tracing
down your cheeks
  Remind me that your face
      cupped in friendly hands
knows my doubts and forgives
It forgives these fears
made larger in the dark
   soothes a joyless life with
snakehand caresses

Look in these eyes
   Am I the blind one?
guilty for the bones
    bleaching in the hills above
    crumbling

Slow your step to mine
give to the leisure pace
earned against this deliberate chaos

God left us alone here
to witness the
       strange things
       the cruel things
           done in his name

From God Left Us Alone Here: A Book of War<br>John Gaps III

# PREFACE

THE IDEA FOR THIS BOOK essentially came about from two haunting photos. Like many people who came of age in the sixties or seventies, I vividly remember the Pulitzer Prize-winning photo of the execution in the streets of Saigon during the Tet Offensive in 1968. To me, it epitomised the violence and insanity of that war. The second photo, which was shot during the famine in Sudan, I saw shortly after it was taken in March 1993. In the image a clearly emaciated and exhausted little girl is curled up on the baking ground while a vulture stands watch over her, ready to pick at her carcass. I have never forgotten the horror of that powerful and emotive image which caused massive aid to be shipped to the ravaged country. On both occasions the images and what they portrayed so assailed the senses that I had no interest in questioning who the photographers were or how these images had affected them.

In 1998 these two images, one of war and the other of famine, both Pulitzer Prize winners and photographed decades apart on different continents, converged for me. That year the South Vietnamese general who performed the execution died and I heard the American photographer, Eddie Adams, speaking with sadness about the image he had made and the pain it had caused. Feeling that his iconic image was a half-truth, he seemed tormented by the belief that by taking the photo he had ruined the general's life. For the first time I began to think about the stories behind the photos or stories of war. At about the same time I became familiar with the story surrounding Kevin Carter's photo in the Sudan. I learnt that the little girl, whose plight had so moved thousands of people around the world, had apparently not moved the photographer enough on that day to pick her up and carry her to the feeding station which was about 100 metres away. Instead, he made the image and left the subject as he found her. This ambitious and struggling young photographer won the Pulitzer Prize in May 1994 for his haunting image and, as a result, signed on with one of the world's most prestigious photo agencies. A couple of months later he committed suicide citing, in part, in his suicide note: 'The pain of life overrides the joy to the point that joy does not exist.'

My initial reactions to the two photos, juxtaposed against my reaction after learning the stories behind the images and what effect they had on the photographers, reminded me of lessons I routinely forget: things are not always as they appear; issues are often complex and multi-layered; choices are rarely simple; and judgments should be left to the righteous. For the first time I tried to look beyond the images and was left to wonder about the people who chose to cover such subjects. Initially I was not particularly interested in questioning their willingness to expose themselves to danger but rather, why they choose to expose themselves to such pain. I could not see how one could witness the insanity and inhumanity of war, disease and famine without being emotionally scarred. Were they scarred? What images did they carry in their heads? Did they actually seek out pain? Indeed, were they insane (for I knew of no other way to explain their choices)?

When I began researching what I had come to think of as 'these people'– the inference being that they were different to me – I found that rather than satisfying my curiosity the list of questions I had about them continued to grow. Thus, out of a need to know or to understand who they were and what was the attraction of the job, the original concept for this book was born and, out of an intense fascination with the journey of discovery, the book *Bearing Witness* was created.

When deciding on whom to approach for the book, I attempted to gather together a group of individuals representative of a cross-section of the industry: journalists, photojournalists and cameramen (referred to herein as photojournalists); freelance, staff and contract journalists and photographers; professionals from the print, radio and TV industries; those who moved quickly in and out of war and those who were stationed in the area they cover; individuals who chose to cover war and those who found themselves covering war by default; and, finally, people who continue to cover conflict and those who no longer do so. All but two of the people I approached consented to interviews while, given the nature of the profession, two of those who had consented to interviews were unfortunately on assignment when I was in their country. All interviews, except one, were conducted in person.

For convenience sake, the collective title of 'war correspondents and photojournalists' or, more simply at times, 'journalists', have been used in this book. Yet, these simplistic categorisations fail to convey the diversity and complexity of the personalities and the profession because these people don't just cover war, they cover famine and disease and often many other issues. Such a title fails to do them justice and, understandably, some reject it.

While the book is about the people who document war, disease and famine, and their experiences, it could not help but become an argument against war, for as James Nachtwey

– one of the world's most famous conflict photographers – says, 'If everyone could be there to see for themselves the fear and the grief, just one time, then they would understand that nothing is worth letting things get to the point where that happens to even one person, let alone thousands.'

Having never gone to war or to a place where famine has raged on a mass scale, and not being from within their industry, I have, in a sense, been what each of these correspondents claims not to be: an uncomfortable voyeur.

# INTRODUCTION

DON MCCULLIN, ONE OF the world's greatest war photographers, recently said of his life's work that he looked at what others could not bear to see. Ironically, and sadly, after over forty years of chronicling history, McCullin wrote that he spends his retirement living with the terrible images of conflict while attempting to eradicate the past. This book is about war correspondents and photojournalists who, like McCullin, bear witness to the human tragedies of war, disease and famine. Through their eyes and voices we are given not only an insight into the people who document history and an insight into their profession, but also into the human costs for those who have chosen to work within the seemingly confusing and alien worlds of human tragedy.

By constantly making choices about the image they will make, how they make it, which one they submit for publication and the text that accompanies it, the photographer becomes part of the process of recording history – no less so the correspondent. Yet we know little about these professionals who write the 'first cut of history', how they deal with what they witness, how their experiences colour the world they live in, and to what extent we see it through their eyes. Although journalists and photographers often profess professional objectivity, what they show us must first pass through the filter of their own experiences, prejudices and value systems, making claims of objectivity impossible. If truth is what they seek to portray, how possible is it to uncover this truth in places of high tension and emotion where chaos and propaganda often reign?

More so than in almost any other job, war photographers and journalists are continually challenged personally and professionally by the issues that confront them: do you pick up the starving child and carry him or her to the feeding station; do you give your sandwich and bottle of water to someone in dire need; do you take the wounded civilian to the hospital? To most of us, these might seem simple questions with obvious responses but, in the presence of devastation and tragedy, which child out of the thousands do you choose to give your provisions to; which wounded civilian do you assist; and can you always predict what the consequences of your actions will be? When do you put down your pen or camera and abandon the neutral witnessing role to lend assistance and when do you decide that the greatest assistance you can give is to get the story or pictures out to the world?

During the Vietnam War, Associated Press (AP) correspondent Peter Arnett made a decision not to abandon the neutral witnessing role when a Buddhist monk self-immolated in front of him in the streets of Saigon. As the monk alighted from a taxi and removed a can of petrol from beneath his robe, Arnett realised that he could probably prevent the monk's death by taking the can away from him. As a human being, he said he wanted to; as a reporter, Arnett said he couldn't. He believed his job was to witness and record, not to become involved. Shaking, he held up his camera and made an image of the man as he burnt to death.

In January 1999 in Freetown, the capital of Sierra Leone, Sorious Samura filmed a young boy desperately pleading for his life with Nigerian peacekeepers. From having witnessed such incidents before in the civil war ravaging his country, he had no doubt that to intervene on the boy's behalf would have led to his own death. As he continued to film, the boy was shot dead in front of him. The images have been frozen in Samura's camera and memory.

Unlike Arnett and Samura, in November 1999 in East Timor, Marie Colvin chose to become involved. Believing that the rampaging militia would overrun the United Nation's (UN) compound in Dili and kill the hundreds of East Timorese civilians sheltering there, Colvin chose to remain there with them. Although she thought she would probably die, she knew that she could not live with herself if she abandoned defenceless people. Her reporting from the compound on her mobile phone galvanised the world and shamed the UN into returning to rescue those it had left behind.

Unlike other participants in war such as soldiers, aid workers or peacekeepers, there are few rules governing the behaviour of the journalist in the field so that the decision of how to act and the ramifications of that decision rest solely with the individual. The complex nature of the job, together with the lack of formal rules can blur the lines between the professional and the personal response, forcing journalists and photographers to choose whether it is ethical for them to abandon their witnessing role or immoral not to do so. Yet, because many of the situations they face are complex and afford these professionals only a few seconds in which to make a decision, the response is often instinctual. Once removed from the intensity of the situation, hindsight and the passage of time can see many, like Samura, questioning their choices and being haunted by the decisions they made and the possibilities of what might have been.

James Nachtwey says there is no photo he would not take, offering the argument that if all the photographers who entered the concentration camps at the end of World War II had turned away in horror from making images – as some did – then essential documentation of that time in history would have been lost to the world. Conversely, Eddie Adams, Penny Tweedie and BBC correspondent and presenter Kate Adie have each argued that there are images that should never be taken and stories that should never be told. Unlike Nachtwey, each has self-censored.

Adams could not take a photo of a young soldier petrified in battle because even though he believed the image 'would have told the whole story of the war' he knew that the boy's life would have been destroyed because he would have been branded a coward and that, says Adams, would have been a lie. Adie has said she has withheld stories, or details of stories, because she believed that if made public they would have provoked revenge attacks and endangered innocent lives. And in Bangladesh in 1971 Tweedie refused to take a photo believing that the presence of a contingent of international photographers and journalists was inciting an execution. Disagreeing with Tweedie's assessment of the situation, photographers Horst Faas and Michel Laurent won the Pulitzer Prize that year for the photos they took of the execution.

On that day in 1971, the media present were faced with questions of professional responsibility and morality. They were there to bear witness yet that very act may have been changing the dynamics of a situation, indeed, causing the deaths of a number of individuals. For Tweedie, the dilemma was complete: she needed to be there to bear witness and she needed to leave to prevent the murders. Within the industry, the different responses to that incident are still debated.

\* \* \*

Is graphic imagery of human suffering little more than 'war pornography' – tasteless and inappropriate viewing material

– or does it provide important testimony to war and as such should be considered essential viewing material by the public? As BBC cameraman Glenn Middleton says, though, the average viewer 'almost discards things that are happening around him because he doesn't want those things to affect him. It is so easy for a viewer to switch channels when another refugee camp pops up, or another warlord or rebel leader in Africa who is in the process of destroying his country.' With photo editors in the West claiming that the general public complains when it is shown graphic imagery of war or human suffering perhaps it is we, the viewing public, who are demanding a sterilised version of human tragedy. Yet how must these professionals feel when they see family and friends switch off the TV when graphic and uncomfortable footage is shown that they know their colleagues risked their lives to capture? And how does the industry walk the seemingly fine line between informing the public through its stories and imagery, and losing the public's attention through saturation or confrontation?

The industry's attempts to overcome this phenomenon of 'compassion fatigue' – the West's seeming indifference to the suffering of others – is a constant challenge. If our desensitisation arises simply through a surfeit of disturbing imagery or repetition of that imagery – that is, another famine in Africa, another suicide bomber in Israel, another targeted assassination in the Occupied Territories – how can these journalists and photographers gain our attention with their work? In fact, how hard is it for them to continually cover human tragedy and is it possible to make an image or tell a story that differentiates one war or tragedy from another?

As *The Guardian* correspondent Suzanne Goldenberg ruminates, 'How do I rev myself to write about something that is almost the same as something I saw last week, because there is this compulsion in journalism to make every event distinctive? . . . Perhaps the point really should be: this *is* reality and this *is* everyday; people have to live like this for months and years. Sometimes you feel that your skills aren't up to the task of describing what you have seen.' And yes, she has felt defeated.

How do such professionals live with the frustration and impotence of reporting atrocities when, as was the case in Rwanda and for a long time in the former Yugoslavia, the world turned its back? If 'desensitising' repetition is inevitable in their work, perhaps there is little possibility of breaking through the public's indifference. Or, as photographer Ron Haviv says, the power of the story or the photography is *in* the repetition – testimony to the fact that humankind continues to repeat the same deadly mistakes.

'Compassion fatigue' may not just be confined to their audience, though. Kashmiri journalist Muzamil Jaleel described no longer being able to feel pain or mourn the death of his own people. In the incessant process of reporting the war in his country he is increasingly 'more caught up in this fatigue' and his 'tears have dried up'. Whereas war photographers and self-professed 'news junkies' like photographer Christopher Morris admit they have seen so much pain that they can no longer bear to watch the news or even edit their own photos. Then perhaps there are war journalists and photographers so sensitised that, as David Rieff comments, 'the edge is just where you want to be . . . anything else would be disrespectful of the reality, which is so moving and terrible and horrendous'.

The legacy of the job is full of contradictions. While journalists live with the horrors they witness and a commonly expressed sense of impotence, they all claim that their job is a privilege and their work has given their life meaning. And while passionately arguing that their aim is to 'make a difference' and give testimony to 'that which should not be', many have refused to become witnesses in war-crimes tribunals. How do they reconcile these conundrums and what can some of them possibly mean when they say war is fun? Indeed, why would someone choose to spend his or her professional life continually drawn back to the next conflict or the next famine while others decide that the risk or personal toll is something they can no longer accept?

In a radio interview, ABC Australia's Rob Raschke spoke of witnessing a massacre in Ciskei, South Africa, in 1992 in an 'altered state' of mind. Having to board a plane directly after the massacre, Raschke says that while he had noticed people staring at him in the departure lounge and on the plane it was not until he went to the bathroom that he realised why. As he looked in the mirror, Raschke saw 'all this body matter and this blood and it was all over the front of my shirt, and on the arms of my shirt'. It was only then that he says what he had just experienced sank in. In her article 'Where is Kigali?', Lindsey Hilsum, the diplomatic reporter for Channel 4 news in Britain, said of the Rwandan genocide in 1994, 'I couldn't stop the smallest part of it ... At the time I could only watch and survive.' At times, covering human tragedy simply proves too much for the human psyche yet at some point in time, whether hours, days, months or years later, reaction can set in. Donatella Lorch, who spent three years in Africa for the *New York Times*, spoke about returning home to New York and crying for six months because there was 'a darkness in my soul' that would not go away.

Ambulance drivers, policemen, firemen and soldiers all receive trauma counselling for post-traumatic stress disorder (PTSD) but it is only recently that media organisations have begun providing professional counselling for their staff (those who freelance or work for the smaller agencies often have no such support). Ironically though, while the journalists often argue they would only feel comfortable speaking about their experiences with someone who has witnessed the same scenes, the machismo of the industry can make that difficult. While many seem reluctant to admit normal human frailties to their colleagues, others feel that admitting to their editor that they are not coping might mean that they will be passed over for the next assignment. In the end, most believe that even if they wanted to talk about their concerns, no one in the industry wants to hear their personal traumas nor do they particularly want to relive them through the retelling. If the result is a conspiracy of silence and pain for some in the industry, why are others left unscathed?

The much-lauded escapades of World War II journalists and photographers like Robert Capa and Ernest Hemingway have seen a romantic vision of the profession proliferating. Because we only hear about the incidents of intense drama in the war correspondent's life, much of the public has come to envisage brave, confident and reckless individuals awakening each day only to travel to the next war. However, when in reality short bursts of high drama and intense fear are overshadowed by longer 'down' periods spent waiting, seeking food or shelter, looking for the next story or photo to make the deadline, or simply worrying, there is little that can be considered romantic about the profession. Conversely, because most of the public cannot understand the life choices these individuals make, conflict photojournalists and correspondents can also be dismissed as damaged individuals addicted to the darker side of human nature.

Although correspondents strenuously reject the label of voyeur, the idea that they are making a living from the pain and misfortune of others is an issue many grapple with. When photographer Greg Marinovich took his Pulitzer Prize-winning image of Lindsaye Tshabalala being hacked and burnt to death in Soweto township, South Africa, in 1990, he explained that as he took the photos part of him 'did not want to be a photographer just then, but as with the killing in Nancefield Hostel [when Marinovich photographed a Zulu mob beating a man to death and had felt like "one of the circle of killers"] I smoothly exchanged camera bodies to shoot slides as well as colour negatives, ensuring I had material for both the AP and my French agency, Sygma'.* Four years on, when Marinovich believed he was going to die after being shot by UN peacekeepers in Thokoza township (see cover photo), he described a sense of relief and atonement because he had always felt like a guilty voyeur in other people's tragedies.

While the moments of actual danger may be minimal, the confrontation with fear is a constant in the working lives of these people. In his autobiography, *War Junkie,* Jon Steele often refers to fear as if it is a dangerous but highly seductive addiction or lover, its principal attraction being its deadly unpredictability. How much is fear, and the associated adrenaline rush, one of the attractions of working in 'a place where excitement never has to be manufactured'? And why do some within the industry, like Steele, toy with fear, daring it to overwhelm them while most others intensely dread the first whisper of its creeping presence? Indeed, is the fear of fear itself the greatest threat to the conflict photographer or journalist, or can fear be their best defensive weapon? Is it true, as

---

***Author's note***: Marinovich had not simply taken photographs but had tried to stop the killing a number of times. In fact, because the killers did not want him to take photos he tried to use this to bargain for the man's life by saying that he would only stop taking photos if they stopped attacking Tshabalala.

psychologist Anthony Feinstein in his study of PTSD amongst war correspondents and photojournalists entitled 'Dangerous Lives' claimed, that their threshold of risk 'has been shifted so far along the continuum of our shared beliefs as to make it difficult to detect'?

By late November 2001 in Afghanistan, no allied soldier had lost his or her life in the West's 'war against terrorism' but seven journalists had. During the invasion of Iraq in 2003, in percentage terms you were more likely to have been killed if you were a member of the press corps than if you were a combatant or a civilian. Since 1990, over 270 journalists have been killed while working in war zones (sixty-two in Bosnia; twenty-three in Kosovo; forty-nine in Rwanda; twenty-seven in Chechnya; nine in Afghanistan; four in the Gulf in 1991; and eighteen in Iraq in 2003). Undoubtedly the profession is becoming more dangerous. Perhaps the increasing pressures from new technology, which may require journalists to file stories three times a day, is forcing them to abandon caution. Perhaps it is because war has become more accessible to an increasing number of inexperienced journalists, or because the proliferation of cheap and easily accessible weapons such as the AK-47, which as Kate Adie has claimed allows any 'bozo high on gin' to become a proficient killer, is making the profession more dangerous. Or perhaps journalists and photographers have now become unwitting participants in war, not because they carry weapons as Hemingway and Winston Churchill did, but because advances in telecommunications have meant that their 'real-time' reportage of events in a war zone can affect the course of the conflict.

Today the international rules of war that hitherto have protected journalists are being ignored, not only by undisciplined militias who often see journalists as the enemy (a price was placed on the head of Ron Haviv by Arkan, a Serbian

## Introduction

militia leader), but by some of the world's most powerful armies. In 1999, NATO justified its bombing of the local Serb television station in Belgrade and the killing of sixteen of its employees with the argument that it had been spreading propaganda. In the first year of the Intifada, the Israeli Defence Forces (IDF) had shot forty journalists and within two years had killed twenty – many of those who survived these shootings believe that they were deliberately targeted. On the day in late 2001 when the US's allies, the Northern Alliance, entered Kabul the US shelled the offices of the BBC and four hours later bombed the independent Arab TV station, Al-Jazeera, killing one journalist. Prior to the invasion of Iraq, the US military exhibited open hostility to independent journalists (they preferred those 'embedded' within the military) telling Kate Adie, for one, that should the military detect telephone or television signals out of Baghdad they would be 'targeted down' – that is, fired upon. On the day US troops entered Baghdad in 2003 the military again bombed the offices of Al-Jazeera and Abu Dhabi TV (despite knowing the coordinates of the two Arab TV stations in both Kabul and Baghdad), and fired a missile into the Palestine Hotel (even though the military was aware that it was the temporary home to the majority of the world's independent press). On that day three journalists were killed.

Although the targeting of journalists by military forces violates international law, the response of the agencies to this worrying phenomenon has been to rely more heavily on the work of freelancers who they pay by the story or photo and for whom they have little or no legal responsibility. Demands by groups such as the Committee to Protect Journalists (CPJ) and Reporters Without Borders to investigate these murders and bring the perpetrators to justice have been to no avail.

With the quick succession of deaths of a number of the journalists in Iraq in 2003, the viewing public began to focus, perhaps for the first time, on the people who risked their lives to cover conflict. Most people would remember the graphic footage of the BBC's high-profile reporter John Simpson as he searched for his translator after the convoy he was travelling in was bombed by US 'friendly' fire; few though would have heard the name of his cameraman, Fred Scott. With one soldier immediately to Scott's right lying with half his head missing and believing that he may have lost his own eye and that another missile attack was imminent, Scott picked up his camera and continued to film even as he had to wipe his own blood off the lens to do so. Why is it that we never hear the names of those who take as great a risk, if not greater, than the famous faces of high-profile correspondents appearing on our television screens?

And finally, how successful are the professionals in making the adjustment between the two seemingly incompatible existences of home and war? How do they move within hours from a place where people are being killed, where there is no running water, food or electricity, to home where the shops are full, the kids have to be picked up from school, the lawn mower needs repairing and dinner is on the table? As noted in the *Columbia Journalism Review*, when NBC correspondent Keith Miller found himself at a garden party in Wimbledon only hours after having left the genocide in Rwanda in 1994, he found it impossible to answer questions about where he had just come from. While the often physical difference between these two worlds of home and war are shrinking, the emotional gulf between them remains almost impossible to bridge (although for Peter Charley it is always easier to shift from home to the war front than from a place of extremes to home).

Is it essential for journalists to devise clear delineations between their working and private selves, as Glenn Middleton does, or is it more common for them to feel as Eddie

Adams did, more comfortable with the soldiers than with the people back home? And how do people like Ahmed Jadallah survive when home and war are the same place? Are intimate personal relationships an inevitable casualty of the profession with men prone to serial marriages or relationships and women to empty apartments? Are the experiences of war and the method of documenting tragedy different for men and women? And, while the bond of friendship within the profession has an almost legendary status and is clearly important, what is the fabric of those bonds, how strong are they and do they survive at home?

When approached to be part of this book one correspondent said that many of the questions raised addressed issues that people in the profession either spent their lives thinking about or avoiding. It is not the intention of this book to find a definitive answer to any of the questions raised. Nor is the book intended as a critique or an apology for the industry with the reader being presented at the conclusion with a neatly labelled package titled *'the* war correspondent' or *'the* war photographer' – there can be no tidy summation of their lives for that is impossible. Journalists who venture into places where war, famine or disease are raging are not necessarily saints intent on enlightening the world and possessing an abundance of bravery and confidence, but neither should they be simplistically dismissed as voyeurs, thrill seekers or damaged individuals, as is often the case. They have chosen their profession for a variety of reasons and possess all the usual failings and gifts commonly found within the family of humanity.

During the course of the interviews I was surprised by a number of observations. Despite the horrors they had witnessed, many of the interviewees expressed an admiration for, as one put it, the gentleness, the kindness and the compassion of humanity. When questioned, the same correspondent replied that to focus on the good within humanity was a choice; to look the other way was a road he did not wish to travel. Although witnessing the most horrific acts of human deprivation haunts many, they have also been buoyed by observing extraordinary and simple acts of kindness, generosity, tenderness and bravery.

Finally, during the interview process I observed an interesting phenomenon. When the photographers and journalists in this book spoke about situations that were obviously painful for them they quite often switched from the personal pronoun 'I' to the more detached and the more distant 'you'. The notable exception to this was when I asked each to relate a story that was important to them, which became their 'story' in the book. In those instances they nearly always used the personal 'I'. Significantly though, they also changed to the present tense as if reliving the story. I found these nuances throughout the interviews infinitely fascinating but for the sake of continuity within the book and so that the reader is not jumping from the first person to the second person and from the past to the present, they are not always presented in the text.

At the beginning of the war movie *Harrison's Flowers*, one of the characters states in dramatic Hollywood style, 'There are two types of people in this world: those who have been to war and seen war close up, and those who haven't – they're not the same animal.' While it is obviously a dramatic statement, it holds some truth. Seeing war close up can warp your vision of the world; it can become a strange and damaging addiction; it can foster introspection and heighten awareness, sensitivity and compassion; it can cause you to close down and withdraw from society; it can bring you great joy and intense pain; it can make your career; and it can kill you. It is anything but the average occupation.

## Introduction

And so a caution: if you have never been washed by the calmness of imminent death; felt the need for silence when confronted by an overwhelming sense of evil; been choked by the memory of the cloyingly sweet smell of death; been outraged or confused by the world's response to the violence of the Hutu killers and its indifference to their Tutsi victims; walked through the death camps of Somalia and the killing fields of Rwanda; or if you have never witnessed mass starvation and the insane chaos and violence that is war, then the only thing you must know with any certainty is that you cannot possibly know how you would react if you were in the place of these war correspondents and photojournalists. You may think that you know. You may hope that you would behave honourably. But you cannot be absolutely certain that you would be the person you would like to be. Not having walked in their shoes, we are in no position to judge the choices they have made.

Former war photographer John Gaps (whose poem is used as the epigraph of this book) stated that no photograph or words could ever give us more than a few grains of understanding of the reality of war. And while we should always remember that photojournalists and the correspondents are not *the story* but rather the conduits of the story, this does not mean that any attempt to understand their profession as a means of gaining a better understanding of war is futile. After reading their words, perhaps you will find that the people in this book will cause you to reconsider your own responses to war and other human tragedy, and your own responsibility and place within society. In doing so, you may be challenged to redefine the act of bearing witness, both yours and theirs.

# CHAPTER 1

# EDDIE ADAMS

## BIOGRAPHY

EDDIE ADAMS, A FORMER MARINE and the recipient of more than 500 national and international awards, is a photojournalist whose career spans over forty years and thirteen wars. He began as a staff photographer in Philadelphia and joined AP in 1961. Eddie's most notable news coverage was in Vietnam where he accompanied American and Vietnamese troops in 150 operations. At that time he was also known for his sense of humour, with Peter Arnett describing how Eddie 'tried his best to smooth the roiling waters of the Da Nang press centre by including marines in a goofy club he formed called the TWAPs: the Terrified Writers and Photographers. He collected five-dollar fees from scores of colleagues, wore a GI can opener around his neck engraved with the words Head TWAP, and demanded secret signs and catchphrases from members.'

Eddie is the only three-time winner of Sigma Delta Chi's

Distinguished Service Award, which honours the free flow of information and freedom of speech in journalism, and the George Polk Memorial Award for courage in journalism. He won the Pulitzer Prize for his photo of the then South Vietnamese chief of police, Nguyen Ngoc Loan, executing a Vietcong in the streets of Saigon in 1968. Although it became one of the most powerful icons of the anti-war movement, Eddie was always uneasy about the photo, which he believed was responsible for destroying Loan's life.

Once a year for fifteen years Eddie has run The Eddie Adams Workshop, Barnstorm, at his forty-acre farm in the Catskills of New York. There, leading photographers and editors donate their time to pass on their skills to young photographers. Entry is free but on a competitive basis. Today Eddie's work encompasses corporate, editorial, fashion, entertainment and advertising photography.

He is married and lives in New York.

\* \* \*

# STORY

I never said that I have really been on a mission like some photographers. I think many of them are full of shit, with how they are going to save the world with their pictures. They go to war because they want good pictures. They want the recognition. I went to Vietnam because I thought the war was a big story. I didn't say I was going to save the world. You know, when I got the Pulitzer Prize it was not for something that I was proud of. I only did one thing that I was *very* proud of – a story about boat people: 'The Boat of No Smiles'.

It was Thanksgiving Day in 1977. I was back with AP for the second time (I would get pissed off and I would jump jobs). Anyway, I went to the president of AP and I said, 'Keith,

*Eddie Adams*

I just read a paragraph in the *New York Times* about people escaping from Vietnam on boats that made me want to escape with them.' At that time nobody was accepting the boat people, no one, not a country in the world. They would land at each port and they would just be towed back out to sea. Keith Fuller said, 'Go.'

But I didn't really know where to go. So I got on the phone and I started calling AP bureau chiefs in Australia, in Malaysia, you name it, throughout all of South-East Asia. I told them I wanted to get on board a boat and they were laughing because nobody really cared about the story in the beginning. (When I first started looking at this issue it was only a paragraph in the *New York Times* but this kept happening every day, so gradually the story got bigger and bigger.) The bureau chiefs said, 'Good luck. But how are you going to get on these boats?' 'Well,' I said, 'maybe I could go on a helicopter and it could drop me or something?' They said, 'When you get there they are all fishing boats, for Christ sakes! You don't know what they look like when you're on top.'

I didn't know what to do so I went back to the president of AP and said that I didn't think that it was a good idea. He said, 'You get your arse on a plane.' I told him, 'I don't know where to go.' He said, '*Go!*'

To cut a long story short, I knew Thailand so I went there and made a deal with the Thai marine police to patrol with them. While I was getting ready a thirty-foot fishing boat, which had been at sea for several days with fifty people on board, arrived. It had pulled in at four or five o'clock in the morning and was being prepared to be towed back out to sea. I stopped them and said I wanted to go with them. I bought about $100 worth of rice and fuel, jumped aboard, and was towed back out to sea. Because it was a small fishing boat and there wasn't any room, nobody could lie down; everyone had to sit up.

When you are a photographer and you go into refugee camps or into a war zone there could be fifty bodies stacked up and if there are a couple of children there they see the camera and smile for it. It is automatic, but it is what you don't want in the picture; you want to get the tragedy, but they smile. On the boat escaping from Vietnam this was the first time in my life that the children didn't smile. It really bothered me. A few days later I wrote a small story and I released a set of pictures called 'The Boat of No Smiles'. Once the pictures ran front-page worldwide the State Department asked AP for permission for the pictures and they presented them to Congress. I was told that it was my photographs that convinced them to let the refugees come to America – 200,000 Vietnamese.

Now I didn't go out to save the world but this did it – something that I didn't know was going to happen – and I think that that is pretty cool. That is the only thing that I have done in my life that was any good and that is why I bring that up. This was nominated for the Pulitzer Prize but didn't get it. But what I am saying is that if I had gotten the Pulitzer for that I would have been very proud of it, in contrast to what I did get the prize for.

## VIETNAM

There are some things in life that are very strange. First of all, let me give you some background. I have lived several lifetimes and Vietnam was a previous lifetime. You have to remember that it was 1965, I had three kids, and I was in my twenties when Vietnam happened. I was sent there for a two-week assignment by AP – two weeks to a month. But when I was there the US marines landed so the two-week assignment turned out to be nine months. When I came home I said that I really didn't want to see Vietnam again.

But something really bothered me when I came back here. Right outside of Radio City Music Hall in New York was a Vietnam veteran who was a cripple. He used crutches; I saw a taxicab almost hit him and nobody gave a shit. I took a personal offence to that, even though I was not military. I went to the AP office and I saw all these guys – you know, the fat ones just smoking their cigarettes and thinking of going out and getting drunk. They didn't care; they really didn't care about the guys. The only people who cared about the Vietnam War were the ones who had a family member there – either a husband, a wife or a mother. That really bothered me when I came home.

I get really carried away; it is my nature. I am the type of person who gets involved with everything that I do. I mean *really* involved to the point where I take a stand and should not. I was totally involved in the war and it was very personal. Like a lot of people at that time I was very gung-ho and very pro-war. You know, we thought we were doing the right thing . . . we didn't know. I didn't carry a gun so I wasn't a soldier but I felt very sorry for them and I felt like I belonged back in Vietnam and I didn't belong with the people at home. That is pretty sad. I was told by friends how fucked up I was and I said: 'No, you are the guys that are fucked up,' because nobody seemed to give a shit.

Anyway, less than two months later I was on a plane going back to Vietnam because I could not understand anybody in America. We talked different languages and although I still had my family here I had become really involved with the locals, the marines and the army in Vietnam. I think I spent altogether about two years actually in Vietnam on that tour. Then I spent about six or seven months at home, once more saying I never ever wanted to see Vietnam again because I was almost killed a few times. It wasn't long though before I was asked if I would go back and I said yes. You know, there was a bond with a few people – photographers – back in Vietnam and living here in the States was difficult. So I went back to Vietnam for a total of three tours.

You wonder what makes you go out there to a war. When I came back from my tours of Vietnam to the States I would read the papers and what I read scared the hell out of me. I would never go to war just from reading the papers but everything always looked worse from a distance. It is not that I didn't think there was not danger – don't get me wrong: people were dying and everything. I knew it was bad but when you are there and you are involved in something, it is a whole different world.

## POWER OF THE CAMERA AND THE PHOTOGRAPH

You know, I am the last person in the world that wants to die. Believe me. But what happens is that when I have a camera in my hands I do strange things. It is only so big but when I raised my camera an invisible six-foot wall of steel came between me and the bullets and it protected me. The bullets used to bounce off it. With that camera I could do anything. As soon as that camera goes down I'm vulnerable to anything. It is all psychological and I know that – I realise that – but that camera really protects me.

I have seen people die. How many times can you watch somebody die? I have seen more fucking people die than most people, more than most military people. All my life it has just been tearing out my heart. I have gone to thirteen wars. I never got desensitised. I cried all the time. I got to the point where I knew what I was taking a picture of and it was not fun so I would be turning my head as I took pictures because I didn't want people to see me crying. So I shoot a lot of actors in my job now – a lot different from what I used to do, but I enjoy doing it and the reason I do it is because it takes nothing out of me. I am not going to suffer over what I see like I did in war. That is the only reason I do it: nothing comes out of the heart and you make money. But, you know, that is sad; it's wrong. You make more money doing that than you do with the other stuff, which just tears and tears at you.

Photography is the only thing in the world where there is instant communication and I think that the still photo is the most powerful weapon in the world, bar none. You could run all the TV shows you want but people don't remember them; they see the show only for that one time that it's put on TV. A photograph is here today; it is there tomorrow; it is in the history books and that image, that split-second image, remains in your mind because you look at it and you study it and say 'Jesus!' and then you go back and it keeps reappearing in your mind. So, when you know what pictures can do, it is a responsibility. I haven't forgotten that, believe me. And although I try to look on certain things as positive so I am happy that the picture in 1968 did what it did, I have said this a thousand times: two people's lives were destroyed in that picture and I don't like hurting people.

So there have been pictures I couldn't take. This one time, things were getting blown away. It was every war movie you have ever seen. I had my camera and I was lying down – you try to make yourself a part of the ground. There were rockets and all this shit coming down and facing me was this marine, about eighteen, freckles, blond hair. This was only for a very short time, possibly a couple of minutes, but if I saw this guy in the street today I would know who he was from all those years ago – it left such an imprint. On his face was fear like I had never seen in my whole life. I like to think that it was the cover of *Life*, the front page of every newspaper in the world. I brought the camera in front of me three times and I couldn't bring myself to push it. I remember it so vividly and I never took the picture. I know why. People read different things into photographs. This photograph would have told the whole story of the war but it would have destroyed his life for being a coward. I knew he was not a coward. I knew that my face looked exactly like his and I didn't want anybody taking a fucking picture of me.

## BALANCING PERSONAL LIFE WITH CAREER

It is hard to balance your personal life with career so that is why I say I have had different lifetimes. When I came back from my first tour of duty in Vietnam, my youngest child, Amy, who was two, ran over to me and gave me a hug and said (I've never forgotten her words), 'Mommy, is that my Daddy?' My wife said 'Yes', and then Amy gave me a kiss. I remember that so vividly. And then my son, who was five, had been telling everybody that I had been gone for six years and the oldest one, Susan, who was eight, refused to give me a kiss until I shaved off my handlebar moustache.

Without question it affects the whole family when you do what I did. I always loved my first wife; she was sweet, beautiful ... nothing personal, we just went different directions, you know. Remember, I was very young and when everybody is young it is career you are worried about – career is very important. I mean, even though you love your kids and your wife your career seemed to take over and you don't realise until later years what you missed.

I also think part of the thing for survival for anyone, including the military, is that if you have a wife you forget her, if you have kids you forget them, a mom, whatever – your mind has to be exactly focused on what you are doing. If people are shooting, you go down; if they are not shooting, you can stand up. As soon as people start thinking and their mind starts wandering, obviously they are going to get hit.

## BLACK HUMOUR

Sense of humour, black humour, is also about survival. It is how you live, and work, and cover the war because you know you could get blown away the next day. We knew that we needed action, we needed pictures, and so if there was nothing happening, what the hell was the good of going out, but when we did we had a lot of quotes that we used to break the tension like, 'If we are lucky today we will get ambushed.' Or you would be ready to leave the office and go out in the field and someone would say, 'Hey make sure we get a fresh head shot of you for your obit.'

We also used to do really, really dumb things because we never knew what was going to happen. This guy had pointed his gun at me, and I said, 'Why don't you shoot *him*?' and the idiot turns his gun over to Peter Arnett! So I said, 'Shoot the fucker for Christ's sake!' I kept saying, 'Go ahead.' I said it more than once. Arnett really got pissed off with me.

## LOSING FRIENDS

In about 1965, Nick Ut [the photographer who took the famous photo of the little girl burnt by napalm running down the road in Vietnam] was probably about fifteen years old when he first worked in the AP office cleaning cameras and all that sort of thing. His brother was a photographer by the name of Huynh Cong La. What happened was that there was a battle going to take place in the delta of Vietnam – I knew it was going to be bad; you know, that's what you look forward to – and I was on my way out the door to go there and the bureau chief at the time said, 'Eddie, I want you to stay here. Send someone else.' I sent Nick's brother and he was killed the next day. I always felt responsible; it was supposed to be me. From that time, Nick and I bonded.

I think of really good friends and guys who were killed while I was there. It is not easy at all because you put yourself in their place. Some of them came to my house when I lived in New Jersey and spent time with the family. We were very, very tight and it is not easy. Every year at the Barnstorm workshop we drink a toast of 250 glasses of champagne for them.

## Bravery

I don't know what bravery is. I don't think that I ever did anything that was brave. I remember one battle when I just kept screaming for a medic – we were with the marines and a guy was hit not very far from me and I just wanted to get help to him. Eventually a corpsman came. About a year later in a bar in Saigon, some guy came over to me, introduced himself and said that I had given him courage. He was the corpsman that I had kept screaming for at this particular battle. Although he was afraid to come and help, he said when he looked at me and saw I had no gun, no weapons, that gave him the courage. Then I found out from the marines that this guy won two silver stars later. And so to me it was pretty cool that I gave him some courage. But I didn't know at the time that I did it, so what I did wasn't bravery.

## Connections

Take a look at what is happening right now in Israel. The Middle East was part of my territory for a while and I am not taking sides . . . well, I am a little bit. I think that the war in the Middle East is very simple. If somebody comes into your house with a gun and says, 'Get out, it is my house now,' what are you going to do? It is that simple. I am not saying that the Palestinians are totally right, but if somebody came to my house I would fight those bastards too. People say: 'Well the Palestinians are invading the Kibbutzim.' Well, where are the Kibbutzim built? On their land! It is simple, it really is. It is wrong what is going on and it is horrible what has happened. People are dying. I can't believe it.

Do you know what is going to happen if this continues? If all these people detonating themselves in Israel are unsuccessful, people are going to start doing the same thing over here in the States. You watch. As far as I am concerned, that is why the World Trade Center happened too. It is all connected. Violence is bullshit and I don't like it, it rips me. I am serious, I get torn apart. People killing each other is wrong. I don't even like somebody to get cut. I have only seen one Vietnam movie in my life – I don't like any war movies because I don't like to see people getting hurt. I don't like it and I never did.

It is the same thing right here. I live about ten minutes away from the World Trade Center and my little boy still goes to school three blocks from the site. The day the buildings came down I was at home here in New York working in the office and we were watching everything happen. I told my assistant to get my cameras ready and then the second tower was hit and I had mixed feelings about going. I was ready three times to go but I made up my mind I didn't want to and I have never been there yet. My wife called right away and she went down looking for our son – we took care of that – but I didn't want to go.

I couldn't understand it at the time. The biggest story in the world was unfolding in front of me and I didn't want to go.

I knew many of those other photographers were going to make great photographs – how could you not? Later on I was trying to figure it all out; in fact, I still am. You see, everything that I have done on wars and disasters has been in another country and now, for the first time, it was here. It was like a bad dream. I didn't want to see it. I turned my back on it. Isn't that strange?

## BARNSTORM

I've had this barn for a while; you know, it is just a country place and there were always photographers there – friends. They were either helping rebuild the barn or were helping do something. So all these friends are there and one time we were just sitting around and we said, 'We have this great space so let's just try a workshop, just for the hell of it.' I said, 'Well, I will try to get all of my friends, people that I want to hear speak, but how do we do it because I have never done anything like this?' At the time my wife (who was not my wife then) said that when she went to school she always wanted to be involved in some kind of photo workshop but she couldn't afford it – most college kids can't afford it – so she said we should do it free. And I said, 'How can we do it free? You can't do it free; it is going to cost us money!' She looked at me and basically said, 'You asshole, you get sponsors.' I didn't know that; I mean, it is not my thing – I just take pictures. And this is how the first one started. We had a meeting with Kodak and within fifteen minutes we had a workshop. What we intended to do was a one-shot deal; it was never intended to be what it is today. It was one time only and it began as a joke.

So every year now we have a workshop, Barnstorm, for young photographers. Everybody is eligible and it is free.

A thousand people apply from all over the world and we take a hundred. Every year, for the past fourteen years in October, the workshop has happened in upstate New York on my farm, but in 2002 we changed the dates for the first time and it was on September 9–13 because I had this dream one night – you know, it was like an original Martin Luther King. What happens is that everybody in the news media – which I hate to admit I am a part of – pushes 9/11 down our throats. The bad guys love it. That is what they thrive on. Well, we are going to ignore them, I thought. We are just going to show that a year later nothing has changed.

So we had a meeting here about six months before the Barnstorm workshop with sponsors and other people. There were about forty people in here and I have never given a speech like this in my life. I told them that for the next workshop, on the anniversary of 9/11 I only wanted positive pictures of New York. All of a sudden, a guy in charge of AP pictures worldwide says, 'Just a minute, just a minute, let's talk about reality,' and when he said that he triggered something in me. He said, 'There are memorials, there's firemen and police . . .' I got warm to what we were talking about and I have never said this before in a group but I said, 'OK, reality. There are forty people here and I have probably seen more people die than all of you together and more people suffer than all of you together. That's reality! Don't tell me about reality. This is going to be a book and a project that is positive. You feed them 9/11; every day you hear it on the news. People have had it up to here with that; people have to live.' I am tired of it and so I went nuts and I just told them what I thought. 'Reality. Give me a fucking break! Look, you get your pictures of your memorial service and your firemen and use them on your AP but not for us.'

One of the deputy picture editors of *Time* magazine, whom

I have known since she was hired, was the only other person to stick up for him and she said similar things. She later sent me a note saying that I knew nothing about journalism and I said, 'I guess you are right. It is probably because any writers and photographers who use their heart to take pictures or write stories aren't journalists, period.' I believe that there is no such thing as what people say is objective reporting or pictures. So they can lie all they want about the great journalist guy who goes right down the middle. That is bullshit. But some people like to live with that belief.

So what we did on the morning of the 11th at five o'clock is 250 editors and photographers got on buses and went to New York City to photograph it one year after 9/11 – nothing but positive photographs. Not one picture of a fucking memorial service. Nothing negative of this city and all the pictures were of the people who lived and worked here. So it was upbeat and we put out a book about that day. It has a little heart on it and it is titled *NYC Life Going On*; it is a valentine to New York City.

\* \* \*

It was not my intention to change the world. I hear these photographers talk – you know, what they are going to do to change things. I mean, give me a break! Look, if they do it that is cool. I am all for it but I know them. The problem is when you know them and you know how they live their lives and how full of shit some of them are, well . . .

Put it this way, I don't have any regrets about what I have done. None. So I would say to people following in the profession – take pictures with your heart.

# CHAPTER 2

# PETER ARNETT

## Biography

Born in New Zealand, Peter Arnett began his career as a war journalist in 1962 covering the Vietnam War for AP and was there to see the fall of Saigon in 1975. In 1981 Peter joined the fledgling CNN and over the next eighteen years became the face and voice of CNN. In a career spanning over forty years, he has covered twenty-one wars but is most remembered for his extensive coverage of the Vietnam War and his live reporting of the Gulf War from the al-Rashid Hotel in Baghdad for CNN for fifty-seven days in 1991.

Never far from controversy, in the late sixties Peter watched a Buddhist monk self-immolate in front of him on the streets of Saigon. His decision not to intervene has always raised ethical questions that continue to divide the profession. In 1991 he scooped an exclusive ninety-minute interview with Saddam Hussein, and in 1997 was one of the first Western journalists to record an interview with Osama bin Laden. Because of government pressure, he was dismissed from CNN over a program he fronted that claimed that the US military used sarin gas in Laos in 1970 to kill American defectors. In 2003 he was in trouble again after giving an interview to Iraqi state-run TV during the war on Iraq in which he said: 'The first war plan has failed because of Iraqi resistance. Now they are trying to write another war plan. Clearly, the American war planners misjudged the determination of the Iraqi forces.'

Peter has received over sixty journalistic awards for international reporting, including the Pulitzer Prize in 1966 for his Vietnam coverage. His autobiography, *Live From the Battlefield: From Vietnam to Baghdad, 35 Years in the World's War Zones*, was released in 1994 (Simon and Schuster, New York).

He lives in New York.

\* \* \*

## STORY

In the course of my journalistic career I have had opportunities to interview all manner of interesting, notorious, abhorrent political figures, military figures, charlatans and so forth: Saddam Hussein, Osama bin Laden, Fidel Castro, Yasser Arafat and Ratko Mladic. On the day that the Serbian forces attacked the UN-protected enclave of Zepa, and following the murderous attack on the UN's enclave of Srebrenica, I had the opportunity to see Mladic – a general commanding the Bosnian–Serb forces during the war in Bosnia who is now one of the most sought-after alleged war criminals in the world – in action.

Nobody really knew exactly what had happened in Srebrenica but some refugees said there had been rape and a lot of people killed. Zepa was the next on the list because the Bosnian Serbs said that they were going to take over all the

UN-protected enclaves – the UN had done nothing in Srebrenica and it did absolutely nothing in Zepa.

So I drove in around noon and there was Mladic at the top of the valley above Zepa bragging about how his forces had successfully captured the town. He said all this talk of rape and murder was rubbish and he would prove to me that it hadn't happened. So we wound down this narrow road to the bottom of the valley and along the way the Serbian military was parked. At each location where there were a hundred or so troops, Mladic would get out and he would raise his fist – sort of like Hitler must have done – shouting slogans, laughing and gesturing as the troops crowded around him. We made our way to the bottom of the ravine where the town of Zepa was and basically half of it was burnt down or burning. He said, 'Well, we only destroyed the homes where the guerrillas were and they all fled.' I said, 'But what about the population, the women and children?' 'Well,' he said, 'we are taking care of them. In fact, we have them right here.'

We turned the corner and there were about forty buses. I looked into these fearful faces of women and kids and I asked Mladic if we could stop because I wanted to ask them a few things. He asked me what I wanted to know so I said, 'What about these terrible stories in Srebrenica? Women are saying that they were raped and there was killing, but particularly the rape. Your soldiers were so brutal.' 'Rape?' he said. 'Rape? I want to show you something.' So he opened the door of the nearest bus and I was hit by the reek of urine and faeces. It stank. I asked how long these women had been there and he said they had rounded them up early that morning. This was mid-afternoon! 'We are taking care of them,' he said. 'We don't want them to wander off.' But clearly everyone on that bus had nowhere to go. The buses were packed with women and children who looked absolutely fear-stricken. Mladic pushed in ahead of me and my camera crew and said, 'Look at these people. Smell them! Do you think my men would want to touch any of these things?'

That was one of the more horrifying moments of my career because he showed absolute disdain and disgust toward people that he had incarcerated and was brutalising. Sure, he drove them away to the Bosnian side of the city and they weren't killed, but the way he treated them was vicious.

Then we got to the famous bridge over the Drina River that winds through Srebrenica and Zepa. Mladic said, 'Come over here, Arnett; I want to show you something.' He looked into the river and he said, 'That's where the bodies were. Young men hacked to death, arms cut off, beheaded. You ask why we are here. The bodies. That is why we are here.'

'I didn't hear about that!' I said. 'Of course you didn't,' replied Mladic. 'You people don't understand. In 1498 the Ottomans came here, kidnapped 500 of our young men and murdered half of them, throwing their bodies in the river. That is why we are here and if you don't understand that you will never understand anything about Serbia.'

I looked at this guy and thought, 'Fucking idiot.' They are still looking for him.*

## GETTING STARTED

When I was in my early teens I used to listen to commentaries about the war in the Pacific during the Second World War and I really admired the journalists who were out in the field

---

*\*Author's note:* Ratko Mladic has been indicted by the United Nations War Crimes Tribunal for the former Yugoslavia for genocide, crimes against humanity, infringement of the Geneva Convention and violations of the laws and customs of war. At the time of writing, his whereabouts remain unknown.

covering conflict. I envisaged journalism as romantic and exciting but I didn't make the connection between doing exciting things and getting shot. One of my motivations in leaving New Zealand was my desire to get as far away as possible from military requirements. I didn't want to go to war: my aim was Fleet Street, the street of adventure, journalists doing daring things internationally.

It was really by pure chance – as all our lives are based on chance – that I happened to go to South-East Asia. I had met and fallen in love with a British-Canadian gal who wanted to go back to England and I decided to go with her. In 1956 we took a slow boat to Asia. It broadened my horizons beyond Australia and New Zealand because they were very insular, provincial countries in those days. I looked at Chinese or black people in a very disparaging way – I was an unsophisticated provincial who knew how to drink a lot of beer and was playing around with journalism. There was no heart in what I wrote. It was just a job to get by.

We got to Bangkok and I understood that this was an exciting, agreeable, wonderful part of the world. I started meeting all these famous American journalists who had covered the Second World War and reported from Asia and who had won Pulitzer Prizes and lived great lives. It was just a matter of time before I started a little weekly newspaper in Laos where I was able to write more colourful stories about politics in a way that I hadn't before. Fortunately for my career, an important coup d'état took place in 1960 and even though I was thrown out of Laos, I had covered it dramatically – by swimming across the Mekong River to get my dispatches out, so I was offered a job in Indonesia with AP and eventually sent on to Vietnam in 1962.

## A SENSE OF GRAVITY

I had reservations about Vietnam. The war with the French had recently ended and there was barbed wire everywhere; a lot of soldiers; the people seemed mean, unfriendly, uptight; and I got a very bad sense of it. It was as dangerous as hell and I was still not interested in courting danger. To my good fortune, several things happened in Saigon. First of all, Malcolm Browne, the AP bureau chief, and I got along just like pals even though he was totally different from me. He was a tall, blond-haired Ivy League graduate, very much an intellectual, and sort of what you would describe as a loner. He had taken up with a Vietnamese woman, spent a lot of time at his apartment reading, was a student of war and the Vietcong, and wrote long, detailed accounts of communism and Vietcong tactics. So I came in and was sort of the guy who did the day-to-day coverage, the action pieces. My energy and enthusiasm and his intellectualism worked and this became important because within a year there was an American build-up and it was really important that we hung together as a unit. He went on to win the Pulitzer Prize for his 1963 coverage; Horst Faas, who was the photographer for AP won it for 1964 coverage; and I won it for 1965 coverage, so we had this tight team.

In addition, I had the good fortune of meeting a group of young journalists: David Halberstam, Neil Sheehan, Nick Turner, Stanley Karnow and various others who did brilliant stuff. My association with these people really rubbed off on me because what I was lacking when I went to Vietnam was any sense of where journalism would take me. I didn't have any sense that I was in an important job but I learnt from these Ivy League graduates about a higher calling and journalism being an integral part of democracy. I gained an intellectual understanding of what the role of the media was, and that it was a reason to risk my life.

In those early years, Vietnam was mainly a political story and not particularly dangerous so our reporting focused on insisting that the US officials be accountable for the money they were spending, the lives that were being lost, and to the reality of what was happening. At AP we came under fire politically from the US government and by the same colleagues I had adored reading in Bangkok two years earlier, like Joseph Alsop. As we started covering more actions, I began to accept that our journalistic role was dangerous, sometimes foolhardy, but really significant. We were there for a reason.

Realising that what I was covering was significant and created headlines energised me into perhaps taking greater risks. First of all I felt that what I was doing was important, that the world had to understand what was going on, but then, if I did a superior job, got more detail and could present it in a dramatic and accurate way, the usage would be significant. So I was marrying the idea of risk with the idea of opportunity. I realised that if the opportunity was there to cover a major development in the war – and sometimes I was able to see major developments where others didn't as I became more experienced – then, to get more of the story and the kind of detail that others would not, I would be willing to take that risk. I used to have the comment that every bullet counts. So whenever I was shot at I would make sure that the world knew – not in the sense that I was trying to aggrandise myself, but that if I was going to take that risk it had to be important and I would present that importance to the public. Many reporters in Vietnam made the most of the action and wrote the kind of stories that were memorable, and a lot saw as much action as I did but didn't come up with the accounts that meant much. Sometimes, though, you risked a lot and didn't even get a story . . .

Of course, the other factor was that we knew that we had to be accurate: the US government was watching everything we did and they were challenging it. I remember AP president Wes Gallagher saying at the time, 'Peter, I want you to do anything that you want to do, write anything that you want, but don't make a mistake. One mistake and you have had it. We can't save you.' 'Well, thanks Wes!' I replied. I figured I would never make a mistake if I only wrote what I saw, although the analysis I did was a little more challenging. I would do my analysis and come up with different viewpoints, but a viewpoint is a viewpoint. The reason I was never challenged on anything was that I basically wrote what I saw and I went and saw everything. I got the eyewitness account or took a lot of pictures that were unassailable. So I realised that that was the way to tell the story and as the war progressed I felt a deep need to cover it well.

After I had won the Pulitzer I said to the AP, 'Look, I want to be the news editor in the bureau. I feel that we should cover the war accurately and I want to run the coverage.' And they said, 'No, you go and report.' I am glad that I did report because I would probably have been a lousy manager. But I really had a deep sense of responsibility for the story and we understood what was going on in a way that others didn't.

## OBJECTIVITY

You are pushed along by the tides of history, which are the emotional and political content of the moment, so you can't be a totally objective observer. We journalists in Vietnam in '62 were all convinced that the Cold War was a threat, that the communists had beaten the French in Indochina, and that the

Vietcong and Ho Chi Minh were probably operatives for the great international Comintern. We were young and we believed these things so in our early reporting we were looking for accountability in terms of the success of the war, not questioning the reasons for the war. At first we were saying the Americans are not winning, they are screwing up, this is not going to work. We felt it was important to present a view that was contrary to the incorrect official view at the time and it was very easy to do because we realised that, by god, we are losing this war. These idiots at the Pentagon and the White House are blind. There is this corrupt government in South Vietnam that is supposed to be our ally but doesn't really care while our guys are dying, the Vietnamese are dying, we are bombing people and we're losing the goddamn war! This is unacceptable. So our belief system was that we were going to make it better.

The older generation of journalists who covered the Second World War and Korea came in and said, 'What are you guys doing? You have got to be patriotic and support the effort. If you say things like it is wrongly directed, it will be demeaning and undermine national confidence.'

Well, first of all there was no national confidence or consensus on Vietnam in the early sixties. No one in America even knew where it was. Young Americans in the embassy would be getting us aside and saying, 'This is fucked up. We are not going to deny that. The US politicians should know this. They should do a better job.' Eventually, we sort of succeeded because the corrupt South Vietnamese Diem regime was overthrown, partly because of the reporting of the Buddhist uprising.

And then we went into a much more critical period of reportage when American troops were committed (1965–1966) and you had the drum rolls of support back home and the flags. President Johnson said this was a holy war sort of thing and all the soldiers coming in believed in the cause. Our coverage was really challenged then by the administration but we were fortunate because we had been there a few years and we knew the lay of the land and had an understanding of the dynamic of the enemy and the failures of the South Vietnamese. While it was exciting to have American troops there, we looked at them with a pretty practised eye. Certainly, in my case, I wasn't an American and so I wasn't caught up in patriotic babble but on the other hand there were New Zealand troops and I had a great awareness that this conflict could be lost because there was far more of a nationalist ingredient amongst the North Vietnamese than I had understood hitherto. We thought they were just puppets of the communists.

An important part of that time was that reporters were not encouraged to cast judgment – you could analyse, but not in terms of whether the war was worth fighting or not – and I didn't feel that it was up to me to decide whether the war was good, bad or indifferent. That was a political judgment. I didn't feel that I had all the answers. I wasn't in Hanoi, I wasn't in Moscow. What did I know?

What I did know, though, was what I saw on the ground so my best service would be to give an accurate accounting of whatever they were doing and to do that it was a matter of getting out with as many units as possible to take the risks they were taking.

Thank god in those days the press had access pretty much to anyone and any place, so we could go with units. But they expected us to behave. You could not be a burden. We were young and fit, we behaved ourselves, we understood the framework, and we got along with the officer corps who were our age. So my job was to go out and chart the progress of the military and that was how I could help the whole debate. That was my specialty. That was what my reporting was all about and I looked at it very pragmatically. I didn't go into it with any illusions of patriotism or anything else because I didn't even understand it in American terms.

Of course, in every story I was recounting the way they would blow away villages, how they would move villagers around to cut off the Vietcong support base, and why they were launching operations. Once I did a 5000-word story on a platoon I had been with for three days: why they thought it was important they were there and what the experience of six months had been like. But the kind of detail Jonathan Schell went into about Ben Suc, the 20,000-word piece on just one village for the *New Yorker*, was beyond us. Good luck to him. That is what the media is about. You have different levels of engagement. My contribution with the AP was to get the facts, the energy of the war, the drama, and present these on a regular basis. That was the standard that I followed and I kept ploughing on and on and on, essentially right to the end. My analysis got very sharp because I had great contacts and I could portray a lot of what was going on. I had the total confidence of the AP in the course of a whole war and we are all very proud of what we at AP did because we laid out pretty much where the war was going.

Now the humanitarian side of the war was not easy to balance as long as American troops were dying. There were the refugee camps and the way the Vietnamese people were being displaced but it was not easy to write about because in the scheme of things they weren't that significant. We couldn't get the stories that were significant, about the degree to which the South Vietnamese population wasn't really loyal to the war effort, because people would not admit that they supported the Vietcong. It wasn't possible to find out what the people really thought – although it became apparent, of course, in the Tet Offensive – but it was sort of a given in the stories that we wrote: 'this is a population that has not been won over, that has been dislocated, dislodged and is not happy'.

## FRUSTRATION AND LEAVING VIETNAM

It was the Cambodian offensive in 1970 when Nixon unexpectedly put American troops in Cambodia that I started feeling this war is a stupid, fruitless thing. For the first time I felt utterly frustrated and believed that Nixon and Kissinger were uncontrollable. It was just an enormous wastage of life going into Cambodia and pulling that country into a war that it has never recovered from. So that was really frustrating to me and although I didn't write it I said it publicly in interviews when I left. It was frustration with the tactics but also the realisation that in the end the writing that others and I were doing wasn't having any impact at all. Earlier writings had somehow moved the consciousness of the public: it was debated, argued, a factor in policy. Not only had I been getting the major awards but I had also been getting noticed and the reporting had made a difference, so I thought after 1970, 'Well, if it doesn't matter and I am risking my bloody life then it is time for someone else to have a whack at it.'

I decided to pull out of Vietnam and within a few months I was in New York. But I wanted to see the end and I felt strongly committed to the idea that the story had to be covered well. There were a lot of good AP people: Horst Faas was still there, and George Asper, and Eddie Adams was coming back and forth – the hard core of AP people. The Vietnamese staff who were really important to us were also still there. I felt that they still needed me and I had insights and opportunities. So I would go back for three to four months at a time. By then I had tapped the main umbilical cord and that freed me. As long as I had this apartment in New York where my wife and kids lived and I could go back and forth, I could retain a detachment that by 1970 I had been quickly losing.

## Post-traumatic stress disorder

I was proud of the fact that I was detached in Vietnam and that I could stand aside while my American colleagues came over gung-ho and left angry at the imbecility of the war effort. I always prided myself on the fact that this was history, that I was willing to do anything it took to record it, and that I was not going to feel about it one way or the other. I'd feel about it in the sense that if I was with a unit and they were blown away, or if there was a village that had been attacked, or I met people that were hurting, I was going to communicate their feelings as best I could within the context of the story. But then I would go to bed at night and sleep OK because the cathartic experience was to explain what I saw. And I saw shocking sights – actions with 300 North Vietnamese dead, 200 American dead – but by writing about the terrible things I had seen I felt as though I had served a worthy purpose and therefore didn't retain those images of brutality . . . or tried not to.

Post-traumatic stress disorder as an issue was never raised until about four or five years ago. I was looking back on Vietnam, the last major *war* that reporters were ever on and reflecting on the fact that the Vietnam War was very different from all subsequent encounters. In Vietnam we were integrated into the military system so there was this protective umbrella that covered us. There was no stress either going in or out. If we were ever injured in an action we would be taken care of. The journalists that died in Vietnam died in action with the troops or they were in planes that crashed, so you never felt that you were sort of flapping out on a limb and getting the kind of nervous fears that go beyond the possibility of getting hurt.

Also, the way the system worked was that when reporters were there along with the military they behaved themselves. There were no reporters anywhere nearby during the My Lai massacre in March 1968. Reporters just didn't see this and word of the massacre didn't reach the American public until November 1969. Whatever the soldiers' proclivities might be, if there was a television crew along they were not going to go and shoot up people . . . well, occasionally they did and we reported a few incidents. I did stories about them blowing away villages and burning them down and they corrected their behaviour. We reported what we saw and they knew that, they accepted it, and they made sure they didn't kill people. The point is, as a reporter you were working towards correcting it and we would discuss it with the military. The military were reasonable people, you know. But most journalists rarely spend much time in the field; they stayed in Saigon which was pretty comfortable. There were a few who went out for a month with a company but most of them did quick shots during the day, went back to Saigon, shipped the tape. The wire reporters and the photographers basically did all the coverage. It hasn't changed much today, really.

The other thing about Vietnam was that the accommodations were pretty good. You went back to Saigon; you had your family, or your girlfriend, or your buddies; there was plenty to drink and eat and a flourishing culture. We knew Vietnamese people. Most of the guys were sleeping with Vietnamese, either lovers or hookers. I married a Vietnamese woman. Also, the GIs were great people and we journalists got along with the officers. I had and still have buddies from the military going back for years. In fact, I had breakfast with General Westmoreland not so long ago. He is an old man and has Alzheimer's but we talked about the good old days. I can still have breakfast with the commander in Vietnam who supposedly hates the media in a war that was lost by the media! So really the climate was one of deep involvement, acceptance, and care between the media and the military. There wasn't the disconnect that reporters have today in the places they go to.

At one level you could say that the reporters were macho but we would still talk through the problems. Guys who would come back from the field and were maybe a little shell-shocked we would send out of Vietnam for ten days. We didn't want any of our buddies to flip out. Some we sent home early because we knew they couldn't handle it. We looked after each other. A lot of reporters had combat fatigue but they basically talked it through; they got angry, they came home, they bitched and moaned, and people were listening. Eddie Adams got scared to death in 1968 and said to us candidly, 'I can't handle it. I am so frightened I don't want to tell AP chief, Wes Gallagher.' I said, 'We understand, Eddie. Send a note to Wes and tell him.' And Gallagher told Eddie to come home. Eddie then came back a year later. I think every media organisation would say, 'Jesus, Joe is looking screwed up. He is drinking too much. We have got to do something about it. Let's get him home, counsel him, get him laid, whatever.' So I think it was all handled in the environment during the Vietnam War. It wasn't a taboo subject, no.

We would also talk about going into action. 'Should we go in further or not?' I remember talking to Neil Sheehan, a reporter with the *New York Times*, about the battle at Ia Drang

Valley*. People were saying, 'God, that's dangerous; all the wounded are coming out,' and then 'Yeah, we will go in anyway.' And we went in together.

Also, all the news organisations were really concerned about the mental and physical capabilities and attitudes of the staff. Because the AP back then was run by war correspondents from the Second World War, these guys loved us. We were doing what they had done and we were the next generation. They were so proud, as I am proud of young reporters I see out there now. I think that it is just fantastic that the traditions are being followed. They really took care of us and would do anything to help us. I would say that within the AP they would have been perfectly willing to give counselling, and probably did. AP would send us out ten days every two or three months to Hong Kong for rest and recreation, free.

In the case of Vietnam, the stresses a journalist might experience were handled at the scene. Compared to the kind of pressure the average GI was under, it was nothing like it. The average GI went to Vietnam for a year without leave. He didn't see any civilisation, was living in a foxhole in a bloody tent, eating poor food, in danger all the time, and he was killing people and watching people get killed. So I think you have got to look at the whole framework of that war for the press. It was a sort of family, a really collegial environment, and that's why of all the thousands who went there not many came out particularly screwed up.

## COMPASSION FATIGUE

I have felt compassion fatigue. For example, I cannot stand any more to hear anything about the Amazon Delta area

---

***Author's note:** The Ia Drang Valley battle in November 1965 was the bloodiest battle fought up to that time.

burning to the ground. I turn it off; I don't read anything about it. The only way I will listen to anything about the Amazon is if someone says things are going to be better. What is interesting about Afghanistan, and what made it a pleasure for me to cover news there recently, is that literally every Afghani I talked to said, 'It has got to get better than this. OK, we are even glad the US bombed our village if it is going to lead to something better. Surely it is going to get better.' And even though Afghanistan is the worst country in the world – the roads are the worst; the smells are the worst; the refugee camps; the society itself is closed, medieval; people stink, there has been a drought and there is no water; they have got a hateful and fundamentalist creed – it is going to get better. I have been to Afghanistan quite a few times and each time I've left I've said, 'Thank god we are getting out of here because it is the worst place,' but I knew with a sense of foreboding we were going to be back. But this last time it really was with a sense of hope. You could actually do news pieces that talked about something positive.

But there are some things you cannot improve. I have been to Africa a lot in the last decade looking for positive stories. There are some places that are fatigued out and the public has got compassion fatigue about Africa. As a journalist, I don't know how to turn that around. Looking for positive signs is fine, but if it is not the reality you have got a problem and people are going to turn off until something turns the situation around.

## Foreign news in America

Most people in America are not going to look at the news on the Internet or buy the *Times* or the *Post*. They get the local newspaper and there is nothing in it. I went to Wichita, the capital of Kansas, and the local newspaper had not one item of foreign news in seven days. The *Atlantic Constitution*, which is a big paper, had a maximum of a column and a half of foreign news a day. You tell this to people and they say it can't be true, the news is everywhere. It is *not* everywhere! I will tell you where they get information. They get talkback radio, which is skewed to the right usually; they look at a bit of television and maybe some magazine shows, and that is it. They don't give a shit. And so they don't know where anything is. They know where Kandahar is now, but only because American troops are there and that is where Osama bin Laden is, or was, but they don't know where Sierra Leone is and will never know and don't want to know. Government decisions are made by an inside group of Congress and the American public largely doesn't give a damn. When they vote they don't vote in terms of international policies; they vote in terms of local issues.

All this is the media's fault. It is the newspapers' fault for not including a page or two of international news every day so that people, like it or not, are going to see it and so that when they get a moment they may read a story about Africa or Asia. There is certainly plenty there – the AP and Reuters put out lots of information – but the newspapers are ignoring information and the more they ignore the less the AP has the resources to put out the information. CNN should be doing more, even though it has limited viewership; it should be doing more than covering celebrity stuff now, which it does domestically. Fox is a joke. There is an ignorance that is growing in America and it is frightening.

Now the way out of this ignorance will be through the war on terrorism. We are going to learn about Afghanistan, the Philippines and Iraq. We are going to learn about the whole world because that is where the US troops are going to go. So actually this war on terrorism is an educational war too. As long as there is American money and American troops involved, the media is forced to be there and are perfectly happy to be there. The government is behind it, the people are sort of interested, so it is a perfect media thing. But don't expect anything from Africa or Asia because Americans aren't interested.

Throughout my career I enjoyed the idea of being a communicator, of actually transmitting a message or a comment from one person to the world at large. That really excited me and that still holds true. Enormously. That I could actually broadcast through the newspaper, and ultimately television, comments that were deemed important, and those comments being a necessary contribution to world discourse and actually influencing what people thought was enormously exciting to me. I think as a journalist it is very frustrating if you realise that there is absolutely nothing that you can do in your work to change anything. Sometimes you have just got to accept the fact that there are situations that are lousy and they are not going to change and they are going to get worse because journalism is not going to change them.

# CHAPTER 3

# MONICA ATTARD

## Biography

MONICA ATTARD GREW UP IN Australia and is one of its most respected news and current-affairs journalists. Although initially not choosing to cover war as part of her career, Monica was posted to Moscow in 1990 for Australian ABC Radio and, as the Soviet Union disintegrated, reporting on conflict increasingly became part of her job. Probably best remembered in Australia as the woman reporting astride a Russian tank in Red Square in her pyjamas as the communist regime ended, Monica is a self-professed Russophile.

After returning to Australia in 1994, Monica wrote *Russia, Which Way Paradise*? (Random House, 1997). Monica has been awarded the Order of Australia for her services to Australian journalism and has received four Walkley Awards, including a Gold Award for Excellence in Journalism.

She is married, has a child, and has recently moved to

Moscow indefinitely where she is now working as a freelancer with ABC Radio and TV.

* * *

## STORY

There are some situations and some stories in a conflict situation that so overwhelm and touch members of the public that it captivates them and they stay with it. Russia in the early nineties as the old Soviet regime collapsed was one of those stories. I reported by completely immersing myself in the lives of the ordinary people so that I could feel their anger, fear and hurt when things were unravelling around them – whether that meant sitting down on the ground with a bunch of protestors and just talking and listening and agreeing, or whatever.

The people who taught me more about Russia than anybody else were a group of rabble-rousing boys who were working-class, neighbourhood kids who became my friends. They didn't speak English so I had to learn about Russia in their terms and they took me to places that I never would have known. I also learnt from my best friend, Natasha, who was very basic, down to earth, didn't speak English, and was at the time a communist. Even the woman who ran the local state-run café taught me a lot – all about what it was to be an ordinary Russian male because they used to come in there drunk. This whole problem of alcoholism, unemployment and the black market I learnt from her. All of the people I knew were extraordinary, ordinary people with no agenda. They loved foreigners who were interested in them but we were different to them and they wanted to make sure we really understood what was going on so we would report it accurately.

Xenya was a very sensitive eighteen-year-old guy who was

just one of those local kids. He was enormously intelligent and a wonderful photographer who worked for a military magazine called *Red Star*. He was always curious about what was happening politically, always asking questions, wanting to go to demonstrations, and always wanting to be involved. It was also very clear that he was not coping well with what was happening politically. And his family, particularly his father who was in the military, was always terribly upset that he was seen to be not conforming to what was expected of a young communist. He had an older brother who was a bit of a brute and his mother was a very downtrodden, repressed housewife.

I remember the elections of June 1990 when Boris Yeltsin was elected the president of Russia. I was going into town to have a look at the voting and Xenya rang and asked if he could come. On the way in I was stopped by the police – they always stopped cars that had foreign number plates – and the officer said to me, 'What is that Russian boy doing there?' I said, 'Well, he is just going in to vote.' 'What do you mean he is going in to vote? Going in to vote with a foreigner in a foreign car?' The irony of being pulled up when he was going to vote in the first democratic election in Russia was just extraordinary. Xenya got out of the car and was terribly abusive to the police. He was very upset and quite teary.

Some people were outraged that I covered the first democratic elections in Russia through the eyes of my mate Xenya and other people wanted to know what happened to him. I think that people stay with the story if you give the human perspective because it means something to them.

Subsequently, the Soviet Union collapsed and things went completely haywire for this kid. The *Red Star* closed down and he lost his job; his father became an alcoholic because the military was so denigrated and it was such a shameful experience to have been through and there was nothing to do; and his brother became an alcoholic because he was a no-hoper and was thrown out of work. Life became completely black for this boy. Several years after my posting I went back to Russia on a visit and I rang his home to catch up with him. His mother answered and said he had committed suicide. Basically he couldn't cope with the mayhem that descended upon his life after the USSR collapsed; he couldn't cope with the old Russia and he couldn't cope with the new Russia. He fell between the cracks. He killed himself because he lived like a pauper and just couldn't cope.

It was one of those things that will stay with me forever. The devastation for the parents of having lost a son in those circumstances when if he had lived in another country, without the trauma of what his country had been through, he would have made it.

Not one of those kids I made friends with did well. One became a drug dealer, another got his girlfriend pregnant and then left her and ended up taking off somewhere or other, another one got a girl pregnant and ended up living with her for a while but that didn't last for very long. Actually, one of them did do all right; in fact, he ended up doing very well. He married a Canadian and moved to Canada, has a young family, is working in telecommunications and living happily ever after. But not many other kids did.

## COVERING CONFLICT

When I applied to the ABC to go to Russia at the beginning of 1990 nobody anticipated the Soviet Union would collapse although wars had already begun. So, in the sense that I chose to go to Russia, I guess I chose to cover situations that I knew had the possibility of being violent. It was not that I covered war in the sense of a Vietnam War. Your personal, emotional reaction to the sort of conflict I covered, whilst it can be dramatic, is not the same as seeing people shot dead in the trenches.

I remember on the way to my first conflict, which was in Georgia in 1990, I was a bit foolhardy. I was a lot younger then, single, and I wasn't a mother. I would probably flip out now but at the time it was both a genuinely exciting and frightening adventure. I was probably going to hear real gunshots and talk to fighting men and all the rest of it. I had to duck because snipers were taking shots out of buildings and they were whizzing over my head. It was exactly what I thought it would be like. Exactly.

But it can be hard to form a clear picture of what is happening when you are reporting from conflict. For instance, I woke up one day in August 1991 and there were tanks all over the city; Gorbachev, the Secretary of the Communist Party who was also the President of the USSR, had been removed from power; and a whole bunch of communist hardliners were in control. People were very, very divided and confused and it was difficult to know what was going on: how serious were these guys, how competent were they? I was so lucky in that situation because David Marr happened to have lobbed in on a holiday. You can't get luckier than that – an enormously intelligent, incredibly clear-headed, amazing man, and he came to Moscow from St Petersburg when he heard about the coup. At the end of the day we would go through theories: maybe this is happening; what about this possibility or that possibility; what is the result if this happens? I think that I would have gone mad without him because there was just an avalanche of material and at times it was so overwhelming. We actually hired somebody to cut the copy and categorise it, otherwise I would never have got out of the office and seen the story first-hand.

When you are in a very dangerous situation it is very easy to sit back in your office and just rip off AP and Reuters. I can't tell you how much that happens. And because television can garner pictures from a number of different sources, television reporters actually don't have to go out and see it for themselves. When I think of great journalism from that time, though, I think of the late Robert Haupt, a brilliant, wonderful Australian journalist who was one of the ones who just got out there and put himself in those dangerous situations in order to cover that story first-hand. Nothing was more poignant to me, in terms of print journalism, than Haupt's material out of Russia. It was just phenomenal; the imagery was so overwhelmingly moving and profound. You can't do that unless you get out there in the thick of it.

There are still some male sexists out there who tell you that women can't cover conflict properly but my experience is that we do it extremely well. Look at Deborah Snow, the ABC correspondent in Russia. She would just get out there and cover wars. She would drag her crew places they wouldn't want to go. 'No Deb, you don't want to go there.' 'Yes, come on, we have got to get pictures. Let's go!' She was at the television tower in October of 1993 when there was this big shoot-out when journalist Rory Peck was killed. She was a lot braver than a lot of male correspondents who I know didn't go out there.

## CAMARADERIE

To the correspondent in the war situation, camaraderie is very important. I found that a lot of times I would not go to places without somebody else – although there are lots of people I wouldn't want to go with, believe me. If I couldn't travel with a journalist, I would take one of my friends like Natasha. Part of the need for company is the loneliness when you are away from home. You are either going to be out twenty-four hours a day covering a story or you are going to be out sixteen hours a day and you need a few hours of normal conversation with somebody. Another aspect of camaraderie is the importance of having someone to bounce ideas off – 'Is this what I think it is?' There is often the safety aspect to it as well: safety in numbers of more than one. I remain really good friends with some of the correspondents who I did time with like Deb Snow and others who are not Australian. There are others who I wouldn't give the time of day to.

## GETTING THE STORY RIGHT

I think a successful war correspondent is one who gets the real story – who covers it accurately and can bring a passion and the human side to it. Rules of behaviour? Keep the microphone running, talk with as many people as you can but let them tell their stories and don't provoke – more than anything, don't provoke. The opportunities to provoke are always there because people's passions are really inflamed. I have seen reporters provoke deliberately as a result of ego. I have seen them ask the wrong sorts of questions, questions they know are going to press a button here or there. You don't have textbooks, or AP or Reuters copy. You have got nothing. You are out there in the field and you have got to find out for yourself who are the bad guys and who are the good guys, although there isn't always that sort of dichotomy. The trick is in determining when there is a good side or a bad side and if that situation arises, having the wherewithal to follow your instincts and following your moral conscience to pursue it.

I will give you an example. In January of 1991, when Soviet troops went into Vilnius in Lithuania, it was obvious who the bad guys were. The USSR was on its way to being dismembered and it was clear that Soviet troops were there to stop Lithuania seceding. So it was clear to me that they were the bad guys. It was just a matter of pinning down who put them there. I can remember interviewing the commander of the Soviet forces in Lithuania and knowing that he was just lying all the way through our conversation. Finally, I just got really angry with him and confronted him with my belief that Soviet troops weren't just keeping the peace, they were there to stamp out Lithuania's independence spirit. He said, 'People like you should really keep your nose out of affairs that have nothing to do with you. Why don't you go cover the Gulf War and leave us alone to sort out our own affairs?' And that was enough to tell me that his orders had come from forces in the Kremlin who were working against Gorbachev.

## BECOMING INVOLVED

There was a strong tradition in the Soviet Union of soldiers doing what they were told to do. When they were ordered at four in the morning to get out of their bunks and drive into central Moscow to occupy their own city in 1991 they did. I found it difficult to believe that the soldiers I was talking to believed in what they were doing, that it was right to oust Gorbachev and turn back the clock to the hardline days. I said to them, 'Do you really believe in what you are doing? You are occupying your own city! Who ordered you here? Oh, the commander. And do you know who the commander answers to? Is he one of the KGB chief's boys? You have got a mother. You have a babushka. Do you think that they are going to like seeing you on television driving through the streets of

Moscow on a tank?' I couldn't believe that these young kids who were all the beneficiaries of perestroika and glasnost would want to do what they were doing. I was so angry and confronting them was the only way I could cope with it. I believed that what they were doing was wrong. I believed that the coup was wrong. At the end of the day I had taken a moral stand. I wasn't objective. A lot of those kids got off their tanks and went home because they didn't believe in what they were doing either. Enough people had come up to them saying, 'Get off the tank now and go home.' And they abandoned their tanks. It was beautiful.

My reactions to events shocked me on two occasions in August 1991. One was the time I've just described because I didn't expect myself to be that emotionally involved. And the other time was again in those three days of the coup when I was overwhelmingly frightened. I had never really been terrified before. I had to say to myself, 'I don't know why I am feeling so jittery about this because Georgia was worse than this. Lithuania was much worse than this. Why do I fear that they are going to mow us down here – that we are going to die in the streets of Moscow?' I think it was fear of the unknown. I felt that if the coup leaders were capable of getting tanks on the street then anything could happen. We were outside the Russian White House and then, all of a sudden, on the other side of the river, you could hear the rumbling of tanks. It was clear that they were coming to get rid of the demonstrators in front of the White House, which was where I was. I knew that I wouldn't leave but I didn't know what to do because I was scared. I was really quite shocked by that reaction.

In this line of work you remember the times that you have been fearful; also certain images stick with you that are really unpleasant – they hurt and you are taken aback by them. One of the images that really sticks with me occurred in a little

Azerbaijani town that was in Nagorno-Karabakh. There had been an Armenian massacre and there were bodies lined up in a row from one end of the town to the other. I can still vividly remember that. I felt a little bit like a voyeur going into these little villages where their dead lay in a row in bags. As I was a radio journalist I wasn't taking pictures, but I had a microphone and I was taken by the people into their bombed-out homes. I felt a little bit like 'I wish I wasn't here and please forgive me for being here'.

I also have this very vivid memory of the barbed wire that the protestors had erected around the parliament in Lithuania after the Soviet troops came in. There were pictures of the dead children and teenagers spiked on the fence. And letters from children to the dead and to Gorbachev telling him, 'take your troops home'. I remember the sandbags that they had erected inside as shooting barriers and the kids in the foyer of the parliament building with Kalashnikov rifles – they were no more than seven or eight years old. Those images are very sharp and unforgettable. You don't know how lucky you are living in a country like Australia until you see something like that.

But I think what really overwhelms me most of all is the passion that is involved in a political fight. When people feel as though they have been oppressed by one particular race, or their future is being undermined, they will kill and there will be no limit to the degree of cruelty with which they will kill. They kill indiscriminately because their passion completely overwhelms them. They kill women (I saw women as victims many, many times but I never saw women kill); they kill kids, bomb villages; they do tragic, horrible things in war because they see their own welfare and their own good being compromised if they don't kill. Whether it is nationalism or racism or downright anger at the political system, they don't see clearly, rationally.

## OBJECTIVITY

Personal judgments of right and wrong influence my reporting substantially. I am a highly emotional reporter and am often criticised for it by people who – I have to be delicate here – mightn't want to do the job I do. At the end of the day I think doing this job well comes down to personal morality issues. You have to be able to take a stand and I think that there are some situations where it is not moral to be objective. I think that David Remnick who was working for the *Washington Post* when I was in Moscow lucidly looks at an issue and is always passionate. His writing is brilliant on that part of the world for which he has a burning passion. He never, never lies or tries to conceal his writing in a lack of passion which is essentially a veil of objectivity. It was obvious that it was really important to him that he took a moral stance – because morality in situations of extreme conflict is really important. It was reading his material that got me thinking about this bullshit about the importance of objectivity. I realised that it was really very critical that we *be passionate*. Alan Ramsey, the political columnist with the *Sydney Morning Herald,* also does it beautifully week after week. He takes a stand and it actually produces a moral, worthy result.

When I came back to Sydney from Russia in 1994 I got into terrible trouble because of a comment I made in a speech that I gave on the issue of objectivity. At the time it seemed to me that there was a terrible lot of political correctness around, which was almost unbearable to live with. If you didn't believe the right things and say the right words then you were ostracised. I commented on this publicly in relation to the way the media covered the Keating years and my point was that at some time the notion of objectivity can be so badly construed as to give an opposite result to that which it intended to produce. There are times as a journalist that you should actually show your colours, take a stand and say, 'This is wrong, this is not right.' Well, I got howled down in some quarters.

I don't think I have done anything that I regret and I certainly have become involved. I have done things like shelter people. My house at one stage became like a refugee centre with friends who were caught up in fighting in Tajikistan and Georgia. If I was in a situation where I saw people being injured I would drop the pretence of objectivity. I certainly never watched anyone self-immolate but if I were in that situation I would do absolutely everything in my power to stop them. You can't say, 'I am a human camera, I will just record it.' I don't think that is moral. I don't know how people do that.

Maybe what they are seeing is so horrendous and so morally repugnant to them that the only way they can justify it is by objectifying it. I don't know. Maybe it is because they really believe that the role of the journalist is to sit there and be a human camera but I can't draw that line between humanity and journalism. I don't think journalists are gods or non-humans, or should pretend to be. You have to have some moral certitude and fortitude and stand by your beliefs. If you don't have those beliefs, if you are so morally derelict that you don't see the immorality in your behaviour then OK, you deserve to be haunted.

## Speaking with people at home

Telling your family and friends at home what is happening when you're away covering conflict is a huge problem. In my case, my parents were absolutely beside themselves with worry when the coup happened. They just didn't know what to think or who to ring. I was ringing them very often and telling them I was OK. I lied a lot to them as well. 'No, I didn't go out there – what are you talking about, Dad? I never ever went to — I know I just said on radio that I had been out to Red Square with all the tanks but I wasn't really there. I was just saying that.' After the coup he would always say to me, 'Please tell me that you won't get into trouble. I beg you, just tell me.'

A couple of years later when the uprising against Boris Yeltsin occurred and he did turn the tanks on the people and started shooting at the parliament, my father was in a hospital bed dying. I know why he was dying and nothing will ever convince me otherwise. He knew I would come home to him and that I couldn't go out into the streets if I was on a plane coming home to Australia. I just know it because I know my father. It was extraordinary. When Peck was killed in the television tower I thought, 'My god, maybe that is what Dad saw. Maybe that was what motivated him to die – so I would come home.' It was difficult from both perspectives. My father was dying and yet there was this incredible story with which I was intimately connected unravelling where I lived in Moscow. So in terms of how your loved-ones are reacting back home, you comfort them by continually reassuring them that you are alive and also by lying to them about what exactly you are doing. I did that for four years. Eventually, the truth comes out but then it is OK. You are safe at home.

## Coming home

I came back from Russia physically, emotionally and intellectually exhausted from four years of constant, unabated revolution. It was an extraordinarily difficult transition. I had anticipated that I would find the slow pace back in Australia a welcome reprieve but it wasn't. I just couldn't cope with it and there was absolutely nothing in terms of the reporting

I could do in Australia that could actually fill the gap. But it wasn't just that. I had to get used to life back in the slow lane, as an outsider, because life became very normal again, very settled. There are no great problems in Australia. In Russia, shopping was a major ordeal; paying bills was an even bigger ordeal; getting a car fixed, huge. Sometimes driving to the city was hazardous because you were always being pulled over by the military for a bribe. There was always an issue! I would have ten things on my to-do list and if I managed to do one I had achieved something, but never more than one. Plus, in terms of the story of what was happening in the Soviet Union itself, it just lurched from disaster to disaster; every day just got a little bit worse.

How do you make that adjustment, moving from turmoil to total stability? I don't know how to do it happily. Perhaps by finding things that are going to fill that hole, that intellectually keep you alive. For me, I found that writing a book was very cathartic. I sat down for nearly eight months and I just relived it and put it all on paper. It was a wonderful thing to do. You go through an awful lot of angst and you pine to go back or to be somewhere else. Oh yes, I have wondered where I really belonged. You consume as much information about where you have been so that you feel as though you are, in a way, still there. It doesn't go on forever, but it feels like it will during the first few months. So basically coming home is difficult for any foreign correspondent but it is especially hard-core coming back from a place where there has been enormous friction and war.

There are people at home who are really curious about me as a person but if I ever got down to talking socially about the nitty-gritty of the coup in Russia or the civil war in Tajikistan, Georgia, Ukraine etc., well, their eyes glaze over. They don't want the detail – which is not supposed to be a negative comment about them that they only want the glamour, but the glamour is much more interesting than the grisly side of the experience. That is very difficult to cope with, very difficult. When my book *Russia, Which Way Paradise?* came out in 1997 the media didn't talk about the substantive issues I covered. They only ever asked, 'So what was it like to get married in Moscow and where did you meet your husband?' Monumentally disappointing!

The curiosity about me drove me crazy when I returned home, but it comes back to the fact that Russia at that time was one of those stories that triggered people's empathy and they wanted to know about the individuals I had included in my reporting. I was overwhelmed by the number of functions I was invited to and the number of speeches I was asked to give. And people knew my friends by their names. It was clear they also felt that they knew me very well and owned a piece of me. The ABC's audience is a terribly loyal audience, it is *their* ABC, and therefore I am *their* Monica. They want to know about you and they feel that they know you intimately and that they can say things to you. When I fell pregnant I got gifts in the mail, which largely made me feel very vulnerable and exposed. It really hit me not all that long ago when I was in the park with my child and I called him and a woman came up to me and said, 'You would have to be Monica Attard.' I said, 'How did you get that?' 'Well, you called your child by a Russian name and you look a bit like her.' That personal/professional divide is a very fine line.

Frankly, within thirty nanoseconds of having reached Australia I would have chosen to go back to a posting where there was conflict but the ABC's policy wasn't to cross post. I think it is a short-sighted policy.

## Legacy

What did I walk away with from my posting? I walked away with an enduring respect for the former Soviet people, the Russians especially, because they had a particular way of life for a very long time that was comfortable though very repressive and they chose to overturn it. Some of them made it and some of them didn't but the ones who made it did so because they were absolutely bloody determined that they were going to survive. Imagine if all of a sudden in comfortable, cushy Australia there was a communist insurgency and the democratic system that we enjoy was overturned and we had a really harsh communist regime imposed on us. How would we all personally muster the strength internally to survive that? It made them have to fight in a way that they had never had to fight before, but they survived it and they found ways around it. I admire that.

I also came away with a loathing of the way the proponents of political systems, whatever they are, use people as pawns in their nasty power games. I think it changed me quite profoundly in a political sense. Certainly I became more acutely aware of the extent to which politics can affect the lives of real people in the way that in Australia politics doesn't. I became acutely aware of how people's lives could be shattered and unravel beyond a position where they could be retrieved. I became very aware of how lucky I was to not be an Azerbaijani living in Nagorno-Karabakh and have my child's bed covered by a huge great slab of concrete because the house had just been bombed. It also changed my attitude to journalism and I dropped the bullshit about the need for objectivity and I then reported very, very differently.

One of the best things I witnessed was people's capacity to survive. To sit with the women who had lost their children in acts of war, and listen to them weep. The worst thing I witnessed was watching in puzzlement as men – and it is always men – carried out completely vacuous orders in order to achieve political aims that they didn't respect, an obvious example being the commanders who ordered and carried out the invasion of Lithuania. The fact that they knew that people were going to be killed, that the people they were going to kill were going to be young protestors – how did they do that? I find that chilling.

There is something in the Russian character that can be a little bit too brutal for my liking. It was very evident in the military but it was at least adequately counterbalanced by the really soft Russian soul that was concerned more with the meaning of life and the fact that life is pretty tenuous and ought to be respected. That spirituality, I think, was brought out by the very thing that tried to quash spirituality in the Russian soul or psyche: communism. That is, the fact that they were all equal, all in the same boat, and they all had to support each other in order to survive: without you for me and me for you we have no hope of overcoming the rigidity of the system. I have no doubt that that communal spirit was reinforced by communism although I think that there were also many historical reasons. Russia is an enormous and not particularly inviting country geographically and the tsars weren't particularly kind rulers. So people have always been left to fend for themselves and an element of brutality arises out of that. But those two aspects of the Russian character – brutality and spiritualism – always fought against each other. I think you could most poignantly see it in the coup of 1991 when those young soldiers got off the tanks and went home. If they hadn't been goaded by their fellow Russians into doing that then there was every chance that they would have stayed in the tanks and gone shooting if they had been ordered to.

Russia is one of those places that if you go to it as a foreigner you either love it or you hate it. There is never anything in between. If you are in between you are no good at covering it and you should get out because what you do is shit boring. But, even being a person who clearly loves Russia, sometimes even I would just crave to have a normal conversation in my own language where I didn't have to read between the lines. Not peppered or short-circuited by the sort of roundabout way that Russians then spoke because of the repression under communism. I yearned to be in a country where I wasn't going to be hit for bribes, where doing more than one thing a day wasn't too difficult, or where getting your food for the week wasn't a huge bloody effort and trauma. I just yearned to get on a plane and go to London or Paris or come back to Australia. But if I left for anything more than two weeks I really missed Russia. It was a real love/hate relationship and it still is to this day. I love Russia so passionately, just like I love Australia.

## CHAPTER 4

# DAVID BRILL

BIOGRAPHY

DAVID BRILL IS ONE OF Australia's best-known TV cameramen/ cinematographers. In 1966 he joined ABC TV in Tasmania and since then has been involved in news, current affairs and documentary filmmaking for Australian ABC, American NBC and PBS, Britain's BBC and Reuters TV. He has also been involved with both paid and volunteer filming for groups such as CARE, AusAID, UNICEF, the United Nations and the Red Cross.

David has covered most of the social and political upheavals that have occurred around the world over the last thirty-odd years including the Vietnam War, the Falklands War, the fall of the Berlin Wall, the Gulf War, and conflict in the Middle East, Russia, Central America, Eastern Europe, Africa and Asia.

No longer covering war, David works for the *Dateline* program on SBS TV in Australia while documenting the world's critical social issues. A biography on David titled *The Man Who Saw Too Much* by John Little (published by Hodder) was released in 2003.

* * *

## STORY

I have been concerned with the spread of AIDS and famines in southern Africa. In 2002 I had been listening to the BBC World Service and had been following the beginnings of a famine in Malawi potentially affecting millions of people. There was nothing about it on Australian TV so I thought, 'I should do something about this.' I got in touch with Mike Carey, the executive producer of current-affairs program *Dateline* at SBS TV in Australia, which was interested in running a program about the famine in Africa. I also spoke to Oxfam's communications manager, Vicki Horne, who did some research with their people on the ground in Malawi to find out more about the famine and the AIDS problem, and we looked at whether we could make a moving television story about the situation there. We hoped it could help the people in Malawi by encouraging donations and make the international community aware of their circumstances. That's what it's all about.

You don't often know what a situation is going to be like and what you are going to be able to film until you get there. The first couple of days are basically spent just talking to people, creating contacts, and looking around; if you don't you can spend days driving around aimlessly and you only have so much time to get the work done. So you need to pinpoint exactly what you are trying to do, which is to bring the world's attention to a human disaster that needs help. In this case it was to bring attention to the famine and to the AIDS situation and hopefully get some international assistance to these people. I did a couple of days filming the drought problems and then we drove out of the capital, Lilongwe, and went down to a country hospital to see AIDS victims. There were a lot of men and women sitting around waiting to die.

While I was there I heard about three little girls, aged fourteen, ten and eight, who lived on their own. Their parents had died of AIDS and their grandmother had died recently. They lived in a little mud hut with a little bit of land and I thought this was a perfect example of what the famine and AIDS epidemic was about. What I like to do is film a very personal and humane story. These three little sisters go to bed in the dark, get up in the dark, cook themselves a bit of food when they can get it, have one hoe between the three of them, and a little bit of land they try to cultivate. Each day, they have to walk a ten-kilometre round trip, two or three times a day, with a huge pot on their head just to collect water.

What I noticed was the incredible dignity of these little girls, their manners and their decency. It is important for me to show the dignity of these people we film. So I spent two days with them as they collected water, cooked a bit of food, said grace, washed their hands, and ate their little meal. They have nobody. They just help each other to survive and I thought that really told the whole story of the double tragedy of famine and AIDS in Malawi. So I built this story up around them combined with the famine and with another family looked after by a grandmother in her late seventies caring for about sixteen children (her daughters had died of AIDS). I felt back home in Australia where kids have a mother and father – at least, most children do – people should be moved by the story. We were.

Somebody said to me the other day, which I found incredible, 'Oh well, there is not much point putting African stories on television because no one watches them.' What I think is so dreadful about this statement is that it is partly true but, as a cameraman, you keep on going because you feel that you have got to get the message across. These people are suffering and they are people just like us; we are all the same basically ... in fact, they are better, I think, because they have much more dignity than a lot of us here in the West and they care for each other more than we do.

Once the story went to air on *Dateline* in September 2002, the reaction was amazing. Journalists who have been around for a long time, who are cynical, tough old journos, rang me and said how moving the story was. It made a huge impact and brought help directly to the people through Oxfam, bypassing the Malawi government. The three little girls were also directly helped. They got an extra bucket and hoe to work their little piece of land, which would have made their lives a lot easier.

I heard recently that they had been robbed. I don't know if they lost their hoe and bucket but Oxfam are spending a bit of time with them now that they have made contact because the girls are alone and they are obviously quite vulnerable. I would like to go back (and *Dateline* wants me to) to see how they are going.

## Discovering the power of photojournalism

When I was young and living in Tasmania before the advent of television, we were very isolated, so I had a great respect for magazines like *Life*. They had wonderful photography and you could see what was going on in the world. I thought, 'God, it is an incredible life these photographers live.' I believed that they did really good work so I wanted to be in photojournalism, or journalism, or do good documentary photography. I didn't know anything about professional journalism or photography at the time or even how you got into this field, but I thought good photojournalism was a very powerful tool with which to communicate.

By 1967, when Tasmania was swept by bushfires, I was a young cameraman at the ABC in Hobart. It was around this time that I discovered I could do some good while filming. At times I put my camera down and helped people by dragging their belongings out of their burning homes and that made me feel a bit better; I didn't feel I was just standing there filming while they struggled to save anything they could. Once the footage went around the world through Visnews, I realised how powerful television could be. It made people aware of what a dreadful thing had happened to Tasmania and a lot of aid and expertise flowed in to assist the tragedy. I realised that television had to be used properly. This job is a huge responsibility but it is also a privilege to be able to get pictures and stories on television that can help people.

I have recently realised that a lot of my early filmwork in black and white is more important now than it was then because it has become history. I captured and documented history, things that were changing. Whether you use a movie camera or still camera, to me it is the same thing: storytelling. The camera is just a tool like a paintbrush or a typewriter that we use to capture a piece of history, to explain what is going on and to make people more aware.

I went to the Sudan in 1993 and I ran into an Australian nurse who was working for CARE as an aid worker (I called her the Mother Teresa of Africa). This little woman, who would have been in her late fifties, was caring for the dying in the famine. She was a very beautiful person. I remember we went into a tent where a woman was suffering from an abscess in her mouth. The Australian aid worker told me on camera that she didn't even have an aspirin to give the woman who was in terrible pain. When we put that to air the next day a pharmaceutical company donated $10,000 worth of drugs, as a result of our story. I could make a lot more money in a day doing commercials than I get for a year doing the work that I do, but as long as I have got my books, music and a few paintings that I like I'm OK. To me, storytelling is a real calling. You can make people stop and think about what is really going on in the world and make a difference, I hope.

## Surviving war

Nothing can really prepare you for covering a war, or famine, or death all around you, but we all have got to start somewhere and you have just got to develop your skills as you go along. But it takes a special type of person to be a war cameraman; you have to be calm under pressure, be good at judging situations, and have a quick mind. It is very dangerous work. A lot of media people, because of the tension in war zones, tend to overreact and panic and rush around. I think that it is important to sit back and observe the situation and if you think it through before you make any decisions you have got a good chance of staying alive and getting the proper footage. For instance, you don't have your head up filming when you could get a bullet through it. What is the point? My job is to do with calculated risks and the instinct that comes with experience. It is interesting because normally I am quite a tense person but in dangerous situations I am very calm under tremendous pressure and I make decisions rapidly. You take calculated risks to go into dangerous places and obviously you become cannier as you become more experienced in this type of work; you become more aware of what is going on around you. I believe I've got good instincts and I feel I am still alive because of that.

It is also very important to work with people you trust because at times you are relying on one another to stay alive. There are some cowboys in our business who are out there for the thrills. I like going out to work on my own, because it means I am not responsible for anybody else. When you have other people with you, you almost have to have a committee meeting every time you need to make a decision – do we stay, or do we go? That can be very dangerous. Who makes the decisions? I like to make my own decisions.

## Professional responsibility

The first thing that comes to my mind when I think of the moral issues involved in the job is filming people who are suffering. Sudan is a very poor country but we journalists and cameramen might be in the Hilton having a beautiful lunch off the buffet. Then we get in the Toyota Landcruiser and travel fifteen minutes up the road to a refugee camp and children are dying in front of us from starvation. That is when I feel guilty. 'Where is the balance? How do you justify filming this?' Then I have to think, 'I am here and I have to eat and I like to have a clean hotel room. I can justify my work and hopefully the film will help stop the suffering – organisations like the UN will see it and do something.' This issue of balance has always been important to me.

I also think reporters and cameramen need to stop and talk to the people first, if possible, and try to explain to them why they want to film what is happening to them. Give the people some sympathy and mean it. I try to be thoughtful of other people's feelings. If I am in the Middle East and people invite me into their home for a cup of tea, say, on the West Bank or

Gaza Strip, and I am there with my camera to film them, of course I am going to stop and ask if it's OK to film. It is respectful of the people. You don't just blow in and blow out. It is simply a case of having manners and considering the feelings of the people who are involved in the situations you are covering.

I have been conscious of my presence both inciting violence and affecting an outcome. The camera is such a powerful instrument that people will deliberately act or make out a situation is worse than it is, or make out that they are going to kill somebody. Most people like being filmed. Those sorts of dilemmas can be difficult but I have always been able to determine if a situation is being set up for me. Again, this sort of judgment comes with experience and intuition. That is why the camera has got to be used in a very sensitive and caring way. Being behind a camera is a tremendous responsibility. There is no bigger responsibility than having the potential to affect somebody's life, and inexperience could push the situation the wrong way. I saw one cameraman in 1972 in Cambodia, after a battle, pay the soldiers US dollars to re-enact the battle, which to me was disgraceful. If a situation is getting out of hand just for the camera then I will walk away quietly, as long as I know that I have got enough footage to cover the essential part of the story.

As journalists and cameramen, we need to challenge politicians. I was in the home of some very educated Muslims in Africa recently while they were watching George W. Bush on CNN. Bush said, 'We will smoke Osama bin Laden out of his cave, dead or alive. That is what we do in Texas.' I found his arrogance and sense of superiority terribly embarrassing at that time, especially while I was in the company of these dignified people. To me, that statement by Bush is more dangerous than war itself. It is also an incredibly dangerous

*Bearing Witness*

way to run foreign policy because it builds up hatred. People may say what they consider to be macho comments but such comments can have a huge negative impact on the Muslim population. We need to challenge the politicians about their stance on war; that's what journalism should be about.

## Risk and danger

There is a notion that some people in my field have a death wish. I think that is just rubbish.

Cameramen and still photographers have got to get out there in the front and get the pictures. Without the film there is no story. The camera can stand out because it can look like a machine gun or a bazooka so you are in a very, very dangerous situation, at times. And you are very aware of that walking up the road with a camera on your shoulder where a sniper could be waiting behind a tree thinking you are a soldier and shoot you.

Probably the greatest danger in war is your vulnerability, things you don't expect – it is not being shot at so much as it is stepping on a landmine or even being in the vicinity of a suicide bomber. What happened to us in El Salvador in 1982 is we were covering the elections there and we were coming back to San Salvador and we got stopped. I was there with the ABC reporter Jim Middleton. We had an interpreter, an American woman who was there for 'the good of the cause'. She was very young and bright but didn't know much about covering war, jabbering on about things she didn't understand. One of the men who stopped us pulled out a pistol and put it to the driver's head and another guy was across the road aiming an M16 rifle at us. I was watching as the interpreter was arguing in Spanish and saw that the man with the gun at the driver's head was getting more and more nervous.

The gunman then went around to the other side of the car and pointed the gun at Jim Middleton. I thought, 'Right, I am taking charge now; this is getting very serious – one wrong move and BANG …' So I said to the interpreter, 'What are you arguing about?' And she said, 'They are just common robbers; I told them I'm here for the revolution.' And I called out to her, 'Just shut up! You don't argue while guns are pointing at people's heads.' Most reporters in war zones carry US dollars with them and I always carried US$200 with me just in case I needed it for such situations. Eventually, I gave the gunmen the money and they let us go. As we took off down the road I found out Jim had a couple of thousand dollars on him. We had got away with only paying a couple of hundred dollars!

Sometimes in this work you are too nervous to think that you could get killed. I never think that I am risking my life. That comes later when you're back in your hotel. That sounds like Hemingway and I don't like to talk like a gung-ho cameraman – I am not – but I remember being pinned down once in Vietnam for about two hours in a foxhole with bullets flying over my head. It gave me time to think. There is a calmness that comes over you because there is absolutely nothing you can do. You can't control what is happening so you squeeze your body as small as you can and you just lie there for however long it takes, hoping nothing is going to hit you. When it stopped I ran up the road and got into a bigger foxhole. We all try to be calm and cool about what is happening around us but everybody experiences fear. Of course you do – we are only human. I will give you an example. In the war in Cambodia, every morning at six o'clock we would go up the road for an hour or two to see what was happening. The countryside always appeared calm, as if nothing was around. I would be in the car listening to a bit of music with an interpreter and a driver but we'd all be thinking that any moment now the other side could open up from anywhere or we could drive over a landmine. You can't help but feel incredibly tense and vulnerable in a situation like that. How do you cope with it? I don't know. Going back to the hotel and having a drink calms the nerves down, makes you forget it, but you know that tomorrow morning you are going to have to go and do it all again.

Fear is a physical feeling, very much so. The theatre of war is an appropriate phrase in the sense that the drama is all around you. War is incredibly powerful: the explosions; people's frightened faces; guns going off; the smell; all those ugly weapons; hand grenades and machine guns and tanks and knowing these are all designed to kill people. War is very hard to explain unless you've been there. You feel so vulnerable.

## Effects of the Job

I think things we see in our work can be very hard to live with. I once saw a Serb soldier kiss a twenty-five-pound round and then laugh before he fired it into Sarajevo to kill people. Dead bodies, suffering children, the plight of refugees can be very devastating to you, but it is not just the dead bodies, it is the overall picture of everything that really gets to you, and how desperate everything is.

I was in Yugoslavia when the Serbs captured two Croats, a doctor and a nurse, and held them in a military camp. This couple had turned left instead of turning right and they got picked up by the Serbs. The Serbs asked me if I wanted to see their captives and then they started to interrogate them. Do I film or do I not film? What is the right decision? I was on my own and there was no one to bounce my thoughts off. If there was a colleague there I could have said, 'What do you think we should do? What do you feel about this?' I filmed the interrogation but I felt very guilty filming it. The doctor and nurse were very scared. They were a very handsome young couple who weren't even fighting soldiers. It was a dreadful thing to witness because I had no power to stop the interrogation. When I left that camp I asked the commanding officer what would happen to these people and he said they would be exchanged for two Serb prisoners but whether they were or not I don't know . . . they were probably killed. So this sense of helplessness is always with you. Always.

I have been asked many times whether I have a sense that all I have seen is accumulating inside me. It is hard for me to answer that. I am very sensitive, even overly sensitive. I try not to be so sensitive but I get hurt over little things. People say that that is what has made me good at what I do – because I feel and care. But it is bloody painful to be oversensitive. It is horrible. It stops you in your tracks. It affects you tremendously. You get hurt so easily over little things that when put into perspective don't mean anything.

There is a lot of drinking in the television industry. Do you go back to your hotel room and sit there? No, you go down to the bar and talk and forget about what you have seen for a while – or try to forget about it. You just can't sit there dwelling on it so you have a few drinks to take the pain away. That is self-destructive, in my case. We all used to go to the bar because the nature of the work is that everyone congregates there to discuss ideas, stories. 'What do you know? Where did you go today? What was it like out there? Is it worth me going there tomorrow?' And so on and so on.

Other people drink more than I did but it doesn't seem to affect them the same way. I used to love having a drink in the bar and talking about what we did. It was terrific. I loved the comradeship dearly. The reason I stopped drinking was because it was affecting my life and the people around me. My drinking got to a stage where I thought I am not enjoying it like I used to. It took me a long time to wake up to it. You think that you can have one or two drinks but it doesn't work that way. I feel much better now for not having alcohol and, after time, you realise that you don't need it.

Seeing the things I have seen has made me more of an understanding person, and a bit more humble and thoughtful, and not so judgmental. You realise those places are hell but here, in our Western societies, we have all this bitchiness, people playing games and you think, does it really matter? We are only people passing through life. Let's just try to get on with each other and be a bit more thoughtful of one another. My experiences have also made me realise that I am a much stronger person than I had thought I was. I feel an inner strength. By going to all these hellholes over so many years it has made me a little more grateful and more understanding of other people.

In this work you make some wonderful friends as you go along. Some of the friends I have made in wars and tough places around the world are my friends to this day because we have gone through so much together. I might not see them all the time but there is an honest bond there, a trust.

## Frustration

There is no way of overcoming people's indifference to suffering in foreign places unless you take people there. The problem is they wouldn't want to go there. So we just keep on doing what we are doing, presenting stories so powerful that as they're sitting in their chairs at home they say, 'God, I have got to ring up and put in my protest about this.'

The way I try to move people is by filming hands, faces, eyes and mannerisms; that is what I like to do – capture the moment of people by touching their humanity that we can all relate to.

In 1971 I was in Vietnam doing an hour-long special for *Four Corners* on the ABC with Rob Sloss and Mike Willesee, which was really just a good look at people surviving the war. We went to film in a hospital and when I was there a little eight-year-old girl was brought in who had had her leg blown off in crossfire when she was three. Her parents had been killed and she and her brothers and sisters were living with their grandmother, and her grandmother used to carry her around on her back everywhere. She just happened to be there to be fitted with an artificial leg for the first time in her life. She was the most beautiful child but she had no expression and just kept staring at me as I was filming her – no emotion, nothing, during the whole fitting of the leg. The artificial leg was very primitive but at least it was something. When she was able to stand on the new leg and she started to walk, she began to smile slightly. She had her independence for the first time in her life. Just the contrast in her eyes as opposed to before – they were now glittering – when she got her balance was amazing. And I thought, 'God, if we could edit this film properly and explain what has happened to this little girl, this is more powerful footage than soldiers firing guns and bombs going off. Through this beautiful girl we have to show what those guns do to people: the hidden side of war, the destruction of the innocent.' This showed a lot of Vietnam – this sequence was an analogy for Vietnam; it was what war is all about. People still remember that little girl and the film is still being shown.

When we showed the film on TV I saw again how powerful television could be because the response the following week to the little girl's story was amazing. People were saying, 'What are we doing in Vietnam? Did you see that little girl?' All of that other footage of guns firing meant nothing compared to what they saw in this one little girl. And so I thought again how rewarding it was to do such amazing work. It feels really terrific when you have done a good story and it has an impact. It is a very satisfying feeling but that satisfaction only lasts for a short time. You feel that what you are doing is so important but in many ways it is just another story and the next day it is gone, forgotten, and you need to move on to the next one. It is very frustrating for me but it is not really anybody's fault – the public just gets on with its own life – but hopefully it might make us realise how lucky we are in Australia.

We can sit back here in Australia in the sunshine, so far away from troubles, we can play our golf or watch the football, and have a wonderful time. But as human beings we should be aware of what is going on in the world, and we in the media should show it. I think that when a reporter or photojournalist says he or she is trying to make a change they have got to believe it because there is power in that belief. There might be limitations to how much we can initiate change but if we keep going and make people aware of what is going on in the world then governments also might change things. That is what I have tried to do for the last forty years. I might be naïve, but I really believe that we can explain to people what is going on in the world.

It frustrates me though when you look back even to Vietnam to see that we, the so-called 'civilised world', haven't learnt from that disaster. I have always wondered and worried and been frustrated about why we haven't reflected on the repercussions of war before we get to that stage of going to war. There is something like forty-odd wars going on at the moment. As a 'civilised world' we can do everything else – we can even put somebody on the moon – but for some reason we can't stop killing each other. If we are meant to be so bright, with all our technology and our knowledge, why can't we stop going to war? No one can answer that question. I think I do, in a way, believe there is a god somewhere but I would like to know who he is when I see some of the dreadful things that have happened in our world, the horrible suffering.

There are some brilliant cameramen and reporters in the world who, while willing to risk their lives to show people what's really going on, don't get much thanks for it in the long run. I wish there was more understanding of their dedication. These are *very* brave people.

There are so many wonderful people and powerful stories in the world right now that are not being covered, particularly on human beings doing really good work – the unsung heroes, people like the Australian nurse in the Sudan and the Oxfam aid workers in Malawi. I would like to go back to some of these places (and I am beginning to do this now) and do some good, positive stories. I want to do filmwork that is special and can help to educate people.

## Adjusting to home

As a cameraman, when you come home here to Sydney you couldn't get a better contrast between some hellhole you've just been in to this place of sun and cleanliness where you can walk out in the street to have dinner at your favourite restaurant. I found it impossible to reconcile the differences between the two environments and so I found it hard to adjust to coming home because, for me, it takes a while to get over the drama of where I have been. Some people I know just get on with living back at home but I have never been able to easily because I get wound up in the injustices of life. You talk to somebody at home and they are not really interested so you get so frustrated you just shut up. I think you have got to have somebody that you can talk to, who has an interest in the world. That is why I like to be on my own a bit these days, or talk about where I have been and what I have seen with somebody I am close to, who will listen and understand, be on the same wavelength or at least who will appreciate what I care about. This is very important to me.

A bit of decency and respect from your bosses or peers is also important. You don't need to be told how good you are but now and then you need to have a cup of tea together and a thanks-very-much, a pat on the back. I would be a very good executive producer because I would care about my staff – my word I would. Every time that they came back from a trip I would take them out to a nice long lunch, talk it through, let them talk. That is really lacking in the industry. As a cameraman you are risking your life and in my own case I have probably gone to more wars than most people in this country . . . My point is that you have got to have an organisation that really cares about you, and provides a bit of support. We all need that; it is just a normal human need but you need it more if you are doing the work that we do.

## BALANCING WORK AND PERSONAL LIFE

You can never say that your work has been worth the sacrifice if you are divorced but if later on in life you can do something positive with the experiences you have had and the things you have witnessed then perhaps you can more readily accept the sacrifice. People say to me, 'Gee, Dave, it's amazing what you have done in your life.' But I don't see it that way. To me, my work has been like the best university course I could have done – being out in the world and living. You can travel around the world but you don't meet the people I have met or see the things I have seen unless you are in this profession where you are right in the heart of life. It is a privilege to be in a situation where history is being made: to have worked in the Middle East, in Africa, in El Salvador; to have been in East Berlin when the wall came down; to have been based in Moscow during Gorbachev's time; to have spent a few weeks with Idi Amin; to have witnessed the fall of Saigon; even to have been there when Australia won the America's Cup in 1983.

Basically though, as you get older, work and personal life begin to balance. For me, the balance started to change about six years ago. I remember being in Burma, which is a beautiful country. The light was lovely and it was peaceful, but I found I wasn't really happy. I was living out of a suitcase, I was in another hotel room, and I started to think, 'Do I really want this? I would like to have a bit of whatever is a "normal" life.' There are times I still feel I want to go and do things but I am not obsessed by needing to go to war now. I feel that there are other important values like, in my case, having a woman in my life, someone I can share with and have good conversations with. I wasn't ready for that commitment before but I am ready for it now. I have done my cadetship in life and I am not as ambitious as I used to be where work came first. No, I have done that. I want to reflect on it and do worthwhile stories that mean something.

## REFLECTIONS

If there was one piece of advice that I could give someone beginning in my profession it would be to be humble and thoughtful of the person you are filming. Don't just rush in there and take a picture or shoot film. Spend time with them, get to know them and find out what makes them tick. It is amazing, around the world people who have very little just invite you into their homes. Try to be a bit better, try to be a bit more understanding. That is what I have tried to do for the last forty years. And be passionate about what you are doing. Be passionate! It is no good going into photojournalism if you think that it is glamorous. A lot of people do go into it for that reason until they get out there and start working. It can be very dangerous work. But you need to really believe in it. If it is just a job you will never be much good at it and you will never achieve a great lot if you haven't got the passion.

Looking back on my life, I realise it has had some wonderful rewards and also some sadness. At my age now, I would like to be able to give back a lot of my experience to inspiring young filmmakers or journalists who would be willing to listen. I am very lucky to work for a great current-affairs program like *Dateline* on SBS that gives people like me opportunities to do stories that might help to educate viewers and really mean something. It is also a privilege to work with really brilliant, dedicated producers at *Dateline* like Mike Carey, Geoff Parish, Mark Davis, Martin Butler and Amos Cohen who consistently turn out valuable information from all around the world. Thank god in Australia we've got SBS and the ABC, two great public broadcasters.

I know I'm repeating myself but TV is so powerful that it should be used properly. I don't think I have done enough. I say to myself that I should be able to sit back and feel a bit more content within myself but I am very hard on myself because I try to be a perfectionist . . . Well, maybe I need to admit to myself that I've done a little bit with my life. I want to continue trying to show through my filmmaking what's really going on in the world because television is *so* powerful.

# CHAPTER 5

# PETER CHARLEY

### Biography

PETER CHARLEY BEGAN WORKING as a cadet at the *Sydney Morning Herald* in 1974 and has since worked for public and commercial radio and TV in both the US and Australia, including National Public Radio, Fox Television, SBS's *Dateline*, Channel Seven and Channel Nine. He has covered conflict throughout Latin and Central America, Africa and Asia.

Peter has won a number of awards in Australia and overseas for his investigative reporting and documentary work, including the John Hopkins University's SAIS-Novartis Award for Outstanding International Journalism in 2001, a New York Film Festival Medal for *Shadows and Whispers* and two Walkley Awards for excellence in journalism, including the documentary *On Life's Border – the Plight of North Korea's Refugees*.

Today he is executive producer of the ABC's *Lateline*. Peter lives in Sydney and is married with one child.

\* \* \*

*Peter Charley*

## Story

We had been filming in Cambodia in 1991 and had been up to the front lines, the northern areas beyond the town of Battambang, with the Cambodian military which was fighting the Khmer Rouge. We were the only team of journalists who got that far into the battle zone and had come back to the capital to finish filming in some of the nearby killing fields. We travelled about half an hour out of Phnom Penh to the largest of many of Cambodia's killing fields – literally slaughter-yards in the countryside where people were herded, butchered and buried in mass graves. In these particular killing fields there were large piles of human skulls stacked neatly together as a kind of monument to the dead. This has become a kind of enduring image of Cambodia's tragedy – giant sculptures made from the remains of the Khmer Rouge victims. There really hadn't been much of an effort made to remove many of the other human remains from the pits into which the bodies had been dumped. We could still see clothes, ribs, leg bones, vertebrae, the remains of hands and feet. Each of the mass graves had been marked with simple signs like '52 headless bodies' or '75 children'. I remember there was a tree there called 'the infant's tree'. It's where babies were slaughtered by having their heads smashed against the trunk. This happened in front of the mothers, I'm told, so you can just imagine the darkest horrors that were witnessed there. It was hideous.

As part of our filming we decided to take a look at the infamous detention centre, or torture chamber, called Tuol Sleng (now called the Tuol Sleng Genocide Museum) through which a number of the killing field's victims had earlier been 'processed'. The torture centre had once been a high school that was taken over by the Khmer Rouge in May 1975 and converted into a detention centre a year later. It was just a lovely old French colonial building with classic, high ceilings, very airy and quite simple architecturally, but the cruelty that had taken place in these rooms was utterly appalling. People were brought there and kept in cages made of chicken wire that had been built in a couple of the classrooms. Other classrooms had been set aside as torture chambers. In the first year it held over 2500 prisoners. Most of them were tortured to death.

When Cambodia was 'liberated' by the Vietnamese they came upon this torture centre and they had – to their credit, I guess – recorded and documented everything photographically and left it just as they had found it. They removed the bodies but they really didn't ever alter it in any other way at all. So it has remained a sort of living memorial to the ghastly atrocities that occurred there.

What we saw there was devastating. Imagine a typical high-school classroom with an iron-bed frame in the centre of the room and on the wall a photograph of how the Vietnamese had found it, including the bed frame with a disfigured body on it. Now imagine the blood splatters around the room. That's how the room was left. We found bloodstains on the floor, blood on the walls – even up on the high ceilings. It makes you wonder what the hell happened in there. The poor souls whose lives were taken in that room must have suffered the most sickening, miserable deaths. In the courtyard of the building there was an insane list of rules the prisoners had to obey. They had been painted on a board in Khmer and English. One of the regulations read: 'While getting lashes or electrocution you must not cry at all.' Another read: 'You must immediately answer my questions without wasting time to reflect.' Then we came across the implements of torture the killers had used on the prisoners: household tools like screwdrivers, hammers, pliers and saws.

They'd been laid out in one of the rooms – like an ordinary, suburban garden shed. Prisoners' limbs were cut off with saws and their eyes gouged out with screwdrivers. There was something in the horror of those everyday tools being used in that way that still remains with me. It is one of the most haunting and disgusting places I have ever been.

For some reason, the Khmer Rouge was meticulous about photographing and keeping records of its crimes – I can only suggest it was because it wanted to record its new beginning. They'd gone to a lot of effort to keep a photographic record of everyone who entered Tuol Sleng. These photos were still there, plastered on a wall. It was tragic, really, to see all those faces. It was haunting and sad and pathetic. Many of the people who'd been photographed seemed to be quite perplexed by the whole process, some were even smiling at the camera, obviously not aware of just where they were or what was about to happen to them. Many of these people were then photographed after they'd been tortured to death. The 'before' photographs showed pretty young women, some smiling at the camera, others looking at the lens as if they were wondering what was going on; the 'after' photographs were of the same faces horrifically disfigured by torture.

I think the most surreal and disturbing aspect of my visit there was the final room we visited where photographs were displayed of the torturers themselves. After seeing what had happened to the prisoners, I suppose I'd built up in my mind an image of the monsters who'd committed these crimes. I expected to see depraved, hard-faced brutes. In fact, the torture-killers were angelic, young boys – pretty-faced children, really. For me, that was the most chilling aspect of the whole thing; it was just very hard to come to terms with. How could it be that such apparently innocent people could be twisted to perform such acts of depravity? I expect the brainwashing and the pressures of that contorted moment in history had turned them. I think that there is evidence in many war-torn or 'revolutionary' scenarios of people turning against their better instincts, perhaps too easily, shifting into the darker side of humanity. There is something intensely and profoundly disturbing about being in those sorts of environments that is very difficult to reconcile, thinking about an individual caged in a dark room, listening to others being tortured, thinking to themselves 'I probably won't get out of here', and then being led into the torture chamber to face such suffering. I don't know what happened to the torturers of Tuol Sleng. I think they would have just melted back into the crowd.

I was at Tuol Sleng with the cameraman David Brill and a field producer, Nick Farrow, and, at one point when we were walking around, someone came up to me and spoke and I said, 'I can't talk just now. I just need to be in silence . . .' I felt I had to be alone in this ghastly place to absorb the enormous, black energy of it all. It was a little bit like being in someone's very personal, very private space – it seemed irreverent to talk. It almost seemed sacrilegious to impose normalcy on such an abnormal place. It was like being in a different dimension – I guess that's the best way to describe it.

I was reminded there of once walking through a village in Guatemala that had been wiped out by death squads who had gone through and killed absolutely every living thing: man, woman, child, dog, cat, chicken. Everything. I remember having a similar sense of being so deeply shifted from my normal axis by the monstrosities that had occurred in that town. It took some days to move on from the images there. In that sort of scenario it seems almost as if the atmosphere has been bruised by the violence. I get this feeling, like at the scene of a fatal car crash, where it is almost as if there has been an injury to the fabric of the atmosphere or something, and that is how I felt at Tuol Sleng. It is as if everything has been ripped and crunched up and distorted and so completely fucked up by what has happened. I imagine, although I have never been to the old concentration camps of Nazi Germany, that they must have the same feeling about them: evil has descended and imprinted itself here.

After that day at Tuol Sleng, I went back to the hotel room in Phnom Penh with David and Nick and we talked about it. It was obvious that we were all burdened by what we'd seen. The only way I can describe how the mind tries to adjust to this sort of experience is that it's a bit like watching the video of the time the second plane hit the World Trade Center, the feeling of 'I cannot believe that I am looking at this'. It just doesn't make sense in the frames of reference by which we measure our normal lives. And that was a bit how I felt looking at this old, converted high school, a place of learning where children would once have played, where there once would have been laughter and hope and all the perfectly normal things that kids go through – you know, high-school crushes and dreams of the future. It is inconceivable that the ghastly tortures, the disfigurements, the electrocutions, the floggings, the lynchings, the drownings, the amputation of limbs, the mutilations, the unspeakable atrocities, happened there. And yet they did. I think none of us, when we returned to our hotel rooms that night, slept particularly easily.

When you see that kind of thing and you think about it for a while, you begin to go through all the usual human imaginings – what must it have been like to have been strapped to that bed? What must it have been like to hear those screams or sobs or pleadings, knowing that your turn was next? How does the human mind process that horror? And what about the torturers? How could they have brought themselves to do it? Surely they must have been under threat of death themselves. What sort of cruel fanaticism or madness drove the leaders to impose such threats on people to carry out such atrocities? How can a whole people be persuaded to abandon human goodness and compassion and kindness – the tendencies that make up our so-called civilised society? How can a whole group of people defy that and do such things to each other? There are no real answers.

## Beginnings

I was working on the Fairfax newspapers in Sydney in the mid-seventies and was selected as part of a small group of journalists to be schooled in all aspects of media. As it turned out, I went into television and that was where I had this sense of just how wonderful it was to capture dramatic images. I think that triggered my thoughts of, 'Well, let's just see how dramatic these images can be.' I was only quite young and I decided to take off and see what else I could gather out there – go to extremes.

I was living and working in New York City where I had gone to basically pursue journalism in a bigger arena than Australia. At the time, the one big story was the civil war in El Salvador, which was tearing the country to pieces. I was very curious to know what it was all about so I went down to take a look at my first war. There were terrible things occurring every day in the city of San Salvador. Journalists were being frightened off from covering certain aspects of this conflict by scare tactics and extreme acts of violence. Tortured bodies were being dumped in the streets – awfully disfigured. The anti-reporter brigade was saying 'beware' and the reporters had a bit of a joke about this. T-shirts were sold with pictures of a whole lot of guns aimed at someone's head and the words in Spanish were, 'Don't shoot, I am a journalist' and all the journalists were wearing these around.

I wouldn't really call myself a 'war correspondent' but more an observer of these moments in history. I've dipped into them briefly, catching moments in the conflict. I witnessed a sort of rhythm that pulses through these situations – long moments of calm and brief moments of tension. That is just something that you don't learn about until you are there. Waves of tension and fear roll over certain situations, these almost palpable, visceral waves of anguish and stress that just surge through certain areas, and then things return to normal again. This is a very bizarre thing.

## SURVIVING IN WAR

When it looks as if things are going to turn ugly I find myself thinking 'I wish I wasn't here' and then 'Why the hell am I doing this?' I can think of a couple of instances when I have thought, 'If I just get out of here alive, *this* is the last time! I'll never, ever take this risk again.' Fear is like a punch in the guts – it's a blunt, cold, clawing feeling. But when it's over, there is such a great sense of relief, a sort of counterbalance high: 'I got through it and wasn't it amazing?!' Sometimes it is hard to come down from the high. You sit around having a few drinks with others who have been through the same thing and there is a real bond. There is a hell of a lot of hard drinking that goes on. Johnnie Walker Black is a friend to almost everyone at times like that.

I think it's pretty clear that some people get hooked on those feelings – surviving danger. There's something in the thrill of those moments that tempts some of us to repeat them. It's like 'this danger *thrills* me. It *changes* me. I *like* it like this. I want more of it. More and more of it.' Then it becomes 'when I'm not feeling this I'm no longer me . . .' I found throughout

Guatemala, El Salvador and Nicaragua that I kept running into the same reporters who had been on the war correspondents' trail for a long time and it worried me a bit that I might become like that too – addicted to the thrill, wanting more of the risk. I guess I'm lucky that I've always had relatively fleeting contact with these environments. Just in and out, really – a very transitory kind of exposure. So I've not really experienced enough full-on, full-time violence or conflict exposure for the addiction element to have taken hold, but still, at times, I could feel that I was at the edge of becoming like that. I recall that 'tug' in San Salvador during the El Salvador civil war. I used to drink at a bar downtown where everyone 'checked in' their guns at the door. I found that very bizarre and cool in a strange sort of way and thought then that a guy could get used to this life; you know, blood on the streets, hard living, good friends who might not be alive tomorrow. I thought I probably should start withdrawing from this world a bit so I don't become sucked into it and have it control me rather than me being able to dip in and out of it.

## Camaraderie, respect and pushing the limits

One of the very attractive elements of life in hot-spots is the camaraderie that develops when people are grouped together in a difficult, tense situation. It's always interesting to see how people perform under those conditions. Certain people emerge as cool-headed leaders, certain people lose it, certain people are helpful, and certain people aren't – that's just human nature. Good and bad are magnified under duress. There is definitely a sense of respect and, in some cases, lack of respect, basically related to the level or degree of experience of the journalist or combat correspondent. One learns to respect the very experienced, calm operator who has been there, done it all, and is able to offer guidance and advice but I don't know if I would always necessarily feel safer working with those types of people. You never know whether one risk is one risk too many.

The Neil Davises of this world have everyone's respect because they weren't afraid to push it that extra mile. (If you have read Tim Bowden's book about his life, *One Crowded Hour*, with its macabre accounts of eating liver of the dead enemy soldiers, obviously you realise that sort of behaviour is not something that most people could even comprehend.) But Davis, probably Australia's most famous war photojournalist, was able to cross the line, I guess, because he had become so close and so deeply ingrained in the fibre of the war and its aftermath. And that transformation is something that one can only respect, because it is evidence of such complete understanding, of such absolute conviction. That's pretty amazing and certainly very impressive, but you wouldn't necessarily go into war with Neil. The irony, of course, is that he was killed in a situation that everyone considered to be so relatively 'safe'. But that says so much about risk and chance and danger. There are never any certainties.

People need each other and rely on each other's information and knowledge. If there are two people, one can watch the other's back. I was briefly in East Timor in 1999 when things were getting messy. Our reporter, David O'Shea, had persuaded the Aitarak militia leader, Eurico Guterres, to let us film him and his men in his bunkered compound, which was a rare and interesting privilege. The whole scene there was totally weird. Guterres' men were half drunk most of the time, killers in a dirty war – one minute the hunters, the next minute the hunted. They were angry and hurt and all muscled-up with a sense of defending the rights of the motherland, Indonesia. They were operating in a place where law and decency had been corrupted by the circumstances of the civil conflict; everything was warped by this nationalistic fervour. It was like 'anything goes as long as it serves our purpose...' Some days these militia thugs would take hits and then there'd be the terrible revenge attacks. Eurico had given his approval for us to be there with him, but we were never quite sure whether his men were going to turn on us. It was that kind of moment – everything was upside down.

In that instance, correspondents who were not in the compound and who would have had good reason to be resentful of us having got the lucky break were still good enough to keep us in the loop in terms of warning us against danger saying, 'Be careful, we've heard there's going to be a raid.' So camaraderie is born out of those sorts of moments and is one of the most important things of all in our job. To some extent, these friendships travel home but in time they sort of drift off a bit, I think. There are some people I have shared some very heavy moments with and I have this extraordinary bond with them. We will always have these memories of what we have been through together but we don't necessarily get together every Saturday afternoon and relive it.

That thing people say about journalists in war fighting and fucking one another is also totally true. It is a very potent emotional human moment when people are thrown together and relationships just become fused. People think this might be our last night together and let's just have fun, let's party.

## Finding the balance

When I am on the phone to home it is just so difficult. The last thing I want to do is freak out my wife, Clare. I have been to a couple of assignments where I haven't really wanted to reveal to Clare just exactly what it was I was going to do because it would be so stressful for her, which would make it even more stressful for me. It is a real dilemma knowing what level of ignorance to leave someone in. For example, when I was on that assignment with Eurico Guterres I couldn't talk to Clare about it on the phone. For a start, Intel (the Indonesian military intelligence) was monitoring the calls so I didn't want to reveal too much to these goons, but at the same time I didn't want to trouble Clare. Is that fair? Is that unfair? I mean, what do you say – 'I'm hanging out with a bunch of pumped-up killers and it's all very unstable'? You don't want to pass on that sort of thing. Clare learns about it all in time, though.

There are a couple of friends who have been through similar things that I catch up with over a few drinks, and I have a very dear friend in New York whom I often talk to when I feel the need to get something off my chest. But I don't really talk to people too much about what I have seen or done. There was a time, though, when I did want to talk about all the things that were troubling me but I found that most people didn't really want to know. I'd talk about the ugly side of the job and some people would be almost offended or turned off. I don't necessarily share my experiences with too many people these days. I'd rather not volunteer the sort of information at a dinner party like, 'Hey, this is the anniversary of when I saw someone shot in the head.' If people ask me I will tell them but I would rather not volunteer the information.

I remember once asking my grandfather who fought in the Somme what it was like. He said, 'It was terrible,' and that was all he would give. I used to wonder why he wouldn't just get it off his chest and say, 'Well, now that you ask . . .' I kind of relate to that now and think that it is just easier not to go into the details.

There does seem to be this dichotomy between life at home and the job. It's hard to know how to switch between the two lives but it is almost as if you have to be a different person because war or combat is such an alien environment. It is not the safe warm home where you are not likely to get hurt and everything is ordered and calm and gentle. It is precisely the reverse – unpredictable, hostile, aggressive, an environment where anything can happen and one just has to think, feel and be different. I think lots of people might grapple with it because carrying the same persona from home into the other life or type of existence can be dangerous or fatal. So it is quite an art, or a skill, to shift from one existence to the other, although I found it is quite easy to shift from home into the field. There is something about stepping off the plane in a different environment. It is almost like you can live out some other side of your life. But it is quite hard coming home.

I often get a feverish sickness and Clare and I can't figure out what causes it. It throws me into bed and I can do nothing but lie there for a couple of days. Clare has seen me struggle with getting back into this life at home again, especially when I have come back from difficult assignments – not necessarily very dangerous ones but ones where I have been exposed to high stress or scenes of death. For instance, up in Papua New Guinea in 1998 I was doing some documentary work for the Discovery Channel and a tsunami hit. There were several hundred bodies trapped in a lagoon that the health authorities weren't able to retrieve. The government had just sealed off the lagoon as a 'no-go' zone to let the bodies rot, to just let nature take its course. We got special permission to enter this 'no-go' area to film the devastation and we were in a motorboat churning through these fetid, bloated bodies in the water, which was absolutely horrendous. It was like being in hell in the forty-degree heat. I remember coming back from that and it took me a long time to settle back into life at home again.

I don't know why it is harder coming home than going out into the field. Maybe it's because you steel yourself to shift into an assignment and once you're there you're straight into it. When you come home there are so many memories and feelings associated with the assignment that are hard to shake off. Once I settle back into the gentler environment of home I often find myself haunted by the aftershock of what I've been through. Sometimes I look at the very bland environment here in Sydney and it just seems so colourless, washed out and passionless, even though in many ways it is lovely and almost Utopia . . .

Sometimes, when I'm under extreme stress on assignment, I prefer not to reflect on the sanity of home. It can interrupt my focus; the contrast can be disturbing with the memory of home exacerbating the difficulties in the field. I remember at the scene of that tsunami we pulled over to the side of the lagoon and got out of the boat to film from the shore. I was standing there with the thought: 'Wouldn't it be lovely just to be sitting in the Botanic Gardens with my wife and little son, sipping a glass of wine?' And beside me a dog was eating the rotting flesh of a young boy who'd died in the tidal wave. The juxtaposition of that thought and that scene was pretty overpowering.

## GOOD JOURNALISM AND COVERING WAR

Journalism is part of the act of recording history while holding out to the public the possibility of changing what is wrong. So I don't think there is anything unethical about journalists trying to set a social agenda when it is patently obvious that something really bad is going on. It would be a challenge to place 'balance' on a report about the Rwandan massacres, for example, or about the struggle by the peasants of Zimbabwe to overcome repression at the hands of Robert Mugabe. Sure, journalists can tell both sides of the story, but in some conflicts there are clearly defined lines of good versus evil, or the oppressed versus the oppressors. Providing a deeper history sometimes gives context to such conflicts – the oppressors may have once been oppressed themselves.

In a war there are many who try to hide the truth and one of the great skills of journalism is trying to peel back the many layers of deceit. So the ideal war correspondent is someone who is able to break through the fear, get into the real guts of a crisis, and put their prejudices aside to just report on what is going on as dispassionately as possible. Having said that, I don't know if it is truly possible to be utterly dispassionate because when you are with one side and see the terrible suffering that is being inflicted on that side, you tend to sympathise with the plight of those people and share their emotions. I certainly don't have a problem with telling a story slanted one way – or portraying it through the prism of one perspective only – as long as it is made clear at the very beginning with a sort of disclaimer like 'this is one side of the conflict as seen through the eyes of one reporter . . .' That can be a very powerful reporting tool. But there are other more balanced styles of storytelling where a journalist will make a genuine effort to tell it from both sides. There's merit to both ventures.

It's difficult not to feel like a voyeur at times, working as a reporter. It is awkward but the job calls for us to step into situations that can perhaps be perceived by some people as intrusive and insensitive. There's no doubt that sensitivities of other people can be part of the collateral damage of journalism. There will always be some who might try to stand in the way of the story, who might view journalism poorly, and some people involved in the situation being reported upon might feel offended, hurt, annoyed or pissed off, but that's just the way it is sometimes. The fact of the matter is that reporters are there to document war, to document history, and that is what has to be remembered. So if a story is there to be got then one just has to get it.

To some extent I do feel judged because of my job – sometimes harshly. It really gives me the shits when reporters are judged as a pack of hyenas preying on misfortune. Sure, misfortune is part of what we record, but often that comes in a context of trying to find the truth of a situation and to report as clearly, rationally and honestly as possible. I think people who hold that view are missing what it's all about. They don't want reporters digging for the truth, but they expect the news to be accurate. That's the galling part of it all – the people who condemn reporters hunger for news as much as anyone. News is that kind of commodity. It's a necessity. Everyone wants it.

## Censorship

When I was younger I was far more radical in what I thought television should be permitted to show. I thought we should broadcast every detail of war in the most graphic form – blood, guts, the whole shocking mess . . . that is, after all, a lot of what war is all about. But after years in the media I've changed my mind on that. I now think that the views I had when I was much younger were, in many ways, as arrogant as the people who say, 'I don't think that we should put anything graphic to air at all.' When making these decisions, you need to determine where arrogance stops and genuine responsibility begins. It is a blurry line. But there needs to be a balance because graphic imagery can be a little like pornography – too much detail can be offensive to some people – and then you risk alienating an important audience.

It's important to tell the truth, but there's a power in the 'evocative' treatment of certain scenarios that can hit home harder than the 'full-frontal' treatment. A shot of a woman weeping over her dead daughter's bloodstained doll or bloodstained bed sheets can be more heart-wrenching and in some ways says more than a shot of the dead girl herself. So the subtleties are important, along with the hard-core. I wouldn't want our editors on *Lateline* to trim away all the graphic imagery of, say, the suicide bombings in Israel and just have a wide shot of a mangled bus. It is important for the audience to see the human damage, but selecting the right proportion of the horror vision is where 'fine judgment' comes in. It's not always easy to get the balance right.

With regard to the photo of the little girl in Basra with her feet shredded [see picture section], at *Lateline* we didn't have access to that photograph because it was a still image and I can only suggest that the newspaper editors who cropped that shot did so because they didn't want to offend by having something too violent in the newspaper. I don't necessarily agree with that decision because I think that is editorialising – perhaps straying too far in sanitising that moment in the war. If that image had come to me in video form I would probably have wanted it to go to air, although it depends on how the image would have been portrayed in video. If the camera panned from the little face down to the feet it could be exceptionally powerful. Yes, if that had been on video I think that I would have shown it.

There are broad rules and guidelines, in terms of the types of imagery that can go to air, on the ABC in relation to time slots. At certain times of day viewers have the right to feel secure that certain images will not appear and there are certain times of day when I think that viewers should be prepared to see more adult content. We wouldn't want imagery like the photo of the little girl being broadcast in the morning because there is a tendency for people to put their kids in front of the television at that time of day. We wouldn't broadcast imagery that was too graphic to someone sitting around the dinner table in the evening either. But, other than those time constraints, these decisions are up to the executive producers. So for the adult audience, if they are watching after 10.30 at night, I think that it is acceptable to have that sort of imagery (with a warning preceding it). In fact, I think that it is desirable because it shows just how ugly that particular war, that conflict, is becoming.

On the whole, I think people probably don't see enough of what war is really like because there is a tendency to over-sanitise war. Yet, for anyone who is seriously interested in what is going on, the Internet and the wider access it gives to overseas news coverage means that everything is out there. At the same time there has always been, and will always be, people who take their chief source of information from the extreme tabloids with the histrionics and the rhetoric that accompanies those kinds of news vehicles. Possibly those people could change their views if you could reach them but it is very hard to get through the firewalls they have around them.

## LEGACY OF THE JOB

I have been in and out of so many places so quickly that it is sort of a blessing *and* a curse. There are certainly moments and images of appalling things that haunt me: the aftermath of very violent moments; what has happened to people when they have been tortured; torture chambers; the terrible suffering from landmines. I remember in Cambodia looking at the many, many people who had lost their legs by stepping on landmines . . . I find that sort of thing very hard to lock away in my mind and I know I won't forget such images. In the end though, I think one does became hardened and images like that – the pain and the suffering – become less shocking, less gut-wrenching. Over-exposure does that to all of us. Sometimes, looking at the graves of those killed in battle, I think, 'Who have you left behind?' or 'I just hope you died quickly' and the hardening evaporates for a moment.

I remember being beaten up badly by some military thugs in Chile. I had received a warning that Pinochet's people were monitoring my reports and didn't like them. A fellow who worked for the local telephone company called me one morning and said, 'You need to know that your phone calls are being monitored and the military doesn't like what it's hearing. Watch out or they'll come around and break your arms.' It was very brave of him – and very good of him – to take that chance to warn me. I thought about it and decided to stay and keep reporting. About three days later some guys came around to my hotel and beat me up. I was pretty badly hurt. I got out after that and followed the story from a different location, moving around a lot. They never got me again, but it wasn't a particularly comfortable assignment.

When I was younger I was much more keen to get as close as I could to the action – something was driving me to get totally into it – but that has changed a bit over time. Clare used to get very, very distressed and unhappy when I went away in case I didn't come back. So I began to feel much less inclined to get as close to the action and now that I have a little boy everything feels different. I have moved on to a different phase. It definitely has made me reassess the level of danger that I want to expose myself to. I think that Clare has saved me, actually, from taking any more very serious risks – at least for the moment.

I suppose there is some truth in the general perception that war correspondents are flawed characters but I don't think all are 'damaged'. There is something very deep and odd and strange about the desire of correspondents to subject themselves to extreme doses of fear and threat. But fear and threat are only part of the picture. This type of reporting also takes in heroism, courage and triumph – the good and the bad of humanity, the essence of all that we loathe and admire. One sees the extreme range of emotion and human behaviour displayed in this arena and I think this is what people find intriguing and attractive about it all. As well as being repulsive and abhorrent, it can be enlightening – even inspiring. But perhaps the most outstanding thing is the compassion and dignity and courage that emerge through the crucible of war. They are the things that stay with me. They will always stay with me.

So no, I don't think that I am 'damaged' from the job . . . knocked around a bit, perhaps . . . a bit bruised in a way that is very difficult to define. But OK. Yeah, just fine.

# CHAPTER 6

# MARIE COLVIN

## BIOGRAPHY

An American national, Marie Colvin reports for the London *Sunday Times*, which she joined in 1986 as its Middle East correspondent. She has reported from some of the most dangerous conflicts zones around the world including Chechnya, Zimbabwe, Libya, Lebanon, Israel, the Palestinian Occupied Territories, Iran, Iraq, Yemen, Kosovo, Sri Lanka and East Timor. In 2001 she was shot by the Sri Lankan military and lost her eye after being the first journalist in six years to spend time with the Tamil Tigers. Marie is probably best known as the woman who stayed behind in the UN compound in Dili, East Timor, in 1999 and whose broadcast shamed the UN into returning to rescue the people it had abandoned.

She has received a number of awards including best foreign correspondent in the British Press Awards in 2001 for her 'unfailing bravery', the Courage in Journalism Award in

2000 from the International Women's Media Foundation, and she shared the 2001 Woman of the Year title in Britain.

Marie's ex-husband, Patrick Bishop (also a correspondent), relayed an amusing anecdote about her from the Albanian-Kosovo border in 1999. Believing her to be in danger, he attempted to form an armed escort to aid a rescue attempt. Asking another reporter where he might find such fellows in the local town, he was advised that if anyone knew how to organise a trip into dangerous territory it was Marie Colvin whom he could find in a bar down the road.

Marie is single and lives in London.

\* \* \*

## Story

The East Timorese people had just voted for independence in 1999 and the UN said it would protect them. What the UN actually did was just outrageous.

I was on the last plane into East Timor and I remember getting off with only two other people as the first wave of journalists leaving East Timor boarded. Within hours of the vote taking place the militias had gone on a rampage and there were fires all over Dili. It was a very extreme situation and we had endless conversations about whether to stay or not. Then the main hotel, where the other journalists were, was shot up. That resulted in my first decision to stay because I believe that what you do as a journalist is bear witness and then hope that what you are seeing can make a difference – that you can stop the madness somehow if you can create enough outrage.

The militias then overran the Red Cross centre and came into our hotel and shot it up, knowing journalists were there. At that point, we were evacuated to the UN compound, which was an unarmed mission. Sniper shots were coming in and we didn't know if the compound was going to be overrun like every other UN post in the country.

Subsequently, the UN made the decision to evacuate the compound in two stages. The first stage involved the twenty-three journalists who had previously been evacuated from the hotel and all non-essential UN staff and their families. About eighty of the essential international staff needed to run the compound were to be left behind for a planned second evacuation. Fifteen hundred East Timorese women and children whose men had gone to the hills were to be left in the compound, but everywhere else in East Timor locals like these had been slaughtered when the UN international staff left so it was clear what was going to eventually happen to them after the UN left.

Because there were some very brave UN people who felt the way I felt and did not want to evacuate, even though the decision had already been made for them in New York, there were endless discussions about whether or not we should leave in the second evacuation. During this time there was an interesting kind of human dynamic happening with the most worried people being the military types who had been seconded to the UN but who were weaponless. It seems that these big guys, who were used to carrying a gun and were now unarmed in the face of armed people, were the most worried and were the people who wanted to evacuate. I remember talking to a sort of political guy there who said, 'Well, it is us dweebs who are being the bravest.' Those of us not used to having the protection of a gun were willing to take more risks. Interesting.

Yet, in the end, I don't think that you ever question someone else's decision. As far as I was concerned, I had been sleeping next to these people; I had been getting rice from them for four or five days; I had been getting their stories from them and so just spending this time with them built in me the feeling that I could not leave them. How could I walk out? I can live with nightmares about being shot but I would not be able to live with the nightmare of knowing I had left that compound and in any way could have done something. In a way it was a hard decision because I had to say, 'I could die here,' but, equally, I just didn't feel that I could live with myself if I left. Everyone in that compound knew that as soon as the last of us went out that door the East Timorese people we left behind were going to be killed. To leave was not a decision I could have made. Luckily, I had quite a few UN people who were supporting my decision and I was hidden during that first evacuation. Though I still remember the sinking feeling as I watched my colleagues and most of the UN people and their families being evacuated on two trucks.

There could be no underestimating the danger. The Indonesian army was supposedly protecting the compound but, in actual fact, they were hand in hand with the militia and within hours of the first evacuation the militia were coming over the walls and then retreating – they hadn't worked themselves up enough into a bloodlust to kill Westerners. At the same time it wasn't possible to escape the compound because on the first night a number of women and the few men who were still there had tried to get out up the back hill in the dark and the militias – and the army, although we could never prove that – started sniping these people and their bodies started rolling back down the hill. Max Stahl [see chapter 18] went out that first night with these East Timorese and joined up with the rebels who were a couple of days' walk away but people stopped trying to escape after that.

Oh god, it was a nightmare. Within the compound it was very, very basic living and I was sleeping outside on the ground, cannibalising everything. One night it would be rations left behind, another night it would be rice with some family in terror. With me, there were two other journalists: Minka Nyhuis, a stringer for Dutch radio, and Irene Slegt, a Dutch woman stringing for the BBC. We just worked completely together. We were sharing food and we looted. All the diplomats who had been evacuated from the compound had only been allowed to take one handbag so one day we went into their store of luggage and we opened up suitcases with crowbars and just looted whatever was in them. (Later, when I had been able to go back to my hotel after the militia overran it, I found these crazed machete-wearing militia had looted all my La Perla underwear and left behind my flak jacket!).

Anyway, it was a very basic level of living: this little sea of families cooking and washing clothes; really quiet; no music; all extremely nervous; everybody watching you, leaving little watchers in their families because they felt that those of us left behind might evacuate at any moment. I noticed that whenever I walked through the compound carrying anything everyone would get agitated because they thought I was leaving. They knew that if the international people left they had no protection. We were like human shields. So our presence, even though we were unarmed, was some kind of protection, albeit a sort of mythical one.

There was a contrast between a strange normality in the compound – people washing clothes and cooking – and waves of semi-assaults. What eventually became clear to me was that the militiamen were trying to terrify us rather than kill us – some kind of line they weren't yet stepping over. The idea was to terrify the international staff into an evacuation rather than killing them.

I had a satellite phone and so I was broadcasting because it was the only way we could get the news out. The story broke and there was a lot of enthusiasm within the compound, a feeling that we were not forgotten. I had CNN calling and the Australian ABC, even the American terrestrial stations. What I tried to do was report what was going on to anyone who would listen. It was one of the times as a journalist I did have an impact and it goes to the issue of objectivity. I wasn't just recording gunshots coming in; I was reporting that the UN decision was wrong. Just being able to channel my fears and sense of impending disaster into some passionate, but equally dispassionate, recounting of what was going on was a release, to be able to get it down to really basic levels of 'these people are going to die'.

Eventually the UN staff and civilian police in the compound waiting for the second evacuation formed a protest delegation to Ian Murray, the head of the compound, and we told him he had to change his opinion. And then the great moment when he announced that the decision had been changed in New York and that every single person in the compound would be evacuated. It wasn't like a cheer or anything; it was just this sigh of relief that we could hear throughout the compound.

Just before dawn, while it was still pitch black, we were loaded into open lorries. There was a lot of fear because many of the people had never gone in a truck, much less a plane. Then one of the last people, a local Timorese who had been trying to help the other people get on, had a heart attack and died. There was nothing we could do. We couldn't take the body into Australia so we had to leave him behind in that compound where we had just all lived together for ten days. It was dreadful. Someone said a little prayer over him and we drove out with the awful image of having left the body lying there in the middle of the compound. I still remember that unnerving drive through the nightmare around us: every house and building was burning. It was like driving through hell. It was about an hour or a bit less to the airport and we didn't know if the militia would come or not so we were all watching for anything to come out of the darkness at any moment. Everyone's adrenaline was really up. I had taken this grandmother with me who was terrified: an ancient old lady who had never been in a car. I was entirely bruised on the ribcage by the time I got to Australia because she was holding me so tightly. I remember stepping into Darwin, Australia, was like stepping into another world where it was sunny and people were walking around and going into restaurants. It was a moment of re-entry shock.

A lot of stuff we do as journalists is incremental and I have witnessed much more extreme things. But the way I look at East Timor is that it had an outcome that I could be proud of. We made a fundamental difference, which happens so rarely.

## GETTING STARTED

In terms of everything from history to what really goes on in the world, there is a difference between theoretical knowledge that you learn at a university or read in a book and actually going somewhere like the West Bank or Chechnya. But I think that my American upbringing was probably, in a way, a good background because I do have a very strong sense of justice. I did not set out with any grand ideas of being able to change the world but I get quite impassioned about injustice in the world.

There are various ways to get started in my profession. I don't think journalism school is particularly useful, other than a place to make contacts. I started on the wire service just doing the journalist's version of boot camp, just turning out stories in New York and working my way up. The other way is to just go out somewhere awful where there are very few staff people and start writing, which is how Maggie O'Kane* started, so it is completely reputable instead of doing all the shit work. But that sort of thing is getting increasingly dangerous because rules are changing. If you don't know the rules, you get killed.

One of the rules I have for myself is not to travel in packs. I believe that if there are ten of you then you are not really making your own decisions because you think that if eight people are going to go then that decision must be fine; but maybe it is not fine. My main rule is: be brave enough to be a coward. Make a decision based on the risks, not a decision based on what other people are going to think of you. I remember in Chechnya being bombed for twelve hours – the Russians were quartering the field so they would do one section, go away for an hour, come back and do another section. I was huddled in the snow with a couple of Chechen rebels – you are often with people whose macho thing is 'I don't care if I live or die' – and one of them said he would rather die warm than live cold. He then lit a fire. But people guide planes in with fire so I made him put out the fire and was then seen by him as a coward because I didn't want to sit by the fire and take my chances with guiding in a bomb. I didn't care if this fellow thought that I was a coward – and I still don't care.

My advice to people who want to cover war is not to worry about things not happening; things always happen. Someone once said to me in Kosovo, 'Well, at least you got shot at today and you have something to write about.' That is not really a

---

*__Author's note:__ With no experience of war, no guarantee of publication and no expense account, O'Kane took herself to the war in Yugoslavia and won the prestigious British Journalist of the Year Award for her first year of reporting.

good attitude. Don't panic, don't worry, and don't get nervous about not having a story because you will always get one. Don't go out and take a step too far. Sometimes it is better to just be completely bored for twenty-four hours. And there are just little things, like if you are being shot at you get into the ditch because bullets go through cars – be knowledgeable about how you might get killed. One other rule that is very important is to be aware of local people who help you. There can be an arrogance in certain correspondents where they think that they are doing some greater good so the lives of the people helping them don't matter. Putting myself in a situation of risk is my decision but it is not one I choose to make for the translator or the driver. No story is worth being responsible for someone else getting killed.

## Changing nature of war

In most of the wars I have gone to in the last ten years they are not between opposing armies. There isn't a front line; everything is sort of a muddle: it is guerrillas, irregulars, civilians – all kind of mixed up and shooting at each other. It is like some barrier has been lifted and wars have become so much more personal, village against village. Your enemies are issues that have been repressed for generations and that now surface to be fought out in really nasty ways. For instance, after a massacre I reported on, I went back to talk with some of the Albanian villagers I had visited earlier. When the Serbs attacked, the men had hidden the women and children and escaped thinking that the Serbs wouldn't kill them. They came back to find their entire families slaughtered. The men had misjudged the depth of hatred the Serbs had for them from generations before, and those husbands and fathers and brothers carry a lot of guilt for underestimating this.

Also it is now a lot more dangerous for correspondents. For example, Beirut 1982 was a really nasty internecine war but journalists had a sort of observer status – neutral, untouchable. It was hands-off; these are the people writing about it. Then suddenly it seemed that they didn't care one way or the other. In the past, if you were a journalist in the middle of conflict you could be killed by accident. But now it has ratcheted up to where people know that journalists are getting the story out to the rest of the world so we are now the enemy: grade 'A' targets.

## Covering war

If you are going to cover the story then you have to take the risk. Just because someone is shot doesn't mean that they have made a mistake (I would say that, wouldn't I?). There is no way to cover war and be invulnerable. I did stupider things when I was younger because to me it was unimaginable that you could be shot. But by the time you have been doing the same thing for fifteen years you start to have a really good sense of how far you can go. I always go in thinking that I am going to survive but knowing there is always a 100 per cent risk every single minute, and every single moment involves a decision about life and death. It is a sort of personal challenge: 'Am I going to be able to survive this without turning into a blithering idiot?'

When you are in Chechnya and you hear the planes coming there is fear but when the bombing starts you find that you are thinking more about how to survive. I avoid thinking about fear because it paralyses you and if you go to pieces you probably are going to be killed. My reaction has always been to get quieter, calmer, step by step. The time that it hits me is afterwards when I have survived and I haven't cracked. You sort of feel, 'OK, I am brave enough to get through that,' and you feel good about yourself. But bravery is still a day-to-day thing, depending on the situation. You don't suddenly discover you are brave forevermore.

We, as war journalists, are flawed in many fundamental ways: we never have to grow up and probably have an inability to deal with life as a monochrome. You don't really have to deal with the details of daily life unless you want to because you are going to be on a plane the next day. To be honest, that's a childish way to live. The duality of this is the complete and utter commitment we have to the story and the irresponsibility in all other parts of our lives. There is always some sense – and that is the bond particularly between war correspondents – that we are all outsiders and this is our strange little tribe of outsiders, passionate about things that are weird to other people. For example, I am not passionate about getting a bigger house or about the jasmine in my garden. I don't sweat the details because I have survived so many larger things. I think that this can be really frustrating to people around us.

As a war journalist, you are also very much of the moment. There is no planning. Probably all of us are very flawed in the sense that we are unable to plan ahead. It is just useless to do so. Why plan ahead when you have absolutely no idea what chaos confronts you tomorrow? In terms of our fears, we fear the known. The unknown is something that we are much more comfortable with because in a war we have absolutely no idea what situation we are going to be involved in. We flee in terror from the known; a normal life gives us the shakes.

Also, I think that the reason why journalists drink too much – which I certainly do – is because at the end of the working day you are not exhausted: you're high on adrenaline. You have just survived something and you cannot go to sleep so you go to the bar. I have never gotten tired in an area of conflict unless it involves something like five days of no sleep. Home is when you get tired. You get off the plane and you collapse because you are now in a safe place with a door you can close and you know that no one is going to come through it. When I get home I sleep for twenty-four hours.

I am furious with arguments about this mythical journalist who is supposed to be godlike and objective. How can you be objective? You can't. It is inhuman. Why are we not supposed to be human? I also think that part of my role is to report on the morality of what I am seeing. When you are physically uncovering mass graves in Kosovo I don't think that there are two sides to the story. If I don't report that, if I can't take a moral position, then I don't see the reason for being there. OK, there are theories of objectivity that you start with in journalism but if you are good you break them. I think it is a dereliction of duty not to at least give your opinion. You can take or leave my opinion; I am not saying that it is necessarily right, but I think that there is a place for journalists to do analysis who have seen what has been happening and know the story.

Also if you are trying to get across a sense of injustice and a sense of the immorality of what is going on, I don't think that you can, in all cases, be a bystander. If you are there where people are dying and you can do one thing to save one person, to me that is just a microcosm of what we are trying to do in a larger sense. I don't have some grand role for myself where I can save the world, but you can try, and if there is a jerrycan sitting there and someone is about to set themselves on fire I would take it away. But you have to accept that you can't save the world. I am not a politician, I am not an aid worker, and as a journalist I feel you have to accept that the power you have comes from what you write. Also, you can't be a walking open wound because you go into so many situations where you are talking to someone who you know is probably going to die. To make anyone in the outside world care about yet another famine in Ethiopia you have to talk to the most dangerously ill people and that is *awful*. I just steel myself a bit and I know that what I write, and the picture I have of this family whose baby is clearly going to die within hours, can have some effect.

I was in one of the few vehicles in a Chechen village that was being bombed and there were thirty people hiding in this village that in the next few days was probably going to be reduced to rubble. You can't get all of those people, or even all of the wounded, out. I find that personally traumatic. The only way to personally get through such a situation is to have some faith. Move enough people by your story and get some kind of outrage sparked. I don't think that there is any easy way around it; you essentially have to sometimes leave people to die and get the story out.

I hate the idea of a journalist as a sort of rapacious person who goes in and just takes. 'I am a journalist so tell me your story and let me get out of here.' You can bruise someone emotionally like that. If I am going to write about that person as a human being, I owe it to him to treat him as a person. Instead of getting a quote from the guy sitting by the river in Kosovo holding his baby girl who is riddled with bullets and blood, I'll sit by the river with him for four hours. The first hour you have a quote but human reactions are much more complex than that and you have to be incredibly patient. You owe it to the person you are talking to who is talking about his or her life. Very often these people are peasants who have had this huge unimaginable event in their lives. These people don't even know what they feel or how to express it. Patience is a key word for a journalist.

The thing that I worry about is giving people a sense of false hope. Sometimes people say to me, 'How can you talk to that man who has just lost his four children and wife and their bodies are lying in front of him?' How can you not? You can give them hope by being a journalist and listening to their story, but you can't let them feel that because they are telling you their story it is all going to change tomorrow. Of course, that is what I am trying to do but you can't leave people with the feeling that you can change their life just because they told you their story. On the other hand, I have never had the strength to sit there and say, 'You know this is awful but nothing can be done,' because I don't really believe that. I find that emotional balance difficult.

I get distraught sometimes, more from feeling powerless than frustrated. I cope with it by just getting on, by having some kind of realisation that I have done the best that I can. My approach is: 'You know you can make a difference here. It is actually not going to be in any way helpful if you break down and get hysterical about this. React in anger rather than being so self-centred that your emotions stop you from doing this story.' I sort of channel it into: 'I can have some effect if I can get on with this and do something.' It doesn't make me a better person or do anyone any good if I am going to stand there and cry. If I break down in tears, it is always late at night remembering things on my own.

## OVERCOMING COMPASSION FATIGUE

It is the profession's fault if people are overwhelmed with conflict fatigue. War is awful and it is beyond a person's imagination but what is the common factor? People! What I try to do is personalise every story within a political/historical context so that people know what is going on and can feel the sense of injustice. I have used everything from a teenage conscript who had absolutely no future, to bravery, which is not necessarily going forward through the guns – it might be an old woman sitting in her basement. We were in Chechnya under Russian bombing and there was no electricity, no water, no medicine and her husband's head had been split open. He was unconscious; you could see his brain; he was not going to live. The house was going to come down on top of her but she just wasn't going to flee. She didn't want him to die alone so she sat in the basement holding his hand. That was love but that was also bravery. Somehow, to overcome compassion fatigue, we have to get across that these are people just like us, who have fears and hopes and dreams, who are dying, not an undifferentiated mass. If someone can feel that, you can create outrage.

Also, I think that as journalists we need to show the individuality and the universality. The issues involved for somewhere like Kosovo are very different, for example, to the Palestinian issue, but there is a fundamental or universal commonality, which is people. People are fighting for their rights, for things that we in the West take for granted. If you can get through to the public that this is about four million people who are occupied, who will never have citizenship, who will never have rights, that this is why they are in this situation then you might move them to overcome compassion fatigue. You may not like how they are fighting but they are actually fighting for their lives. They are trying to escape lives that we in the West would not accept as living.

You see a lot of injustice working in this profession and I get very passionate about that but sometimes I am also overwhelmed by what I see. Yet I don't believe that I can't do anything. I *have* to have faith that every little bit that I do helps. Within the industry we have discussed this endlessly. Even people in the middle of a war say to you, 'Why should I talk to you because it is just going to be printed in a newspaper and no one cares anyway,' but that is just giving up. The way I overcome any compassion fatigue I might feel is by having faith in humanity further down the line. I look at my job as not just getting the story into a newspaper but having faith that if I can write this story strongly and clearly enough then someone out there is going to care and somewhere something might be done. It then comes down to democracy: little things like people writing letters, email, gathering in Trafalgar Square . . . So, my hope doesn't have to be 'I can solve this' but that I can build outrage and move people to say, 'This is awful, it has to stop.' I think politicians can then react to that.

## HOME

If I had figured out my personal and professional priorities in life I would probably be less tortured. I think that I try to balance them but somehow with personal relations I always come up short. But I am not sure I always wouldn't come up short because I notice in other relationships that people always want more. Is anyone ever really satisfied? There must be happy families somewhere but I don't particularly know any. Being a war or foreign correspondent is probably the most stressful thing for a relationship and what I have stopped trying to do is be everything. When I started in my profession I kind of subscribed to the myth of the woman who can have it all. But I've learnt that you can't have all of anything so I have made a kind of mental list of what is important to me. I passionately care about the job and I feel very lucky, but I pay for the privilege.

People who care about me get furious with me because as a war correspondent you are constantly at risk. You are talking down the phone to someone and there are explosions in the background, or they read your story and they say, 'What the fuck are you doing?' That puts a strain on relationships. You are also just jumping on a plane with little notice – twenty-four hours notice is good – and then you are gone for three months. I can't be the wife that is going to cook supper every day. If that is what someone wants then it is not me. I used to torture myself about that but I don't any more. I think one of the real differences between male and female correspondents is that men always seem to have wives, albeit sort of sequential because they always have four or five wives – and I am going to be really sexist here – but they sort of have wives very often that they can go home to and who keep the home fires burning. We female correspondents don't have wives. What we need are wives. You know, it would be very nice to come home to someone who is always there.

When I am in a war zone covering a story I am completely and utterly involved in it and can block off home, but the job does leak into life at home. I am agitated when I come back or quite intense about things but in terms of my experiences colouring my world I try not to let it affect me. Home is very important to me, in the sense that there is a wider, sane world where people care about things. And I just don't want to bore people going on with things such as, 'I have just come back from a famine – why are we eating steak?' so I have tended to get more realistic. Do what you can to the best of your ability and don't think that you can change, or have any right to change, everyone's life. If somebody is comfortable in the way they are living, I don't think that it is my right to judge. If somebody is happy having dinner parties where we are all supposed to show up on time, I am not knocking it. I think people have respect for you, but god, I wouldn't want someone at my dinner party boring on. I don't want to be the kind of person about whom they say as you move up to the bar, 'Oh god, here come the experiences in Beirut again.' I don't want to think about war all the time and I don't want to hang out with others in the profession all the time just as they don't want to hang out with me all the time. I don't want my life to be 'the foreign correspondent' and nothing else.

## Post-traumatic stress disorder

It is interesting how your brain works. For me, I never relive the pain of being shot: it is always the decision I made, which was to yell. I was lying in a field and the Sri Lankan military came out of the base shooting flares, obviously on a search-and-destroy mission. So the decision was: should I yell and alert them that I am there or will they stumble on me? I just thought that if they stumbled on me they would kill me. Not a great choice! I was uninjured until I yelled 'journalist' and then they fired the grenade. The nightmare for me is always that decision about yelling. My brain leaves out the pain. I think that the walk was the real nightmare – when I was not a person. They were about fifty yards away up on a road and they made me walk to them. I knew that if I fell they would shoot so I had them put a light on me before I would stand up, but I lost so much blood that I fell down, literally. I would stumble and fall and they would shoot over me or at me – I don't even know. I replay that whole walk endlessly in the nightmare. I know that it is my brain trying to find a different resolution. 'This body didn't have to be shot.' I used to have nightmares every night but now they just occur once in a while.

I notice that most of us don't ask for help. I have an innate resistance to counselling and that is probably part of that culture of the war correspondent, but equally I just don't know ... sitting down in front of a psychotherapist who has never been through anything that I have been through ... It has got nothing to do with my father, nothing to do with my childhood. It has got to do with an extremely traumatic event that I know about. I don't think there is any problem with my brain. I know why I am feeling this way and I would rather just get through it. So I have talked about what I went through with colleagues and friends. To me, it is much more healing to talk it through because the nightmares I had were always about somehow wanting the outcome of the incident where I was shot to be different.

Most of the male correspondents are very closed off. I remember one male colleague who was waking up with nightmares and was found by his wife crawling across the floor because he thought he was under fire. I have been married twice but my second ex-husband, who was a war correspondent, recently killed himself. That is awful because I know part of that was caused by whatever PTSD is. He was someone who could not talk to anyone about anything. He was very macho and proud – 'I am not weak' – and that was part of it. In a way our profession has a macho culture but we all know what we have done so there is no question of, 'Oh, you are weak.'

## Spiritual belief

I have a very deep belief in a spiritual being, something beyond this world, which is challenged and threatened constantly – the question being that if there is a god how can he possibly let these things happen? You know, the line in the Bible 'God created man in his own image' has always made me question the kind of god that must be when you see what men do. It is probably one of the attractions of the job that you see such tremendous bravery in the smallest person but you also see what madness is in the human soul. War is dehumanising but you see such extremes that you have to believe in God. Equally, the idea of this all-powerful, all-good god, seems to me to be a total contradiction. You cannot exaggerate man's inhumanity to man. I go round and round with the question of how people can do this. That is really a fundamental question for me but whatever answers I come up with are not enough.

## DOING THE JOB

My whole approach to anything, not just being a foreign correspondent, is: I can do it. I think that as a woman you are underestimated when you start out but you prove yourself and then it is absolutely fine. There are no issues at all now when I am out in the field. I can certainly cover wars just as well as anyone. But I don't think that I could do the job if I didn't care about each person. It hits me every single time. You have to leave yourself raw and open but it is probably true that I am no longer shocked as I was by the sight of my first body and I am trying to become a bit more of a camera – maintain some kind of distance. I think that the whole importance of our job is to be a witness, to testify, to say this is what I witnessed and to be almost forensically exacting about what I report, and feel it.

I think that I feel comfortable enough with the notion that I am not going to a war zone just to feel a heightened sense of reality. But there is no denying that feeling; you see such extremes and it is addictive. Yet the ranks of war correspondents begin to thin above a certain age and I think that we are all slightly superstitious. Mostly people who stop covering wars feel that they have taken one risk too many and the idea of walking into a situation that puts your life in danger is one you physically can't do again. That survival instinct hasn't yet made me stop, but I suppose someday it might.

# CHAPTER 7

# ROBERT FISK

## Biography

ROBERT FISK WAS THE Belfast correspondent for *The Times of London* between 1971 and 1976 and then moved to Lebanon to take up the position of Middle East correspondent. In 1985 Fisk completed his PhD on Irish neutrality during the Second World War. In 1988 he joined London's *The Independent* newspaper as their Middle East correspondent.

Robert has covered conflict in Ireland, Afghanistan, Iran, Iraq, Lebanon, Algeria, Israel, the Palestinian Occupied Territories and Bosnia. He is Britain's most highly awarded foreign correspondent, having won the British International Journalist of the Year Award seven times. He is probably also Britain's most controversial journalist.

Robert is author of *The Point of No Return: The Strike Which Broke the British in Ulster*; *In Time of War: Ireland, Ulster, and the Price of Neutrality 1939-45*; *Pity the Nation: Lebanon at War*, which has been updated and expanded into *Pity the Nation: The Abduction of Lebanon*; and *Night of Power*.

He lives in Beirut.

\* \* \*

## Story\*

Before the massacre in September 1982, people in Beirut were saying there would be a massacre but nobody quite knew why. I had been a little bit nervous when I had left Beirut to go on holiday in Ireland because my instinct told me something could happen. Travelling down the coast of Ireland, I

---

\* **Author's note:** On 6 June 1982, Israel launched an invasion of Lebanon with the intention of driving Yasser Arafat and the Palestine Liberation Organisation (PLO) out of the country. Menachem Begin was Israel's prime minister at the time and Ariel Sharon, then Israel's defence minister, oversaw the invasion. Within two weeks, the Israeli military (IDF) had surrounded West Beirut where many of the Palestinian fighters were living in refugee camps such as Sabra and Chatila. It is estimated that over 15,000 Lebanese (mostly civilians) died in the invasion. In August, the US brokered a cease-fire with the proviso that Arafat and his PLO combatants leave Lebanon. In return, they promised that their families left behind in the camps would be protected. By early September the international peacekeeping forces (including the Americans) charged with protecting the Palestinian civilians had left Lebanon. Within days, Sharon announced a 'mopping up' operation of the camps. The Israeli military set up roadblocks. When the Israelis had finished, the Phalange militiamen (Christian militia group aligned with Israel), and possibly members of the South Lebanon army (a creation of the Israelis to combat the Hezbollah in Southern Lebanon), moved into the camps. The Israelis watched the massacre from the roof of a nearby high-rise building and at night shot flares into the air so that their proxies could continue their work. No civilians or media were allowed to enter or leave the camps for three days. It is estimated that around 1700 people were killed in Chatila and Sabra.

Robert, along with fellow journalists Loren Jenkins (from the *Washington Post*) and Karsten Tveit (from Norwegian radio) were the first journalists to enter the camps.

Robert's story, as told in this chapter, was related to me as we walked through Chatila.

went into a bar with a television and saw bombs dropping in the Bekaa Valley: on a Syrian position west of Beirut. I thought the war was over but there is an Israel attack on a Syrian position! That night it was reported on the BBC that Bashir Gemayel, the then Lebanese president-elect and leader of the Christian Phalange (enemies of the Palestinians in Beirut), had been assassinated in a bomb explosion in the Phalange headquarters. I put a call through to Beirut. Gerry Labelle, a New York AP staffer who had only recently been sent to Beirut, said Gemayel was alive and it was OK. In the morning I turned on the BBC – their report had been true: Gemayel was dead.

I learnt later that publicly Ariel Sharon said that the Palestinians killed Gemayel, which was a vicious thing to say because the next morning Sharon brought the Phalange into West Beirut and sent them into the Palestinian refugee camps of Chatila and Sabra. As soon as I heard that the Israelis had brought in the Phalange, I knew there would be a massacre. But apparently Mr Sharon did not know that, right? What did he think the Phalange was going to do?

My editor at *The Times* in London said, 'Don't worry, Robert, the Israelis are only going into Beirut to keep law and order.' I said, 'They are not!' I had to get back. I drove to Dublin, got on a plane to Switzerland then a plane to Syria (no visa), had to wait overnight in the airport, caught a taxi to central Damascus and a taxi to Beirut but the driver got as far as Chtaura, forty-four kilometres from Beirut and lost his nerve when an Israeli plane went over. I got another driver and he lost his nerve. I got one more who said, 'I will take you to the line where you cross into Beirut.' There was a line of cotton through a field of wild grass and that was the way though the minefield. So I followed the cotton with the driver whose brother was on the other side and the brother took me to East Beirut. I wasn't allowed to cross into West Beirut because of roadblocks so I called up a Phalange official and said that I needed a driver who would take me to West Beirut. For $500, they took me.

I had this theory that the Israelis would bring tanks and armour through the port so I got down there and, sure enough, there was a line of Israeli tanks. I said to the driver, 'Get behind that tank and before this one.' There was shooting at the tanks as we were going along and the driver was taking his foot off the accelerator. I said, 'No, follow the fucking tanks!' – he was more frightened of me than the last shell that went over. I hadn't slept for two days so I was pretty irate. We drove past my house on the Corniche straight to the Commodore Hotel where journalists gather and Gerry Labelle was there and just stared at me, saying, 'About fucking time!' My American friend Loren Jenkins, a big, bearded guy from Colorado who worked for the *Washington Post*, walked up to me and said, 'Something is going on in the camps. I have just been at Saeb Salam's house [the former elderly prime minister of Lebanon], and this woman came in and said someone has just put a knife through the throat of her husband.' The Phalange was in the camps and the massacre was still going on.

The next morning I decided to go with Jenkins and my friend Karsten Tveit to the camps. We had travelled together during the Lebanese civil war and had been in great danger so I knew they were very tough guys – you travel with people you know are survivors; you do not travel with people who are frightened, new, young, aggressive, boastful.

When we got to the entrance of Chatila, where Jenkins had tried to get in the previous night and had been stopped by the Israelis, he said, 'That house had been standing yesterday and now it has been blown up.' That is how we knew something was still happening. We found an Israeli officer and I asked, 'What has happened in there? It is like Treblinka!' They were the words I used. He said, 'I don't know; I only came this morning.' Jenkins said to him, 'You fucking liar, you stopped me last night when I wanted to go into the camp. You were here last night!' The Israelis all knew what was going on; they were on the roof of a high-rise building overlooking the camps. That was their command headquarters and Hobeika, the Christian Phalangist commander and chief of Lebanese intelligence services, was in a Mossad (Israeli intelligence) office in one of those buildings. They were all watching what was happening in the camps.

You have got to realise that the Sabra and Chatila camps had been bombed from the air by the Israelis for two months and many Palestinians had already died. After the bombing, the surviving Palestinian fighters had left. When the Phalange militia came into the two camps most of the people left were old men, women and children so they were the ones the Phalange killed. An independent inquiry in Israel held Sharon personally responsible for this massacre.

Nobody stopped Jenkins, Tveit and me going into Chatila so we were the first people in there. On the morning of Saturday 18 September 1982 all the houses on each side of the road entering the camp were flat. The Phalange had been killing for two days and the place stank of corpses. The Israelis must have been smelling the stench and pretending they weren't. We first went up this little street and found two women lying on the road with a dead baby beside them – shot in the head – and, very oddly, some dead horses. There was a bulldozer standing right here because there was a mass grave on the left. Up here, I tried to climb over this massive embankment of earth but while I was on top I realised it was moving up and down. I looked down and I saw the breast of a woman, an arm, and a leg, and I had to clamber down holding onto people's heads. I was trying not to be sick because of the smell and I was covered in flies that were going from the living to the dead.

There were little children still alive and some of them whose parents were lying dead said, 'That's Mummy.' They thought their parents were asleep, maybe. I found an old man, Mr Nouri, lying dead on the road with his stick. A kid was identifying the dead and I was taking the names from him. (Afterwards, we found some film shot by a number of television crews at the gate of the camps and saw ninety-year-old Mr Nouri wearing his pyjamas and walking out of the gate with his stick pleading to be allowed to leave. The Phalange ordered him back. He was forced back to death. Karsten and I kept replaying the film, making him come alive again.)

We got very frightened at this point because we could hear the armoured vehicles of the Phalange moving around inside. I stuck with Jenkins because I thought they might kill a Brit but they wouldn't kill an American, but I think that they would have killed anyone. We walked up a side road and heard them coming so we ran into the backyard of a house and hid. As we turned around, there was a body of a young woman lying on the ground surrounded by a halo of clothes pegs. As she lay there, we saw her blood trickling across the concrete. She had only been dead for a few seconds. We were very frightened, as you can imagine, but went around and found more bodies.

During the first night of the massacre in the refugee camps, the Israeli army were dropping flares from aircraft to help the Phalange move around the narrow passageways of these tenements. The people who lived here had no idea what was happening. If you had a little house down here you stayed inside because you would have heard shooting and then the first thing that you would have known was that there was a gunman coming through the door. The houses in the camps were full of the dead. In most cases the family had obviously retreated to the far room – the bedroom – and their bodies were all over against the walls with usually the woman on the bed, almost always raped. There was a lot of rape in the camps at that time. The Phalange were here for two-and-a-half days.

I think that you are making a mistake if you think that what happened here was an insanity. The Phalange has been brought up to believe by all the elderly, sick, Christian leadership and aristocrats of East Beirut that the Palestinians were the cause of the civil war. So when they came into these refugee camps it was revenge. You can't go into a house, rape a woman in front of her family, and then shoot the lot of them without having something a bit wrong with you. Among all the discarded Israeli uniforms – because the Phalange was wearing Israeli uniforms – were a lot of whisky bottles and I think probably a lot of them were on drugs.

Sharon and Menachem Begin said they never imagined that this would happen. Give me a break! One of the accusations against Sharon is by a woman who has acknowledged that she was raped. I know her. She still lives here. She was crippled after they raped and shot her. She pretended that she was dead but they came back and shot her again, yet she still survived.

When I was in Chatila during the massacre, many of the victims were still alive but were murdered two weeks afterwards, once they were handed over to the Phalange by the Israelis. The Phalange took all these prisoners, thousands of them, to a stadium and they were all put in the underground changing rooms. I actually went in there with one of the

Reuters correspondents and we recognised one of his telex operators and got him out. We didn't know we were saving him; we thought the prisoners were only going to be interrogated but almost all the men whom we saw held there were never seen again. We know where some of their bodies are but nobody digs up graves in this place. You dig up a grave and you are going to pour more blood into it. That is what happens here.

Do you know what was on the front cover of *Newsweek* the week after Sabra/Chatila? 'The Anguish of America's Jews'. Now a sane person might have thought the anguish might have been rather more serious amongst the Palestinian survivors of Sabra and Chatila.

## WHY THE MIDDLE EAST?

I don't like war, believe me. My fascination for it doesn't come from guns or weapon-firing – I think they are frightening, evil things, if one thinks evil exists – but instead I am interested in history. My father used to talk about what it was like to see the German bombers coming over Kent in 1940 and my mother was a radio repair operator on Spitfires at Battle of Britain aerodromes in the 1940s, so I grew up with the idea that the First World War was not very far away from me and the Second World War was very close. I grew up reading all the great books on the First World War: Siegfried Sassoon and Wilfred Owen. I have heaps of my father's own photographs and postcards he bought during the First World War and I used to watch and read everything about the Second.

If you look at the history of the twentieth century it is really a history of change through violence, not through social, political movements. In many ways the history that I have had to witness in my life has been the direct result of my father's First World War. The frontiers of Northern Ireland, Yugoslavia and the Middle East were all shaped by the victors immediately after the First World War so it has an intimate connection to us now. The promises that the victors made in the First World War – the Balfour Declaration giving British support for a Jewish homeland in Palestine and the declaration to King Feisal of the Arabs that we would give Arab independence – were promises in total conflict with each other. They couldn't both work. So what you realise is that the First World War has an intimate connection to us now, here, today. Lebanon would be Syria if it weren't for Britain and France's victory in that war. So I grew up conscious of history over my shoulder and, with that as a background, the attraction of being a foreign correspondent for me is to be a personal witness to history. I am watching it. Unfortunately this part of the world is rather afflicted by the thing called war.

In the new edition of my book *Pity the Nation*, I described why I stayed on in Lebanon. I think this country is like a book you can't put down. All night you would read and, 'oh god, it is ten o'clock, just one more chapter'. And then you realised it was one o'clock in the morning, 'but just one more chapter' and then you see the dawn coming through the curtains. When the last Israeli soldier left Lebanon I went down to Southern Lebanon. All the Hezbollah (or the Party of God that arose out of the Lebanese Shia resistance to the Israeli presence in Southern Lebanon) and their families were marching beside the border fence and at dawn there was Galilee and the fields of Galilee in Israel. That was the dawn of reading the book; you have finished the book and you put it down and open the curtain. The end. But of course it is not the end and it will go on.

*Bearing Witness*

So one difference between me and other correspondents is that I have stayed on station while most reporters are moved every three years – just when they begin to learn something. I was very fortunate because *The Independent* said they would take me if I stayed in Beirut. What has happened is that I have accumulated a store of knowledge covering over twenty-five years. I don't need books – I read them, keep them, check my memory; I have an irrefutable knowledge on things like the camps. I know my way around, I know where people live, and I know who they are. Mind you, for my work I have a huge area to cover – from Afghanistan to Algeria, including the Balkans – but I had the great fortune to stay in Beirut because, as I said, Lebanon is like a good book although I think that Ireland is actually my main subject. I probably know more about Irish history than the Middle East.

## THE PALESTINIANS

When I came to Beirut the Palestinians were in South Lebanon which was Fatah land – Fatah being the military wing of the Palestine Liberation Organisation (PLO). Every time the Israelis came over the border, the PLO ran away to Beirut and went to the cinema. And when I first went to Jerusalem, Palestinian collaborators wore uniforms with black berets and the West Bank was submissive. Well, not any more. Now if the Israelis come over the Lebanese border, the Hezbollah is driving as fast as it can to Southern Lebanon to get them. In the end, it drove the Israelis out. They won. It was the Hezbollah who showed the Arab world that you can fight the Israelis partly through religious strength but also with a good deal of nationalism. The Hezbollah isn't primarily an international terrorist organisation: it is a Lebanese resistance force.

So what you have got increasingly today with the Palestinians is a radicalised and non-frightened society. Once you lose your fear, you never get it back. Sharon does not realise that. As Israeli prime minister he has said, 'They must incur bigger losses.' Wrong! Once an enemy loses his fear he has won and you have lost. That is what you learn in wars if you want to know a war correspondent's viewpoint – apart from the fact that war is not about victory and defeat; it is about death.

## BEING AN HONEST BROKER

The Israeli writer Amira Haas told me that the purpose of journalism is to monitor the centres of power. That is a brilliant definition of journalism. A journalist is also someone who is allowed to tell the truth. Now, there is no such thing as the truth per se – we know that you can't buy it on the supermarket shelf like people think that you can – but I think that we can try and tell the truth as we see it, as honest witnesses. But that is about all.

I am not biased. If you are biased you can't cover the Middle East. At one point I was going to make a film with a British producer around Sabra and Chatila. Over lunch he said, 'Look, I will tell you that I am Jewish and, honestly, I think of my Jewish background.' And I said, 'Not while you are working with me you don't.' When I go on a story I don't think about my Protestant, Anglo-Saxon, English background. When I was in Northern Ireland I was attacked by the army for telling the truth about what they were doing to Catholics. I didn't let my background of being an English Protestant interfere with it. Amira Haas doesn't let her Jewish background interfere with her work. Her mother was a Jewish partisan in Yugoslavia captured by the Nazis but Amira is living and working in Gaza. Of course, you are subjective, but you are an honest witness, and an honest witness can also be moved to passion and anger. Absolutely. But you have given an honest witness's account of events, of people's thoughts, and of your own thoughts. I don't want the version I am given by the government. I talk to people, investigate the story and then try to tell the truth as a journalist, which involves saying, 'I am going to sit back now and this is what I think happened.' But you are an honest witness.

I am not a crusading journalist either. I am a journalist who believes in campaigning for an end to landmines, massacres and the death of kids, but I don't go on a moral 'crusade' about it because my job is to send the story back to London. That is all I can do. I am a nerve ending of the newspaper. But because editors in London are telling many of my colleagues on other newspapers what the story is for today, every so often you get someone new on the desk and you have to tell them, 'Look, I am sorry, you don't understand. I am telling you what the story is. I am here. Right?' I am not just getting information out; I am getting my view of the Middle East out and my authority as a reporter is much greater if I stick to that rather than turn up on political platforms. I don't politicise; I give lectures at universities, but I won't stand on any political platform.

In fact, although I am a British citizen I have never been interested in voting in British elections. If I had become an Irish citizen I probably would want to vote in Ireland because I am very interested in Irish politics. But I have never been interested in British politics at all. Probably also because my father was a country councillor for the Conservatives I would be tempted to vote Labour and that is the wrong reason.

Also I only do radio interviews live so I can't be edited and that is actually a very disciplining experience because you can't afford to slip on the topic of the Middle East. This is white-hot incandescent territory for a journalist, especially the Palestinian/Israeli conflict so I go in passionate, tough, and if they attack me I raise my voice a fraction and go back at them because the moment you say 'I am sorry, I think that you are misunderstanding me', that is what they want you to say. So you must say exactly, carefully, what you mean. I was on a live BBC interview recently with an Israeli spokesman talking about the Occupied Territories and he said, 'How can you call these lands occupied? We gave the land back after Oslo.' And I said, 'Oh, I'm sorry. So you mean these soldiers who stopped me between Jenin and Ramallah a few days ago were Burmese or Swiss? They looked Israeli to me.'

One of the interesting things that has happened recently is that a whole vocabulary of lies has been built up, clichés that journalists are taught to use: 'terrorists', 'disputed land' and now 'neighbourhoods', not 'settlements'. Language is meant to liberate us but that kind of journalism imprisons us. The Americans have been imprisoned by words on the subject of the Middle East for decades: Israel builds colonies for Jews on occupied Arab land, which is against international law, and we call them 'settlements'. Now my colleagues are calling them 'neighbourhoods'. You see what has happened? A Palestinian shoots at a settlement, we denounce it as horrific, but we know why – because they are on his land. But if he shoots at a 'neighbourhood' he is a mindless 'terrorist' because there is no reason to shoot at a 'neighbourhood'. We call it the Occupied Territories but as soon as the US State Department said it is in future to be called the 'disputed territories', so did the American press.

The American people have been given a false picture so that they don't understand, by people who do understand. Noam Chomsky is American's finest linguist and linguistic philosopher but he doesn't have a column in an American paper; he doesn't have a voice. Do you think that if the late

Edward Said had been offered a weekly column in the *New York Times* he wouldn't have taken it? Ever since 1967, there has been an increasing campaign in the States to make sure there is no criticism of Israel. You have to say to yourself, fight, fight, fight, when you are doing what I do because people want to shut you up. There are very powerful Israeli lobby groups and anyone who dares criticise Israel is immediately labelled anti-Semitic. It is an outrageous claim to make; it is a disgusting, libellous, slanderous accusation and I threaten anyone with legal action if they say that about me. In Britain you can't go around calling someone a racist and get away with it; in America you can.

So what happened was that the newspapers and television in the US simply found it easier not to attack Israel. But there is a big problem now for that lobby group because we (*The Independent* and *The Guardian*) are getting into America via the Internet and we have broken through the curtain. It is going to take years to change but you should see the letters I get from ordinary Americans saying, 'Thank god we can read the truth at last instead of our own bloody papers.' Some of the people who are saying this are American Jewish people.

# QANA*

When I got into the UN camp at Qana, I was walking through literally streams of blood. There were people on fire; a baby

---

*****Author's note:** On 18 April 1996 the Israeli military shelled the UN peace-keeping headquarters in the Lebanese town of Qana. One hundred and five civilians who had fled to the compound for shelter from the bombing were killed. Although the Israeli military initially denied it was aware that it was shelling civilians in a UN compound, Fisk's evidence was proof of culpability. Not only did Israel have an unmanned drone flying over the area, enabling them to clearly identify the target and the damage being inflicted, but the UN soldiers had repeatedly pleaded with the Israelis, informing them that they were shelling a UN compound.

burning; a corpse up a tree on fire; a young woman holding an old man in her arms who was dead, rocking him back and forth saying, 'My father, my father.' The Fijian UN peacekeeping soldiers whose camp it was were overwhelmed because they were picking up dead babies whom they had held in their arms. With my mobile I had this story on the line, live, around the world immediately before anything came out of Israel. Calling my paper in London I said, 'We need the whole of the front page, the second page, and the third page,' because at that stage my duty was to get that story into print before it was misunderstood or tampered with by propaganda.

Coming back from Qana to Beirut, there was an Israeli gunboat firing at the bridge above Sidon, stopping all traffic. Two cars were on fire and the people were burning inside. This ship was always shooting at the main road so I had previously taken a photograph of it and wired it to London to get *The Independent*'s defence correspondent to give me the gunboat's firing capacity. I got to the bridge and I called him up and he said, 'I have got some bad news for you. It is six thousand rounds a minute.' I said, 'Fuck!' My driver, Abed, then asked me how many shells it fired. I said, 'Oh, don't worry, Abed, let's get moving.' He said, 'Are you sure?' I said, 'Abed, I have just watched an atrocity. We have got to get that story to Beirut.'

The gunboat was shooting shells on the road, 'boom-boom' every fifteen seconds. I said, 'Abed, it is going to take you more than fifteen seconds to cross so I will tell you what we are going to do and you will do as I tell you. We have got to go before the next 'boom-boom' and as you are on the road you will hear it, but it won't hit us.' I had to trust that they weren't going to change the firing times. 'We are only going to be safe if we go when you hear that boom. Don't worry, we want to hear it when you approach the bridge.' So we approached the bridge, full speed, and then 'boom-boom' and we went straight down, a shell bursting in front; we went through, 'boom-boom' behind us. That is how we got the Qana story out. If you do a job you should do it well, as Father and Mother used to say to me. You have got to have resilience, and you have got to want to write – and I do. I came back to my flat in Beirut and wrote and did interviews all night and we had three pages in the paper.

    A lot of people told me there had been a drone, a pilotless plane with real-time TV, above Qana. In other words, if there was a drone then the Israelis knew what they were doing – they say they know everything until something happens and then, 'Oh, we didn't know it.' I went down to Qana for the funeral for the victims and the Fijians pulled me up with them on the broken roof of their UN compound. They were in tears. One of them said, 'I think there is a film showing that the Israelis had a drone over the compound but it has been taken by the UN Secretary-General Boutros-Ghali and we have been told not to discuss it. Nobody made a copy.' Boutros-Ghali wanted to be re-elected secretary-general and the Americans were pressuring him, demanding that no inquiry be published, although the UN had had a secret inquiry.

    I came back to Beirut really upset but within two minutes my mobile phone went and a voice gave me a map reference in Southern Lebanon. I knew it was the same guy. I raced back to Southern Lebanon and a UN jeep pulled up. He was a very brave man; he could have lost his job but he didn't – they never found him. He threw the video tape onto the seat of my car. He said to me, 'I carried two children dead in my arms at Qana who were the same age as my own children and this is for them. I copied it.' I went back to Beirut and banged the videocassette in and there was the drone. I could hear the UN radio operator saying, 'Qana. This is Qana under fire!' I could hear the shots from the gunboat and when the camera panned up there was the drone. A UN soldier took the video on his private camera and had handed it over but this guy, my friend, had sneaked a copy before it was passed over to UN authorities. So it was my property now. You know what I felt. Gotcha!

I caught the first plane to London and called all the senior news editors on a Sunday morning and said, 'We are going to give copies of this tape to every television station, with copyright *The Independent*. You want to see this! Here are the still photographs; you can print them in the paper. Here is the video; watch it; understand what is happening.' It went around the world and it was free. We gave it to Israeli TV as well and they showed it. On the same day I was flying back to Beirut on the aeroplane watching my film on the Air France television news. That night I sat on the balcony in Beirut and had a big cigar (I never smoke cigars), looked at all the stars and said, 'Just stay like that.' The next day there were interviews all day. The UN made a statement that there was a film and they would make the inquiry public. That was the one great exclusive story I am delighted I did.

## Lessons of war

I was in Northern Ireland in the seventies and I think Belfast is quite a good training ground for anyone who wants to cover war because you are threatened by everybody there. But just in terms of rules for survival for a war correspondent, I think that the first thing is, if there is violence then self-preservation is all you think about. I remember in 1982 coming back from the airport area in Beirut. I was very frightened because we were surrounded by the Israelis and there were shells falling all across the road. As I was walking to the car, two young Syrian soldiers called from two gun pits – it is rare for Syrian soldiers to want to talk to a foreigner but they were just young kids. Perhaps I could have wandered across and said, 'How are you?' and shaken hands and talked to them a bit but I was frightened because I could hear the planes coming back. Plus there was a T55 tank behind them that wasn't properly camouflaged so I got in the car and left very fast. I went back the next day and it was just ashes. You don't want to die. I am afraid you think 'Let it be the other person' (unless you have someone with you whom you know well and then you have to protect them).

Also, you do try to help people when you can. During the Israeli invasion of Lebanon in 1978 we were under fire and some farmers begged us to take them out and even though there were shells falling down on us we stopped and took them out. You do try to help people but, you know, when I was on the bridge at Sidon, coming back from Qana and there was a burning car on the Awali River, I didn't stop to see if the person inside was alive because I am sure they were dead. They couldn't still be alive in that car. It was a cremation bed.

In terms of behaviour in famines, I haven't really covered enough famines to know. I did have a man come up to me in Ethiopia and ask me if he could drink the ink in my fountain pen though.

In December 2001 I was beaten up. At the time, I was the only Western journalist in Taliban Afghanistan. I got permission from the Taliban to go to Kandahar because they know people I know, and they know I know bin Laden. The last thing that bin Laden said to me when I interviewed him in one of his camps (it was a twenty-foot-high air-raid shelter artificially built into living stone on a mountaintop in Afghanistan) was, 'Mr Robert, from the mountain on which you are, we destroyed the Russian army and helped to bring down the Soviet Union' – pretty accurate I would say – 'and I pray to god that he permits us to turn America into a shadow of itself.' Anyway, I was on the main road to Kandahar with Taliban men and they were frightened. They didn't want to die for Allah; they didn't want to be 'martyrs'. One of them turned to me and said, 'How can we protect you when we cannot protect ourselves?' That was when I knew the Taliban were beaten.

Later, returning to Kandahar, our car broke down in a village called Kila Abdullah, close to the Pakistan-Afghan border, which had become home to thousands of desperate Afghan refugees. Initially they had been friendly but when the first pebble passed over my shoulder and bounced off the shoulder of my friend Justin Huggler (my colleague on *The Independent*) and he looked around at me with concern, I knew the situation had changed. I still remember that pebble. Pretty quickly I was being punched and that's when I knew things were very bad, very serious. By the time the people who had gathered around us were picking up stones and banging them into my face, I remember thinking, 'How long does it last?' That is what I asked myself, thinking I was going to die.

I hate people fighting but you have to be tough and I remembered what a Lebanese person had taught me: 'Whatever you do, don't do nothing.' So I thought, 'Well, if I am going to die, fuck them!' And then I started fighting back. I couldn't see the first guy properly because I had blood in my eyes but the second guy I punched and felt his nose collapse underneath my hand. The third guy I hit in the mouth. I saw him spit out his tooth and he fell on the road. And then, amazingly, they all fell back and this religious man came through the crowd, took me by the arm, and led me away. He got me down the road to a policeman (who really didn't want to help), who got me down to a Red Cross convoy (which I fear had seen me being attacked and had gone past me). I first thought I would clean myself up and keep going but when I saw myself in the windows, before I had been patched up, I realised that I couldn't possibly go on because I was losing far too much blood.

Another thing you learn in war is that actions are messages. Most correspondents, except my friend JC [Juan-Carlos Gumucio, who was Marie Colvin's husband] and myself, had fled Lebanon because of the kidnappings in the eighties. At that time, I interviewed Ghazi Kenaan, head of Syrian military intelligence in Lebanon. After he gave me an interview, he said, 'Why don't you come jogging with me tomorrow morning?' He, of course, is not touched. He is an Alawite and is a good friend of the Syrian president. Anyone touches Ghazi and they flatten Beirut, right? So I went jogging with him, just the two of us, and the purpose, of course, was to show everyone that you don't touch Robert Fisk. It was a very thoughtful thing to do. He didn't have to do that; he could have let me be taken. Actions are messages.

I wore a flak jacket in Bosnia but I don't in the Middle East: it is too hot. The flak jacket came in after the psychobabble about how you 'cope'. Obviously it is for protection but I am very mindful of the fact that one of my BBC colleagues was shot by Croatian soldiers, possibly deliberately, and the bullet went through under the arm and was kept inside his body by the flak jacket. It spun around and around destroying his body. In the Iran-Iraq War it was 129 degrees Fahrenheit but when an Iranian offered me a flak jacket I put it on because shells were going off all over the place and frankly I didn't want to die in a place like that. I was with boy soldiers ready to go over the top on motorbikes into minefields with coats on so that when the mine blew them up they wouldn't be blown to pieces and their mothers could have the bodies back.

## WHAT DO I CARE ABOUT?

Human rights are fairly high on the list of the things I care about. I don't mean to sound like a journalist who goes on campaigns but injustice is the issue that moves me in the Middle East. I will tell you one thing about human rights: I have never had to do so many stories on torture and summary arrest and executions and people living in fear as I have recently. I am very angry when I see massacres like Sabra and Chatila and Qana. I was very angry at the Israelis and I still am. I remember my American friend shouting 'Sharon!' out loud in the camp among the bodies. So we get angry. I think that as a journalist you should be passionate. Massacres such as those are crimes. They are wickedness.

Why are there more atrocities in the Middle East now or during the last fifty years? I think because of the failure of American stewardship. The big problem with the US is that it has decided that everybody in the world wants to be an American and America must take precedence over all else. Whatever America wants it has a right to have and nothing will stand in its way – and nothing does stand in its way. Those whom it chooses to reward, it will reward; those whom it will crush, it will crush. Any amount of rubbish can be produced to justify it. And the UN is always the elderly carthorse that is forced to step in after somebody, especially the Americans, have been smashing up the world in some new adventure. Poor old UN. I think that intrinsically it is an excellent organisation but the trouble is that the sum total of its parts is not what we think that it is. It is not an institution of wise men. It is riddled with all the hypocrisy and deceit of the countries that make it up.

Although I have no religion, I do believe that we have souls and that is why I object to words like 'evil'. People can be wicked but when you say 'This person is evil', you are dehumanising them. The people who flew the planes into the World Trade Center did not believe the people in the WTC had souls. I believe the people who flew the planes had souls because I am not going to be like them. When you start saying he doesn't have a soul, you become the suicide flyer.

The thing I am chiefly interested in is being a journalist. I love my job and I do think that the presence of a series of reports by journalists can have an unstoppable power to convince. Does an individual article change the world? Watergate and the *Washington Post* investigation clearly brought down Nixon. But I think that it is very easy to be romantic about journalism and there are obviously great moments of satisfaction when you can crack a story but, by and large, one shouldn't get a big head – or a big nose as they say in the Arab world. You shouldn't believe that your journalism changes the world. The institutions and governments and people that we write about are massive things and if we think that something is wrong all we can do is chip away at the bottom of a mountain and just get a little bit more stone out. Maybe we will get a fracture and at some point, with many other people chipping away, circumstances changing, public opinion altering, maybe we can bring down the mountain. But all we can do is chip away. Doing journalism properly is very hard work.

So my job is to get the story out and tell people what is really going on. What's the point of getting frustrated or upset if they don't read it or if they hate it? I just want to make sure that no one could ever say, 'We didn't know. We weren't told.'

# CHAPTER 8

# SUZANNE GOLDENBERG

## BIOGRAPHY

BORN IN CANADA, Suzanne Goldenberg worked as a freelance journalist in India before joining *The Guardian* in the UK in 1988. She has covered political events in India, Pakistan, the former Soviet Union and the Middle East. In 2000 she became *The Guardian's* Middle East correspondent in Israel and in the following year her highly acclaimed coverage of the Palestinian/Israeli conflict earned Suzanne the Press Club's Edgar Wallace Trophy for reporting of the highest quality, the What the Papers Say Journalist of the Year Award and the James Cameron Memorial Award for her 'consistently impartial reporting'. In 2002 she shared the Journalist of the Year Award from the Foreign Press Association. Her reporting has also earned her vilification and denigration within some quarters of the ultra-orthodox Jewish community (Suzanne believes much of the criticism levelled at her arises from the critics' expectations of her because of her surname).

Suzanne has said she went to Israel to write about peace but ended up covering war and in late 2002 left Israel to cover politics in Washington. She also spent two months in Iraq covering the troop build-up and then stayed for the duration of the invasion in Baghdad.

Suzanne is author of the *Pride of Small Nations: The Caucasus and Post-Soviet Disorder* published in 1994.

She is single and lives in Washington.

\* \* \*

# STORY

It is hard to pick just one story that has remained with me or is special. I remember images more than stories.

One image that sticks in my mind dates from the siege of Ramallah by the Israelis at the end of March 2002 that continued into April. All the journalists were cooped up in a hotel because of the shooting, and it was unusually cold and misty. I remember we went out of the hotel in a convoy of soft cars. We were trying to follow up on stories about Israelis summarily executing Palestinian policeman and other people in uniform pinned down during house-to-house searches.

We were on the way back through the centre of Ramallah – a built-up section – and there was a lot of shooting very close by. We, and the reporters in the car behind us, looked for cover and very quickly turned into a driveway that had a high wall. So there we were: two carloads of journalists huddled behind a wall and squeezed into the space between the bumpers of the two cars while a tremendous battle went on nearby between the Israeli army and armed Palestinians evidently holed up in a building. The Israelis were using anti-aircraft guns and tank fire, and chips of stone were flying into the driveway. It seemed to go on forever.

There is no question that we were scared, some people more than others, and there was the problem of trying to make a group decision. We realised there wasn't much protection from either the cars or the wall so we tried to break into one of the buildings to at least get some shelter because the only way out would have been to cross an open road. But it turned out we were in the driveway of an insurance company or a bank, and we couldn't break in. We lined up there and just waited – the waiting always seems much longer than it is.

I was with Tracy Wilkinson from the *Los Angeles Times*, who is a tremendous reporter. It was wet, we were soaked through, and we crouched against the bumper of one car, waiting. An Italian TV crew decided to do a stand-up commentary of what was happening for TV. So we became a backdrop to the TV reporter. Tracy obligingly lay down to get out of the frame, and the TV reporter put on her helmet and began reporting on the dangerous battle now taking place all around her while we just sat there.

It is these kinds of things, the absurdity, that I choose to remember rather than the traumatic or terrible things I have seen.

## Covering conflict

I always wanted to be a foreign correspondent and I definitely see my job as a privilege. I love it, I am rewarded well, and I think I have gained a certain understanding over the years about what human beings are capable of, good and bad, and I value that tremendously.

Generally, what inspires me is the story itself, and probably a fair measure of anger. What is interesting about covering conflict is not the armies, or the hardware, or even the battles themselves, but seeing what is happening to ordinary people. It is hard not to be caught up by it. But as much as I found and still find it compelling to report about what happens to people whose lives are overtaken by conflicts, if you live in a conflict zone for too long it is difficult to cover it with any sort of freshness, without your sensibilities being overwhelmed. It becomes repetitive. In Israel, after a certain point, I began to feel: 'How do I rev myself to write about something that is almost the same as something I saw last week?' because there is this compulsion in journalism to make every event distinctive. Perhaps the point really should be: this *is* reality and this *is* everyday; people have to live like this for months and years.

Because of the intensity of my experience in Israel, I thought when I came here to Washington in 2002 I wouldn't be capable of reacting to less violent situations. It was interesting for me to find that during the sniper shootings by John Muhammad and Lee Malvo (in the autumn of 2002) I could appreciate the drama of the situation, and the fears and emotions of people despite the fact that the dangers were not as extreme as in the place that I had come from. In terms of covering the invasion of Iraq, compared to covering Israel, Iraq was a much bigger story, it happened so quickly and it was all-consuming. Unlike Israel, in Iraq I only ever saw a part of the story at one time, but everything was so extreme that each little piece was huge. It was overwhelming.

Journalism is one profession where there isn't much in terms of a defined code of practice, unlike with doctors or lawyers. There is not the possibility of sanction for malpractice as there is with a doctor; disbarment from the profession doesn't really exist. So I think conduct generally is established on an individual level. It comes down to how one behaves. In this regard, I suppose everyone has belief systems of some kind or other: what you believe to be right or wrong or moral.

I wouldn't say that my beliefs are spiritual or religious, but I try to behave with sensitivity toward people, especially those who are suffering. In terms of guiding principles, I am pretty firmly of the belief that if you are covering a highly emotional subject, one in which there are fiercely held beliefs and a lot of rhetoric, there is not much to be gained by writing emotionally for one side or another. That does not mean that you should not write with compassion. But the whole point of journalism in such situations is to convey another reality, or to bring a degree of rationality to impassioned debates. The job is to help people understand what is going on, and I think it is more effective to do that through reporting and detail rather than writing polemics or giving vent to my own sense of outrage.

At the same time, I don't subscribe to the notion of objectivity as a goal of journalism. I think the word to strive for is 'fair'. I think the idea of objectivity is one of those journalistic myths and, more often than not, is used as a way of maintaining the status quo, and to suppress ideas that challenge the view of the world put forward by the forces in power. I think objectivity means parroting views that are conventional and that don't upset people because they side with the forces that are in power.

There were a number of attacks on my reporting from Israel by lobby groups, and almost invariably they hauled out the charge that I had not been objective. In the beginning the attacks came as a shock to me, but after a while I ignored them because I realised the vast majority of the angry emails were cut-and-pasted complaints that had been copied off a web site set up by a pressure group. It wasn't like anyone had ever read my work. No one wrote, 'you actually got this wrong'. They were just slavishly following someone's direction. I think criticising people for lack of objectivity is often code for the critic really saying, 'This doesn't correspond to my point of view,' or 'This doesn't correspond to the prevailing dominant view.'

The controversies did affect my relationship with the military in Israel. Talking to individual soldiers was fine because I speak Hebrew and we got on well. I was rarely invited on press trips, but then neither were a lot of other journalists. I think the public-relations people in the army decided at one point that: 'If we don't like what you say, we are going to freeze you out.' But I never saw that as a huge problem because those kinds of tours are meant as propaganda. In terms of calling up the military spokesman, I had no problems and if I wanted a special briefing it sometimes happened, but not with regularity.

In terms of the larger picture and the nature of the relationships between the press and the military, it is certainly true in Israel that the old values of respect for journalists are disappearing. The Israelis, on a number of occasions, have shot at journalists who they clearly knew were journalists. But then the whole nature of war has changed, and with the spread of conflicts involving militias and different irregular forces rather than professional armies, journalists can't just sit in army headquarters and be briefed about what is going on, or at least I don't think that is what reporting should be about. That has probably had an effect on the way the military views journalists nowadays – or journalists who are not travelling with their troops. It also makes the job more unpredictable, and more dangerous.

So tenacity is essential in the job – especially because militaries respond to the changing relations with the press by cutting off our access. For example, during the offensive on the West Bank in 2002, we were the first into Jenin City. We had heard that something had happened in the Jenin refugee camp. Palestinian officials were talking about a massacre, but from the outside there was no way of finding out exactly what had gone on. To get to the camps took us three or four days but everyone had problems: the press, the UN and the Red Cross. The checkpoints were a nightmare. It was the most frustrating situation. But it was also a valuable experience. Things aren't exactly what you see on TV and you have to be able to make up your own mind in conflicts and trust your own judgments and your own ability to go out to see if, indeed, something is true or not true. And because the changing nature of war can mean armies see journalists in an adversarial way, it forces journalists to get to know people across the spectrum: the actors in the field, officials and grass-roots people. Establishing those contacts and talking to them to get the information takes time. It doesn't take years but certainly a few weeks or months. But in the end that leads to better understanding and better journalism.

Of course, those are some of the larger issues, but on the job the concerns are much more immediate and have to do with private codes of behaviour towards the people who I am using, essentially, for their stories – stories that can convey the horror of a situation. I try to recognise that the people I am interviewing have just gone through a degree of trauma and I try to be respectful of that and not get so caught up in the mechanics of getting the story that I can't see what is really going on with them. There is something heartless in asking people to relive a horrible situation and then just saying at the end, 'Well, thank you very much, goodbye,' and not acknowledge them as a human being – to just extract that information from them, that quote, that image of them crying. I don't think it is right to do that.

It is understandable, however, that anyone would question the ethics of the profession because you do find yourself doing things that you wouldn't see yourself doing in normal life. For example, after suicide bombings in Israel the authorities would allow all the journalists into emergency rooms to talk to people. I am not sure they always asked the wounded if they wanted to talk. There was just this expectation that people who were slightly wounded would make themselves available to the press. That was disturbing because it was showing off the wounded for a specific political purpose, without regard, perhaps, for their individual rights. But I did the interviews. On the other hand, there is no point going to see someone whose house has been bombed just because you have got nothing to do that afternoon. That is obscene. And you don't have to interview someone groaning in agony because his leg is blown off if somebody else was there and saw just as much. Those are the kinds of micro-decisions you can make. On the other hand, I also don't see any conflict in helping the people you come across. If you are sleeping in a hospital or somebody puts you up then you give them money. If you meet somebody who you think is perhaps talented in some way, you put in a word with someone and help them.

## CAMARADERIE, FRIENDSHIPS AND SUPPORT

There is a jokey thing among journalists to refer to non-journalists as 'civilians', which I think reflects how relationships between journalists and others outside the profession can sometimes be difficult to sustain.

In terms of non-civilian relationships, the support network between journalists, people that you know around the world, is a good thing in small doses. Personally, I don't want to live my life entirely inside that group because after a certain point it becomes limiting. There is also the illusion that these friendships that you have formed in conflict areas are close and real. Sometimes they certainly are but it may just be the intensity of the shared experience. They are probably not lasting friendships. I mean, when you are seventy-five are you still going to be friends? Can you really sustain a friendship with somebody on memories of the two weeks you spent together in some horrible situation? You might come out of that hopeless situation to more ordinary, everyday life and you have nothing to talk about. You will certainly come out with strong memories of that person, but I don't think that is the same as friendship.

Some of my good friends are journalists and some aren't. It depends on where I am. In Israel almost all of my friends were journalists. In India, where I was posted before that, some close friends were journalists but many were not. I knew a lot of academics and NGO (non-governmental organisation) types and filmmakers – not war photographers but documentary makers or people who make fiction films. And I have only just moved to Washington so I can't really say yet.

But in Israel I felt I couldn't tell people what I thought. I just couldn't and it limited friendships because I felt I couldn't speak freely without provoking some degree of friction. In such a polarised situation people didn't want to hear what I had to say. So if I wanted to maintain acquaintances or friendships I felt it was best not to talk very much beyond a certain point. It was so bizarre; the situation that so dominated life and was the biggest conversational topic was something that I didn't feel I could really discuss. I would go out in the morning to Jenin or Ramallah and see my neighbours on the doorstep – and they were nice people – but when I would come back I couldn't tell them what I had seen because of the fact that I was crossing, physically, to the other side. Of course, the reverse also held true for my discussions with Palestinian friends.

So socially it was also easier to allow people to talk about what was going on in their lives. They might say, 'Oh, I read this story and it sounds horrible,' and I would just say, 'Yes, it was horrible,' and let them talk about what they thought of the situation. I would talk to my partner, but otherwise I like to keep my personal life or home life separate from my work life. When I visited friends outside Israel I didn't often want to talk about the situation because people found it disturbing, and seeing people from outside Israel was a joy because it was an escape. If you are trying to escape it then why talk about it? Also, I didn't want to be holding forth when I could be catching up with friends on what was going on in their lives.

My experience is that journalists talk about what they have witnessed all the time with each other, and it sometimes makes me uncomfortable. At a gathering of journalists you often get people talking about what they have seen; it is just that they change the perspective to make themselves the focal point. This horrible thing happened and *I was there*. These people were all killed and *I was there*. That is their whole point: *I was there*. Certainly a lot of boasting happens whenever journalists get together, which is pretty distasteful – this reliving of events and somehow reworking them so that the journalists assume some sort of heroic stature by the fact that they were there. It is just so arrogant. That is just not what this job is about.

As for relationships on the job, certainly there are little tribes where the correspondents, by and large, tend to hang out together. These things all break down at some point though. People also tend to work in small groups, although you also have larger networks of friendship or collaboration when you are in the field. The groupings were not so intense in Baghdad as in Israel, at least in my experience, because there were so many journalists from around the world staying at the Palestine Hotel. People think that there were very few people covering the war but, in fact, there was quite a large press corps – maybe over 200 people – and so with that many people everyone tended to stick to their own language group.

Essentially though, I only like to travel with people I know and it is preferable to be with at least one person that you know well and have worked with before for safety and also for companionship. I think it can be dangerous working in a group because decisions can be hijacked. You don't travel with people who you don't know because are they going to do something that will antagonise the people that you are interviewing and perhaps provoke violence against you? Are they going to be too afraid to move? Are they going to be foolhardy?

## UNDERSTANDING WAR

War is something that exists; it is an abhorrent behaviour, but it exists. Especially in this century when there doesn't seem to be a reliable means of stopping it all the time and there doesn't seem to be an overwhelming commitment to the powers of diplomacy and negotiation, or good faith when those things are being deployed. Once a conflict erupts, or even in the lead-up to war, I think all societies are prey to some darker human impulse that essentially makes it possible to deny the humanity of their opponents. That still surprises me and revolts me – the process of transformation that allows people to discard absolutely any sense of identification or regard for 'the other'. It continues to be shocking, but it happens, it exists. People are capable of much more than you can ever imagine – for good and for bad. Human beings always have the capacity to surprise.

Does the most graphic photo convey the horror of war? Does the most gruesome description convey it? I don't know. How much can a reader, or a viewer, absorb? When I was in Baghdad I would see some of the footage that Reuters TV couldn't put out. It was interesting talking to the photographers about what you could cover and what you could not. They said there is so much that they could not send out because people could not stomach those pictures. So I guess if the viewers' only reaction is: 'This is too disgusting to look at' – the image has gone beyond the point where it can bring home the horrors of war. It is not effective to display horror if it so disgusts the viewer that they focus on the picture being sickening, while missing the idea that what people are doing to each other is revolting. And, in a sense, the most frustrating thing is confronting your limitations in conveying what happens during war – the external as well as the internal transformation of lives. There are horrors so great that sometimes you feel that your skills aren't up to the task of describing what you have seen. Yes, I have felt defeated.

Self-censorship is one area where there are always running discussions. For instance, at *The Guardian* there were ongoing debates while I was in Israel about how much physical description to include about the suicide bombings. What do people really need to know? I would argue, just let it rip: let it go. I was all for fuller descriptions: this is what a bomb does to people; this is what a rocket does to people. If it blows out their brains then let's just say it. And in suicide bombings I would say, 'These things eviscerate people,' and I would talk about entrails. But the people back at the newsdesk would say, 'Tone it down. People can imagine the rest,' and they would take it out. I am not sure what is right. I think that my point of view is right but I can accept the other point of view.

I can't remember all of the stuff I wrote in Iraq in 2003

because I wrote in a blur; what I was experiencing was so much in the moment, especially on the worst of days. Given that Baghdad is a city of millions of people and is quite spread out, I could only really know what I could see for myself. I didn't see Al-Jazeera's footage or what others were writing, especially during those last days of the ground war in Baghdad. There was no electricity, no mobile-phone network, no communication. The effect of all of that was that the reporting was by necessity more descriptive and that again produced debates about how graphic the detail should be. In Iraq I probably was more graphic in description than in Israel, and it generally appeared in the paper. In Israel I probably wrote more graphically than was printed.

## Bravery

There is also a fine line between intuition and experience. You know, saying 'this feels bad' may feel like intuition, but I think something can feel dangerous because you have been in a similar situation before and you are reading the signs. In terms of operating on the ground, I think there is also a fine line between courage and stupidity, or between a sensible amount of fear and being too afraid to work in a situation. I think the notion of fear and how dominated you are by your fears is common for everyone, and with the entry of more women into the profession I think it has now become OK to admit that you are afraid. You don't have to be like Hemingway any more and censor any thoughts of fear. I think that is a healthy thing.

For me, at a certain point my hands shake and I can feel my heart beating. That is the physical part of fear. In that situation I just try to slow myself down. Seizing on something very small but tangible can help. Where I have had to cross open areas and I have been afraid of getting shot I always say things to myself like, 'I am wearing a pink shirt and red sunglasses and everyone can see that I am a woman; nothing is going to happen,' and play it over and over in my head like a mantra to keep me going. There hasn't been a time where I have become frozen and been unable to think what to do. Looking back, though, I might not have done the right thing at the time, every time, but I have never been frozen to the ground, unable to move. I do feel, in retrospect, that I put myself in too much danger sometimes, but that has also come about because situations can change so rapidly.

When I'm operating on the ground, while I am working, I don't really think about death. I have never gone through what Marie Colvin or Tracy Wilkinson (who was injured in a Baghdad suicide attack) have gone through and I have never been beaten up either so I have not had an experience where my life flashed before my eyes. Actually, I have to say that my big fear is going off to a place of conflict and having a car accident. Statistically, I think driving in a dodgy car in a dangerous situation is more risky than hiding behind a building with a flak jacket on.

## Baghdad

You can't detach yourself from places where you have seen things, where you have been experiencing intense times. There is a complex mix of emotions and I guess that is what prevents detachment: anger about a continuing situation or sympathy for the people who have to live through it. Definitely, when I left Israel, I had a sense of abandoning people – and some said as much. I also felt an affinity with the people in Iraq because I was there covering the troop build-up for quite a long time before the war. If I had left before the war started I would have felt like I was abandoning the people I had been with for nearly two months. When it was clear the UN was going to evacuate people were saying, 'OK, you are going to go too,' and I would say, 'No, I am staying.' They were happy and said, 'If you need anything we will help you.' Total strangers. Once the war started I wrote a piece about how I didn't know what happened to people who had become my friends. I was struck by how things that had become part of my routine there had broken down, that people I used to pass in the street were not there, that people whom I considered friends I couldn't see or I couldn't reach on the phone any longer because the phone system went down during the bombing.

I wanted to cover the civilians during the war so I wouldn't have wanted to be embedded with the military in Iraq; it just wouldn't be my thing to travel and work with them. Of course, there are restrictions with both. I don't deny that. In Baghdad, before the war the biggest restrictive factor was the Iraqi regime. The main instrument of control was the minder who was also, in many cases, the translator appointed by the Ministry of Information. He would accompany you saying you can do this, but you can't do this; you can go here, but not here. All of our drivers were also reporting on our movements to security agencies so we were always trying to escape them. Before the war, we could go off the leash, and I did quite regularly. We could go shopping by ourselves, to restaurants, or just generally go out on our own and not tell them where we were going. I would say, 'I am going shopping,' and then I would see people but even then it was difficult to really openly talk to people because, 'What do you think of Saddam?' was just too bold a question.

I guess I would divide the coverage in Iraq into three stages, and that was the first stage: living under the regime.

Then came the war, and then the fall of Saddam and the American occupation. For me, the worst time in Baghdad was not the bombing but the ground war when the Americans were there. In the bombing you could feel quite detached and I really didn't have a sense of fear – or, at least, I wasn't overwhelmed by the bombing. If you look back at *The Guardian*, you can tell that the worst time for me was before the statue came down, which was forty-eight hours after the American forces began their entry into Baghdad. People were just dying all over the place and what you saw in the hospitals was just horrific. Those were the worst days.

Also, when Reuters was hit by American tank fire in the Palestine Hotel it was scary. Right up until that time most of the buildings and sites being destroyed had been across the river although there had been small arms fire in the area of the Palestine Hotel. When the shell hit Reuters in room 1503 I was in suite 902–903, which was exactly the same position six floors down, and I really felt the blast. I had been sitting in the suite having a cup of tea with somebody and all this debris started coming through the window. I was very scared but my first thought was that my colleague had just gone off to her room to sleep so I went screaming down the hallway to see what had happened to her. She was covered with dust but was fine. We went downstairs because we knew the building had been hit but we didn't then know if it was the first hit, or why it had been hit, or who had hit it. So those were the worst days for me and probably the worst days for the city – it was just so brutal and violent at the end of the war.

Then came the third stage. I stayed in Baghdad for a few weeks after the war ended. There was a lot of looting and a lot of unrest, but before the war the Iraqis had made huge efforts to protect things. I found a filmmaker who took pictures of everything in the museum before the war started and before it was put in the vaults because she thought it might be looted. A woman in the Foreign Ministry moved all the computers to the ground floor where the staff thought they would be safe in case the building was hit during the war. Well, of course, effectively they had just moved them closer to the exits for the looters and all the while the US soldiers were just standing there watching.

They were the power in the city and the only people who could have intervened to stop the looting and yet they did not. They made a choice not to. I suppose I could have gone up to them and said, 'What are you doing?' but there was no point. We should have known. Everyone predicted the unrest would happen but I had no idea that it would destroy the whole city – more of the wider city was destroyed by looting and burning than by American bombs. It was also during this time that the hostility to foreigners began to creep in.

But I have to say that for me, unlike most of the other media, the focus was not the looting of the National Museum – that was just part of a larger picture of an entire city that had become lawless – but the suffering of the Iraqi people. Banks were being looted where middle-class people had their savings accounts. It's hard to think how they are surviving now.

## Dealing with trauma

Looking back over the years, I suppose I have become more sensitised but I don't know if that is because of what I have seen or because of the process of growing older. I think a lot of it is because of growing older and becoming more aware of my own mortality. At the same time, I think I have become more aware of the process of blocking things out. I am convinced that everyone blocks things out. It is a normal human mechanism to enable people to cope with dangerous situations and to remain functioning until they reach a point where it is safe to collapse. But even then, what I find extraordinary is that among the people I have met the majority have generally continued to function even after terrible things have happened to them. Probably psychologists would argue that nobody really blocks out horrors forever and that the memories and images will return to haunt the people who have lived through wars and the reporters who have covered them. But I think the ability to suppress horror is crucial to being able to function as a reporter covering war.

I once interviewed a doctor on post-traumatic stress disorder who said, 'Well, when you leave Israel you will be overwhelmed by your memories.' I haven't really seen that. It's true that when I came out of Iraq the only person I wanted to talk to for the first few days at home was my partner. Normally, if you have been away for three or four months, you would think you would want to call up your entire circle of acquaintances but I did not do that and I did not really go out at first. I met a couple of close friends but my re-entry was slow and gradual. People were very understanding.

## Caution

I am ambivalent about the glorification of the notion of 'war correspondents'. By 'war correspondents' I suppose I mean that elite section of people who only cover conflict and are based in London or New York and are parachuted in to cover big stories. I understand the attraction, the adrenaline rush. It is addictive, there is no question, and yes, of course, there is an aspect of fun. Extreme situations are fascinating, and there is this additional aspect of being all pumped up on adrenaline and fear because of the intensity of the experience. There is a huge amount of excitement. But I suspect people who want to experience that all the time are damaged characters. It is an addiction – this sort of very powerful illusion that here you are, happy people having adventures all around the world. For some people, war does fulfil a romantic idea. But there are also reporters – local reporters – who cover conflict all the time because the conflict happens to be taking place where they live yet we glamorise the other breed of journalist. I am uncomfortable with that.

There are certain skills required for going into dangerous situations and writing about them but in many ways writing about conflict is the easiest kind of reporting because it is right there in front of you. A journalist who can't make a good story out of a horrendous experience is really lacking in some pretty basic skills. I think it is much more difficult to make a compelling, gripping story out of mundane life. This kind of reporter has to make phone calls and do research that is maybe not so glamorous and may not attract a lot of attention, but is still important and useful journalism. A war correspondent's job is simpler – writing what they see that day. This is also a skill because it requires paying attention to absorb what you are seeing, but in some ways it is a less complex task.

The reason I was able to give up covering Israel and go to Washington is because I don't see myself as a war reporter, or at least not exclusively as a war reporter. I see myself as someone who wants to report on the human condition. I think that reporting on war is limited – the world is bigger than that. So I would say that my job still centres around the same mission that I had when I began reporting from India all those years ago: to just connect, to let people see the connections between people far away and themselves. My mission hasn't changed.

# CHAPTER 9

# ROY GUTMAN

## Biography

BORN IN NEW YORK, Roy Gutman has been a journalist for over thirty years. In the sixties, while studying international relations in London, he decided he wanted to be a foreign correspondent, or 'our man in somewhere'.

After working for Reuters for eleven years, Roy joined *Newsday* in 1982. From 1989 to 1994 he was their European bureau chief covering the fall of the Berlin Wall, the reunification of Germany and the disintegration of Yugoslavia. In the Balkans he was the first to expose the Serb concentration camps and practices of ethnic cleansing, including the policy of systematic rape of Muslim women by the Serbs. His extensive coverage of the conflict earned him a Pulitzer Prize in 1993 for international reporting. He has also been honoured with a number of other prestigious awards including the George Polk Award for Foreign Reporting in 1992, the Selden Ring Award in 1993 for investigative reporting and the Edgar

Allan Poe Award from the White House Correspondents' Association in 1992. He has also received a special Human Rights in Media of the International League for Human Rights Award in 1992 and in 2003 won the National Headliners First Prize for Magazines.

After leaving Europe, Roy worked as *Newsday*'s national security reporter in Washington for eight years and in 2001 joined *Newsweek*. Today he is director of American University's 'Crimes of War Project', adjunct professor at the Medill School of Journalism and senior fellow at the US Institute of Peace.

Roy is author of *Banana Diplomacy: The Making of an American Foreign Policy in Nicaragua* (1988) and *A Witness to Genocide* (1993). He is co-editor of *Crimes of War: What the Public Should Know* (1999) with David Rieff. He is currently writing a book about the war in Afghanistan during the 1990s.

He is married and lives in Washington.

\* \* \*

## Story

My stories about my career tend to be of things I didn't do. I have so many stories – such a horrible list of them that it is hard to decide which one to tell you.

A story that I didn't understand until five years after it happened helped lead me to focus on the concepts of law as a way of looking at and reporting war. It was in the middle part of the Croatian War, maybe October 1991, and I was in Zagreb. I didn't know what else to do that day – you never do really – and I heard that the European monitors who were collecting information on human-rights violations were going to Vukovar as part of an aid convoy because the town was completely under siege by the Serbs. There must have been about thirty vehicles, twenty food trucks, my little rented car and the rest were press vehicles. As the convoy got to the outskirts of Vukovar, the Serbs stopped the column, deliberately fired on its flanks and kicked out the press. (Actually, the aid trucks got stuck there for three days and never got the food through because the Serbs said they were carrying weapons).

I had to do something so I followed a colleague's car to a hospital nearby in Vinkovci, which was the front line of Croatia and Serbia – in fact, the hospital *was* the front line. We discovered that the entire hospital had been moved to the basement because every ward and every ambulance was destroyed, every red cross painted on the building was basically used for target practice by the Serbs and every window was broken. But I got a good little story about a multi-ethnic tank crew whose vehicle had been destroyed by someone who was now also a patient in the same ward: a perfect vignette of the war. I wrote the story about the crew, the people, and said this was a sign of the tragedy of Eastern Slovenia. It was a genuine and interesting story that actually recapped what had happened only two days earlier and it was in a setting that was right out of hell. But what I didn't realise until years afterwards was that the real story was the destruction of the hospital – that was a war crime.

At the time I didn't even think to ask why the hospital had been destroyed but six years later, when I was working on the book *Crimes of War*, I called up the International Committee of the Red Cross in Geneva and said, 'By the way, what was going on there with this hospital and had this happened elsewhere?' It turns out that five other hospitals had been destroyed by the Serbs. Five hospitals deliberately destroyed! This was one big story that I missed because I realised I could have rung an alarm bell right at the beginning of the wars in the Balkans with that story if I had only approached it within a legal framework rather than just the human-interest story of the multi-ethnic tank crew.

Years later, when I realised the significance of what had happened to that hospital in Vinkovci, I asked the Red Cross why they hadn't announced at the time that the Serbs were destroying hospitals. I believe the answer to this is they never make any such announcements because it would jeopardise their work. I worked with the Red Cross often and used them for fact-checking but I never quoted them. For instance, if I had been to a place but I wanted to make sure that I wasn't putting the story together wrongly, or missing some big element, I could ask them if I was correct. And they could say 'yes' or 'you are off in this regard'. As a journalist, you have much more confidence in writing your story if you have one of the world's best observers of human rights and international law as your source. But even they don't know all the laws. If they find a violation in the field do you know what they do? They call up their own legal office in Geneva and the legal office has an interesting yardstick: if it stinks it is probably a violation. The same yardstick we use as journalists.

So my point in telling this story is that I discovered a hospital that had been destroyed before some of the worst atrocities by the Serbs in Bosnia and Croatia took place. It was a test by the Serbs. It happens in every conflict. Sharon today is testing us to see how far he can go and so is Arafat. In every conflict, one side or the other is testing whether we – the international community, journalists, governments – are watching and it turns out that on the whole we aren't because war crimes and atrocities happen again and again. I could have rung alarms bells with that story if I had have only approached it from the angle of the legality of what was happening. It doesn't take that much to do so.

What I discovered, or rediscovered, in the course of the later Balkan wars, was that I could be an investigative reporter in war (I had only really ever been a diplomatic reporter until then). In regard to the story about the hospital, I should have got all the versions: the hospital's version of what happened and the Serbs' version of why they did it, and then the story would have been 'in a systematic violation of agreed international law the Serbs have targeted and destroyed five hospitals. They say what they are doing is no violation at all'. And I would solicit a comment from the International Red Cross to confirm that what happened was a violation of international law. In this instance I believe they would have no choice but to say it sure looks like one. Now that would have been a good investigative story.

## GOOD JOURNALISM

The American media are doing a pretty good job of covering America but in terms of covering the world, hell no. Since the end of the Cold War there has been a diminution of interest in the rest of the world because of the perceived lack of a security threat. I thought 9/11 would change that but the change has been fleeting and superficial. So obviously something is wrong in the American approach to journalism right now. We are missing stories and we don't understand that we're missing them.

September 11 was a case study in missing a story and I was one of the people who missed it. A terrorist movement took over a state (Afghanistan); that is a pretty serious development and nobody told the public! How did this happen? In 2002 I got a fellowship from the United States Institute of Peace and I want to do a book about how the media missed that story. My thesis is that if you were watching the war going on in Afghanistan and Kashmir, you would have probably discovered that al Qaeda had taken over the war. Now that would have been a hell of a story! How on earth did we miss it? I wouldn't say the fact that we missed it was scandalous, but it is quite surprising considering this is a world that is interconnected, where I can get anything I want on the web, and yet I didn't know that al Qaeda had taken over Afghanistan.

If we really look at the events since the end of the Cold War, we can see that this is the pattern – small wars produce monsters, and the media, on the whole, are not able to cover these wars in anything beyond a superficial manner because we don't know the rules. I am focusing now on what we are missing, what we have got wrong, and my feeling is that we in journalism – editors, publishers, reporters – have got to be out there where everybody thinks there is no story. Even though these are small teacup wars that don't affect us directly, it is out of these wars that monsters grow and worse wars arise.

Rwanda was a bit different: it was an example of a story that journalists went to but didn't understand. Many journalists got it wrong for a long time and the public was confused. Was it a genocide, or wasn't it genocide? Lindsey Hilsum, Britain's Channel 4 foreign correspondent, was the first journalist on the scene and was one of the first to leave because she was so baffled and overwhelmed by what she was seeing. She said, 'For god's sakes, I have got to understand the rules of war because that would help me understand what I am seeing.' To do that you need to define, at least in your own mind, what you are seeing within a legal concept.

Let me give you examples. Somebody may destroy a church during a war. The only question you have to ask yourself to understand what the crime is, is: 'Was this church being used as a military installation?' Either the people attacking it were attacking a religious building that is protected under the law and are therefore commiting a crime, or it was being used for military purposes, which is the crime. Either way, you have a crime. Too often, television just shows this destruction and doesn't tell you another thing. A case of this is what happened in Goma* (then Zaire) – the scandal of our age – because that is where everybody said, 'Here we can do something in providing assistance to the victims.' But we were in fact helping the people responsible for the genocide. Why did we help the *genocidaires*? Because nobody defined that the crime of genocide had taken place in Rwanda and that these people we were now helping in Goma were the *genocidaires*: the killers.

I do not view myself as a war correspondent by vocation, although I covered the Balkan wars, which ran, with a break, for a full decade; covered the wars of Central America in the 1980s; did Beirut, Cyprus and some others. I don't seek wars. On the other hand, photographers such as Gilles Peress and Ron Haviv do seek them and they have the frustration of taking great pictures that create an impact, which then

---

\* **Author's note:** In the African Republic of Rwanda in 1994 the Hutus turned on their friends, neighbours and relatives, the Tutsis, in what turned out to be approximately 100 days of mass slaughter, which in the majority of instances was performed at close quarters with machetes. Anywhere from 800,000 to over a million people were slaughtered. At the end of this period the *genocidaires*, or those who had been the killers, panicked and retreated across the border to Goma where they amassed in camps. As disease and malnutrition began to take their toll in the camps, the governments and aid agencies responded with assistance. They were, in fact, in most instances keeping alive the killers while for months before they had ignored their victims.

What happened in Rwanda is, of course, far more complicated than this. A good account of the genocide can be read in *We Wish To Inform You That Tomorrow We Will Be Killed With Our Families* by Philip Gourevitch, Picador, 1999.

disappears. But wars do matter; they change history. And our reporting makes a difference, though on the whole we think it's not enough of a difference. A group of us journalists and photographers who had covered the Balkans met in 1996 to review what we'd done there. And we were all asking ourselves: 'What are we doing wrong? What did we miss? How is it possible that in 1996 the international community still hasn't arrested a single war criminal; that everything that we covered seems to have been in vain? There must be something more we can do.' We all sort of knew that the law was going to be important in finding a solution but we just didn't know how. Then it occurred to us that we didn't even know international law or how it relates to war – there was no guide.

So Gilles said, 'We have to have a book or something to explain the law to us,' and that is what the *Crimes of War* book is. We have ninety authors in the book, people who came to us in some cases because they were furious about how our governments don't live up to their international responsibilities. David Rieff, my co-editor, is a really tough cookie (I think the world of him but I disagree with him greatly on a lot of things) and his contention, and the reason for doing the *Crimes of War* book was: this international law we have is inadequate but it is the only thing the world has to keep some sort of order, so we journalists really should understand it. And because journalists are probably the first line of defence during war we should know enough about the law to be able to report to the world, 'Hey, there is a war crime over there, goddamn it!' Who else is going to tell the public?

We know that the general public expects, through their governments, to be living in a relatively orderly world, although everybody knows that there is disorder in many places. What the public doesn't know is to what extent their government has a responsibility to do something about that disorder and that's where international law comes in. Law sets certain outer limits of human behaviour and these limits have to be upheld by the major powers, starting with the US, but everybody else as well. The moment our governments walk away from those outer limits is the moment they give a green light for atrocities and that is basically the moment you walk away from world order. That is what happened in Rwanda and the Balkans.

We have great journalism schools in the US but there isn't really one that tells you how to cover a war (well, there's an exception as I just taught a course in war coverage at the Medill School of Journalism, Northwestern University). Every good journalism school should have a course in war reporting and journalistic safety: first aid, weapons recognition, how to react to kidnapping, and the rules of war – what is legal, what is illegal, what is criminal. I feel this with a passion. It is not that you have to cover war as a journalist or even want to cover war, but war does happen and you may have to cover it. If you can do the toughest thing under the worst situations, probably everything else you have to face on the job is a lesser category. But, on the whole, the American journalism schools are living in another world; they focus on the front page – it is like vocational school.

So out of this book on war crimes then came the 'Crimes of War Project' at the American University – since moved to Medill. In 2000 the project had a seminar on covering war and war crimes and I invited foreign editors plus reporters. We brought together the best photographers we could – three photographers: Ron Haviv, Steve Lehman and Gary Knight – and had them tell us, with illustrations, what it was like at the front line. The stories they told were hair-raising. These guys really dodge bullets and rocket fire. Then we brought in the guys from Centurion (a private risk-assessment company that provides hostile environment training) to explain how to minimise risk, and we also brought in Chris Cramer, the president of CNN, to testify about PTSD. Everybody was gripped but the truth of it is that we didn't have any impact on the industry... no, I shouldn't say that – it has had impact. When Kurt Schork, one of the best buddies and best colleagues I have ever had in this business, was killed in Sierra Leone, Reuters turned to us and asked, 'Who are your contacts for PTS?' This demonstrated there had been a breakthrough at a certain level.

My feeling is that war coverage is more important today than ever before and we need better war reporting. So here is my contention: if, as journalists, as journalism students, we are given a general picture of how wars occur, how they develop in this new era, and if we learn the framework of international law, we can report the war in a way that readers are going to relate to. How do we do it? Firstly, we need to look at the crime and look for what our government says about it. Then we should get lots of people to comment about how this should not be happening but how governments are letting this happen. That gives the reader something to get angry about rather than just seeing suffering people but not knowing why they are suffering.

## COVERING THE BALKANS

I had gone through six months of trying to write the story about the war in Croatia for *Newsday* and I know I did more than a creditable job. But, at the crucial moment, I couldn't go to Vukovar when it fell because we had a babysitter problem at home. I was responsible for covering stories for all of Europe for *Newsday* and I missed the fall of Vukovar! I wanted to go a week later but *Newsday* were not interested. In fact, they felt that my preoccupation with the whole story was misplaced while I felt that it was the most important story in Europe and could be one of the most important stories of the decade. No one really knew what the war in Croatia was about at this stage: was this a civil war, a religious war, an ethnic war, a war of aggression, or was this a war of post-communist succession? I went through all of these five categories trying to explain the war but, by explaining it in all these different ways, I didn't explain anything. There are times you can't report something with great depth because it just hasn't reached that point. By the time I figured it out, my editors had lost interest.

So I went through a whole period where my editors were either disinterested in what I was offering, or even mocking it. I'd been really burnt because I felt my judgment must be off. So when the war in Bosnia happened I was very wary of it and I thought, 'I don't want to go through this again because I have better things to do with my life than write stories that are not going to be printed.' That was the sentiment that preceded my coverage of Bosnia so I waited until my editors suggested that I go to Bosnia. I am afraid of things like dying, a bullet crossing my path, or getting into a situation I can't get out of, so in this sort of instance you don't really volunteer, but you are driven to do it because your editors ask you to, because the competition is doing it, or just because the story is there. Anyway, my number-one problem in Bosnia was figuring out how I was going to tell the story so it really made an impact. I didn't want to go through the frustration again of feeling like I was sort of being laughed at by my own editors.

What drives me as a journalist is when I see something that should not be, something that totally repulses me and would repulse my wife or anyone I know. In Bosnia I came across such a story quite by accident. I had been interviewing people in a refugee camp when I was told by the matron that there was a train full of refugees from a village in Bosnia coming into the nearby station. It was a sealed passenger train that had been shuttling back and forth to the Hungarian border because the Hungarians didn't want the refugees. This was something that hadn't been seen for fifty years and thoughts of the Holocaust came straight back at me.

I find that when you know something terrible has happened you are driven, something takes over and you hope that your professional background allows you to think things through logically in order to get the story. But I could not bear to be frustrated again about what I thought was a massive story so I took my editors along step by step until they recognised that this was something very big. Gradually the story unfolded, first the sealed deportation trains, then expulsion in freight cars, until I discovered the Omarska concentration camp.

I had first heard about these Serbian-run concentration camps when I visited Banja Luka in July 1992.* In the course of a conversation with one of my Bosnian sources there I said, 'Is there anything else going on that I should know about?' – an innocent question. He said, 'Yes, there is a network of camps.' From that moment on I had a burden on my shoulders of not just writing about these camps, but writing about them accurately with the maximum of fact-checking. Writing about such a subject without proof could destroy everything that you had done. But at that stage, on that first trip to Banja

---

\* **Author's note:** Banja Luka was Bosnia's second largest town and became a centre for Serbian power under General Ratko Mladic in April 1992. In an attempt at ethnic cleansing, the Serb forces initially terrorised and disenfranchised the Muslims and eventually moved thousands out of Banja Luka via sealed trains.

Luka, I did not have witnesses, only hearsay. I levelled with the public, my editors, everybody, that I just hadn't been to any of the camps because the Serbs wouldn't take me. I was very careful because I felt they existed and I didn't want to exaggerate. I sent the story to somebody at the White House; somebody at Freedom House, which is an organisation that works for human rights around the world; a friend connected to the CIA. I sent it everywhere and the story didn't register. What I wrote made *no* difference! People in Washington knew me as a very serious and solid reporter ... or so I flattered myself ... and the reaction to my ringing of the alarm bell about the concentration camps was zero. Well, that really gave me the feeling of a tremendous burden. That was about as much pressure as I have ever felt on my shoulders in my life. I had to find a way to do this story again so it would make an impact. I am convinced that a strong story, well told, well framed, well presented, will have impact, but the point is you don't give up – maybe this is my illusion but I believe it. So I talked to my editor and said, 'You know this story is true but I cannot figure out how to get it across so that people will take it seriously.' He had a very simple suggestion: find a survivor of one of these camps. Then somebody turned up in Austria who had been imprisoned in a camp and that just drove me bats because then I realised there really *is* a network!

So I devised a formula. I wanted to find either two people who had been in one camp, or one person who had been in each of two camps. It was a formula that came to my head as a way of putting across that these camps are systematic and widespread. I said to one of my editors, 'Can't we hire the satellite and take a picture of this place because I am convinced of what I am being told is true, that people are being mistreated and tortured?' Today you can hire a satellite to do anything but you couldn't then. I was thinking, 'For god's sake, the CIA have the capability to do this!' In fact, they did have the capacity and the images but they didn't know what they were seeing – they didn't have the intelligence to allege what was going on and for that reason they did not know how to package it. This is what a journalist has to do: you package it to present to the political leadership. You have to tell it in a way that people can actually relate to. The CIA didn't have the analytical tools and it was only after I wrote my story, or so I heard later, that the CIA was able to put together the much bigger picture. When I finally found the Omarska camp I wrote about it as a concentration camp. In fact, I quoted the Red Cross saying that it was a 'death camp'. They didn't say that straight out, of course. They put it in a question form by asking, 'If this isn't a "death camp", why won't they let us in?'

I felt in my bones that putting a spotlight on the story about the concentration camps would have impact immediately, but we journalists are usually very wrong about predicting impact. We throw ourselves into something because we really feel it matters and it will change people's minds but on the whole we get it wrong. This is why I am so critical of the industry. It is only after failing and realising that we haven't figured out how to tell the story that we can come up with a formula that helps us next time. So I think that we really do learn from our mistakes and we ought to be more analytical and willing to look at ourselves.

## JOURNALISTS AS WAR-CRIMES WITNESSES

Courts of law have a different purpose than the domain of journalism. Their job is to nail somebody, to prosecute, to sentence, and to incarcerate, but a journalist should just report what he or she sees and let the chips fall where they may, with no further agenda. So on the whole I don't think journalists should be testifying. What I do believe though is that we should be helping the courts in every way we conceivably can within our profession.

In some ways, the Yugoslav tribunal would not have come about but for the mass of material that was provided by the media. At one point, I was told that some of my stories were like a road map for the court and that is what journalists' reports should be – not to necessarily put people behind bars. But equally it is not to see an injustice done. A friend of mine, Michael Montgomery who was with the *Daily Telegraph*, did brilliant research in Kosovo and Montenegro about the people who killed the civilians in Pec and his stories provided the road map for the prosecution. I don't mind helping the courts find a couple of the detours or road signs that they may have missed – because we can do things in journalism that the legal profession can't – but we have different jobs and I think that we journalists have to watch our step about testimony.

Also, there is a difference here between testifying in an international tribunal (international journalists can cover war crimes in an international setting because informally they have a kind of immunity in that the courts don't have the power to subpoena them) but what if you are a journalist from Angola and there is a domestic court set up in Angola to try war crimes and they want you to testify? Would immunity work in a domestic setting? How dangerous would it be for you to work in your own country after that? On the whole, this is one of the reasons why people shy away from covering war crimes in their own country because they know there can be an aftermath. Richard Goldstone (the first prosecutor at the International Tribunals for the Former Yugoslavia and Rwanda) who wrote the foreword in *The Crimes of War* really made the most solid point: reporters do so much to make these courts function that the courts should not ask reporters to step over that line. But everybody ignores his advice.

I have been asked maybe half a dozen times by the Yugoslavia War Crimes Tribunal to testify and I have turned them down every time. My colleagues who have testified at tribunals have had a very mixed experience. But, in the end, I cannot stand an injustice and I don't want to see impunity – that is one of the reasons that you go into this business of journalism – so I think that if my testimony would make the difference between some major criminal walking free or being put behind bars I would have to very seriously reconsider my stance on becoming a witness.

## COVERING WAR

From my coverage of war, which goes back to the Turkish invasion of Cyprus in 1974, I believe that there are really two styles of reporters. The first type is the old-style romantic guy with the safari jacket and the equivalent of a notch in his belt for every war he has covered. But you have got to ask yourself did he really cover it or did he just happen to be there? That thing that some reporters have of being at as many wars as possible is really mad and I don't think it is healthy or even necessarily proper journalism. Then there are the people out there who try to cover what is really going on in conflict, which is much more meaningful than just, 'I am here.' Kurt Schork of Reuters was not just looking for bang-bang, he was out there looking for the story in Sierre Leone when he was killed. Now, whatever gets thrown my way I cover. If I feel really strongly about something my editors will often listen to me, but on the whole I have to listen to them and cover what they want me to.

In Bosnia I felt that it was a situation of such immensity and awfulness and there were so many stories that I needed a team.

Andree Kaiser, who was born in East Germany and served time in their political prison for showing disrespect to the regime, called me at one point and said, 'Can I come with you?' I had met him covering the reunification of Germany. It was one of those marriages made in heaven because he is a great photographer; his style was very unusual, like a Cartier-Bresson. He could be silent and wait for that moment when nobody was looking and then get the photo. This man has such a pair of eyes! He saw things I didn't see. A good photographer is like nothing on earth. I took Andree on the first trip out of my own personal budget but after seeing his images, my photo editor at *Newsday* said to me 'you can take that photographer on any trip from this point on'. I said, 'Well, my only deal is I want to get him life insurance.' Photographers usually work as freelancers and if they get killed it is the courtesy only of the organisation hiring them to return the body to their family.

I also had a wonderful translator. I have always made it a principle to try to hire a journalist who may not have perfect English but who offers me another pair of eyes and journalistic judgment. Seska Stanoljovic is a very brave lady who had been working for a Croatian daily and who came out with me on the trip to Banja Luka. I was there for two days and I got six stories out of it. I could not have done it all myself because Seska saw things that I didn't see, or heard things that I didn't hear. So I had my team – not that we really saw everything eye to eye, but we tried to figure things out. I have found that as time has gone on I am able to assemble teams which may not have total rapport, but which I can make work. One of the reasons for this is that I tell people, 'I want to trust you; I really want to listen to you; you are part of the team, and I am just one of you. I have got to make the decisions, but you have got to contribute to this thing.'

I've found that I do not work well in packs with other

reporters. I think that working with other reporters is the death knell to investigative reporting. Every time I tried to go out with people – and I love my colleagues – I would often wind up in fights with them about what we were seeing. I remember having a five-hour debate about whether what we were seeing was genocide. At the end of the day I didn't want to hear their views. Also, if you're in a pack with other reporters, you have to all decide what you are going to do and then you seem to go with the weakest view in the car, or the view of the most cautious person. It is a disaster on wheels when you go in with a pack. I think, on the whole, in this profession we are all loners.

## FEAR

When I feel fear the first thing I usually think is, 'This started off as a good day. How the hell did I get into this?' Or, 'I am not like a photographer; I don't need to be dodging bullets so what am I doing here?' and I have to figure out how to get out of the dangerous situation safely. When I first covered the war in Lebanon in 1982 they had a green line, a no-man's line out in the field. Here is the trick to getting from one side of the green line to the other: act as if you do it all the time. You know, I am just walking through here and here is my pass . . . nonchalant . . . cool as possible . . . just show no nerves and usually that cools people down. Then you say, 'A piece of cake.' That's my phrase when I have crossed one of those things. But it isn't a 'piece of cake'.

I was once in a situation that was so bad – my motto is 'how long does it take before I can tell my wife about the story' and in this case it took me about six weeks: a long time. I was in Mostar, in the southern region of Bosnia–Herzegovina, with Andree and we wanted to go to East Mostar, which was the

Muslim zone, but we had to drive in through the Croatian area because the Croats were besieging the east. To get to East Mostar, we had to drive through the airport in West Mostar. So I drove down the road in the airport and it came to a dead end where there were men standing around with sub-machine guns. Clearly that was not the way into East Mostar. So I figured I must have done something wrong. I went back to where I started and drove the other way. I got down to the end of that road and again there was a no-man's land: a place I shouldn't be. Then I drove down the first one again, and then the second one, and at one point I was in the middle of the airport driving around thinking, 'Where is it?' Finally the Croat soldiers arrested me. I was so relieved!

I said to them, 'Listen, here is my problem. I want to get into East Mostar but I can't find the road.' They drew a map and so I drove in there and, you know, 'a piece of cake'. It turns out you had to drive down the runway itself and at the end of the runway was a little road coming off it. How could I have expected that? I have never driven down a runway before! That was pretty scary but in a sense we were well protected because we were making open movements; we were not driving fast; I had TV marked all over the rented armoured van we were driving; I had all my passes (you need every press pass for every different military faction in a war but you have to be sure to show only the right ones); I had a rough idea of where I should be; it was a day when they weren't shooting; and I kept my cool. There is a big element of luck in these things.

I was at risk in Sarajevo once. It must have been in 1993 and the UN had put up a sign-up sheet that said they were driving to Grbavica (a Serb-held area of Sarajevo). Did anyone want to join them in their own vehicle? So I went with ITN to join the UN and we drove to the Serb checkpoint. The Serbs asked for everyone's passport and they said to me, 'You are a dangerous guy. We would like to talk to you.' I was well known by the Serbs because I had done so much coverage of ethnic cleansing and so I was marked – Milosevic was on my case. To cut a long story short, I was just standing there for about three hours. The Serb military said their boss wanted to see me and so I was keeping my cool, not talking much, but I said to my friends from ITN, 'You have got to send the word to the UN, please, and to whoever the hell else, maybe the Brits, that I am being held here and I do not want to move. I will not get into anybody else's vehicle. They are going to have to drag me and I want you to photograph what they do, but let's just really keep cool.' I understood from one of the ITN translators that they were sort of mentally slicing me up, you know. So that was a case of winding up in a situation that was so bad I *never* told my wife about it.

## DEALING WITH TRAUMA AND SHARING

I try to avoid scary, dangerous situations but they cannot be avoided. If I am in such a situation my motto is to get the hell out of here – this is not what I am supposed to be doing. The combat photographer though is supposed to be doing scary, dangerous things and so I think they have a huge burden beyond what we print reporters do. You have got to have the world's strongest psyche. I admire combat photographers immensely. I love them. Ron Haviv has told me that there is this group of twenty, no more, and they call themselves something inane like 'the group'. This is the most unusual group on earth – they *choose* to go into the most horrendous situations and I think that is why they shouldn't have the PTSD quite in the same way as we normal reporters who don't actually choose to cover war. They have chosen to do it; it is their volition. Also, I have found photographers to be much more articulate than some of us print guys. Gilles Peress and Ron Haviv are really eloquent, articulate, impassioned speakers.

I have seen dead people; I have seen blood. I haven't actually witnessed, like Ron did, executions in front of my eyes but I have found that when I have been able to put together a good team they are the best people there are with whom to discuss what you have seen. When we were in Banja Luka in 1992 sitting opposite a man from the Muslim party who was giving us this list of trains going through the station with how many wagons and how many people on them – cattle cars basically – I remember Seska sort of saying, 'My god,' under her breath to me. She repeated that phrase maybe about 100 times on that visit because we completely believed what the man was telling us. You know, that is pretty traumatic so I tend to want to tell people almost immediately when such things occur.

That same day, Seska and I met some other journalists over dinner and I started talking about what we had seen at the Manjaca concentration camp that day: guard dogs, barbed wire, men being humiliated in front of us. It is not quite the same as seeing somebody's throat slit in front of you but, boy, it is pretty traumatic. My inclination over dinner was to say to the other reporters, 'You should see Manjaca!' but Seska said to me, 'Roy, shut up. *You* have got the story. Don't talk about it.' Her point was that I was giving away a story but I am not protective of my stories . . . I mean, I want to be there first and get the story right, but then I want to make sure everybody else has it too. I am pretty competitive, in the sense that we have to be, but if you are dealing with something so horrible, so huge, that the only thing you feel is going to make a difference is coverage . . . I mean, there by the grace of god go I . . . I wouldn't want some reporter hiding the story.

So yes, I have been jarred and shocked by some things – that happens – but it may not have been war coverage, it may just be a story I have missed. I guess what would really stress me out more than anything else – and I don't mean to be flippant – is getting something wrong. For me, that would be huge stress.

For instance, here is a case where we had to take real risks, significant but unknown risks, perhaps one of the most frightening things I have ever done. In August 1992 I had heard this story of the systematic rape of Muslim women in a little village near Tuzla (Bosnia-Herzegovina) by Bosnian-Serb soldiers. The soldiers had been ordered to rape the women; it sounds incredible, but the women were processed: they were raped once and then released across a minefield. Just to get to Tuzla involved a four-day drive into the interior, where no journalist had travelled in the three months since the war began. Then there was the question of how do I actually get rape victims to tell me their story? Well, the mothers and daughters, like so many other internally displaced, were encamped in a high-school gymnasium. I have never covered rape before but I brought the mothers and the daughters together (they had been separated from their husbands and fathers; no one knew where the fathers were but they had been loaded on buses and probably sent to Brcko Luka, one of the worst of the Serb-run detention camps). Everybody in the room was in tears except me. I was *angry*. I had this sort of pseudo motto for myself: 'Don't get angry, get even.' And so what is 'even' for them? I think getting even is to tell their story irrefutably, strongly, so nobody can dispute it, but get the thing out! The fact that Andree was with me and being his usual unobtrusive self, waiting for the moment and then silently shooting the images – this made all the difference in the world in convincing the public that this really happened. But a British TV guy wrote that he had gone to Tuzla and couldn't find these girls. He said it was a phoney story about rape. What an idiot. How could he have done this? He could have called me up and I would have said, 'Here is who you go to.' The problem was not being first with the story or even having the story in the first place; the problem was having it right and then having it believed. And having it believed means more than your own story. For that reason, in this situation, I decided I would share my sources, nearly anything with my colleagues, and my colleagues shared with me too, and we don't usually do that.

People ask me how do I stay sane because some of the things I end up covering are so very painful. One of the great aspects of journalism is that you have written about it. If you have done a good job and you get people's attention, you can sleep well. For me, writing about atrocities is working through the pain of seeing them. For people of any other profession dealing with civilian atrocities there is usually no end stage because everybody knows that they always come too late, they can do so little, and there is no way to undo the damage. But journalists, by telling the story and putting it out to the general public, are performing a useful task. For the victims, you have confirmed that their story is true and given it a life beyond the person it has happened to. And if you are writing a story about war crimes, in particular, you are reminding the authorities that it is their job to stop them. You may prevent things happening further down the line. So at least you have done those things and, on the whole, you can't do very much more as a journalist. People sometimes ask you to do more but you really can't and shouldn't. I operate in a framework of hope, but I am a realist too. You should go on to the next story but you can at least look back and say, 'I did that story.'

# CHAPTER 10

# RON HAVIV

## BIOGRAPHY

AS A PHOTOJOURNALIST, Ron Haviv has covered conflicts around the globe since 1989 in places such as Panama, Afghanistan, Somalia, Iraq, Russia, Rwanda and Columbia. He also spent ten years covering the break-up of the former Yugoslavia. It was Ron's images of the first killings of Bosnian civilians that informed the world of the horrors to come and for his efforts he was placed on a death list by the Serbian warlord Arkan.

Originally with the Saba Press Photos, Ron is a contract photographer for *Newsweek* and in 2001, along with six other photographers, became a founding member of Photo Agency VII.

He is the winner of numerous awards including the Overseas Press Club Award (1989, 2001), University of Missouri Picture of the Year (1989, 1991, 1995, 2001), the Leica Medal of Excellence (1989) and World Press Photo (1989, 1991) and is the subject of a documentary for the National Geographic Explorer Channel. Ron is the author of two books, *Blood and Honey: A Balkans War Journal* (TV Books Inc, 2000) and *Afghanistan: The Road to Kabul* (de.MO, 2002) while his pictures are featured extensively in a number of books including Peter Howes' *Shooting Uncle Fire: The World of the War Photographer* (Artisan, New York, 2002); Giorgio Baravelle's (ed) *Rethink: Causes and Consequences of September 11* (de.MO, New York, 2003), and Photo Agency VII's *War* (de.MO, New York, 2004).

Ron is single and lives in New York.

* * *

## STORY

In March 1992 I was in Yugoslavia to follow up on a story that I had been doing on the fall of Vukovar. While I was there it was apparent that the war in Bosnia was going to start but nobody knew exactly when or how. Tensions were rising, people were getting nervous, but there wasn't really any military fighting.

I was in Belgrade one day when a friend got a message that fighting had started just across the border in a small town called Bijeljina in Bosnia. By the time we arrived, the town had already split into Muslim and Serb sections with civilians starting to shoot each other. Within hours, the town butcher was fighting against the town carpenter, the police had split up and everyone had weapons, trying to organise themselves in a military fashion to protect themselves. This was the beginning of the war in Bosnia and I spent several days documenting its beginning. Just like the war in Croatia the previous year, civilians were fighting while waiting for troops to arrive to bring the battle to another level. On the fourth day, as I was standing around the town centre, a few vehicles pulled up and well-armed, professional-looking soldiers led by a warlord named Arkan jumped out. They were the 'Tigers', a paramilitary unit with quite a reputation in Croatia for brutality – executions, robbery, other war crimes – all done under the guise of Serbian nationalism.

I was photographing them as they came off the bus and Arkan walked up to me and asked who I was and what I was doing. I explained that I had already photographed him the previous year – a portrait that had become very popular of him holding up a live tiger cub with his troops. I said that I would like to go with one of his units as they fought through the town so he assigned me to a small group of about fifteen guys who I ran off with as they began to organise themselves for battle.

A few hours later they started to move through the town, street by street, fighting their way to the town centre. We reached the centre where the mosque was and I heard a bit of a commotion in a room where soldiers were interrogating a young man. They told me that he was a Muslim fundamentalist and they were going to take him prisoner. I then heard some more commotion and walked across the road to where soldiers had pulled a middle-aged gentleman and his wife out onto the street. The couple were standing up against the brick wall, the soldiers were screaming at them, and the woman was screaming. This went on for a few minutes until shots rang out and the husband went down on his back. At this point the soldiers then turned to me and started screaming at me not to take photographs.

When you are around soldiers that are in the process of fighting, or in this case starting to execute people, tensions are quite high: everybody is very jumpy, very nervous. The adrenaline is so high that it is almost as if everybody is on amphetamines and you have to be careful not to upset anybody because somebody could quickly turn and shoot you without thinking. So it was a very nerve-racking situation but I had previously made a promise to myself that I would never watch somebody be executed in front of me again without taking a photograph. (When I had been in Croatia, Serbian soldiers had executed some civilians and had put guns to the heads of me and my colleague to stop us from taking photographs. I always felt guilty that I wasn't able to do anything to help those people and wasn't even able to document their deaths. So I made this promise that I would do my utmost not to allow that to happen again. Here it was happening again in front of my eyes.)

By now it was quite obvious to me that there was nothing I could do to stop what was happening because there was a large group of soldiers intent on what they were doing. Things got more confusing, more soldiers were shouting, and I kind of slunk off into the background, looking for a place where I would be able to take some photographs. I found a truck that had crashed in the middle of the street and I walked behind it. From there I was able to see the woman trying to comfort her husband and stop the bleeding. I took two quick images of them together and then I walked away from the truck. As I did, more shots rang out. I looked up and the soldiers had just shot the woman. Moments later they brought out another woman and shot her. Then they brought out a young man. He was absolutely terrified and at one point, broke loose from the soldiers' grasp and tried to escape but he ran into a wall he couldn't climb over. As he turned back to where the soldiers were, one shot him. Of course, at this point I was also being told no photographs and, as I was in the midst of the soldiers, there was not much I could do. They started to march back to their temporary headquarters taking the first man that I had encountered with the Serbian soldiers as a prisoner.

Even though I had the photograph of the woman and her husband, I realised that I really didn't have the evidence of Serbian soldiers in the same image with the victims. When most of them had left I stood in the middle of the street hoping to get a frame with the soldiers and the bodies. As I lifted the camera I saw three soldiers coming from my left so I put my frame on the victims. One of them lifted his foot back, sunglasses on his head, cigarette in his hand, and appeared to be kicking the bodies as if checking to see if they were still alive. I took several images and put my camera down. Just as I did they turned and looked at me and I smiled to them and I said, 'Let's go.' They didn't realise that I had taken any images and we ran up the street.

As we did I encountered the original man they had taken prisoner so I ran up to take a photograph of him just as a Serbian soldier pushed him down to his knees. I bent down to take the photograph and as I did he put his hands up in the air and looked at me. He didn't say anything but he looked at me as if asking could I please help him to get out of what he thought, and probably correctly so, was going to be his eventual death. I looked at him and with eye contact showed him that I was helpless as well. The soldiers then marched him off into their headquarters.

As I was standing around waiting for permission to leave, getting very nervous that the unit I was with was going to tell Arkan that I had taken photographs, I heard a great crash and the man who I had just photographed came out of the third-floor window and landed at my feet. The Serbian soldiers came out, looked at him crumpled on the ground, roughed him up and then picked him up by the scruff of the neck and doused him with water before dragging him back into the house. I tried to talk to the commander to help this man but it was pointless. The next day I went looking for this man but he had disappeared.

Arkan arrived a couple of minutes later and one of the soldiers whispered something to him. He then came up to me and demanded my film. I thought that they had told him what had happened during the fighting but in fact he was asking for the photographs of the prisoner coming out of the window. I argued with Arkan for several minutes about how I would never betray him and how he had nothing to worry about, but he told me that he would process the film and if there were any pictures he didn't like he would take them. I argued with him that the processing labs in Belgrade weren't good and it would be better for me to process the film. We had a ridiculous conversation about film processing and I think he thought that because I was arguing so much about the film in my cameras that the film in them was all that I had. However, I had managed to hide the film that I had taken earlier of the Serb soldier kicking the dead woman and her husband and also the man pleading for me to help him. Eventually, I gave him the film in the cameras and left.

## GETTING STARTED

I was studying to become a journalist but in my last year at university it just didn't seem right. I had started picking up a camera as a hobby and it came to me that maybe it would be interesting to use the skills I enjoyed as a writer for photography. So I freelanced in the streets of New York. I was the youngest person working and other photographers were very helpful, leading me from place to place and giving me advice.

One of the people that I met on the streets was Chris Morris who was a pretty well-established photographer at that time. I was kind of in awe of him. I knew he travelled overseas and I asked him, 'Where are you going next?' Chris said, 'Panama.' So I said, 'Well, I am going to Panama too.' I didn't even know where Panama was but I thought if Chris was going there it had to be good. Chris looked at me kind of strangely and said, 'Oh great. Maybe I will see you there.' We ran into each other a few more times in the next couple of weeks and one day Chris said he had a free plane ticket (the airline had a buy one, get one free special) so I could have it if I wanted, stay in his hotel room, ride in his car, and we could hang out together. It was totally amazing! It really was just like a gift from the heavens.

So I hung out with Chris in Panama as he taught me about working in dangerous situations. Manuel Noriega had just lost the democratic elections and nullified them. Chris and I were following the winners as they were trying to bring people out on the streets in an uprising and Chris said, 'Whatever you do, stick with the candidates because if anything happens that will be the story.' As the day went on Chris and I got separated. I stuck with the candidates and took photographs of the vice-president being beaten up and covered in blood as he was attacked by paramilitaries and several people were killed. The story and my photos made the cover of all three newsweeklies. It was amazing!

At the time I was only thinking about it in terms of it being really great for my career and not about the bigger picture. It wasn't until a few months later when President Bush announced that he was going to invade Panama and began his speech by discussing my photographs that it clicked for me. It wasn't that I agreed with his reason – that wasn't relevant – but I realised that photography could seriously affect the world. It was the clearest connection. Until then I had been interested in the world but I was looking at things with normal interest, not getting upset, not becoming involved, just finding my way through life. But when the President of the United States was using my photographs as a justification for invading a country it really solidified my ideals that I could play a role in effecting change. That was in 1989 and it was a great time to start being a photographer because the whole world was changing.

## Being a photographer

Anyone who uses the word objectivity with photography or with news is being unrealistic. Photography is not objective but what photographers need to deem, and what the public needs to trust, is that they are being fair and that they are not misrepresenting a situation. As simplistic and clichéd as it sounds, I think the basic idea of trying to be fair to everybody and trying to help the defenceless has shaped my beliefs and carries through to my work and the way I act during war. But on another level this work is completely selfish. To be able to see the history of a country happening before you is an incredible privilege, watching amazing events like the Berlin Wall coming down, Nelson Mandela walking out of prison. To be able to document these events and show people my vision of them is a privilege. And to be able to play a role, albeit a small role, in the process of disseminating information and affecting decisions made by the person on the street and the powerful politician is truly inspiring.

Photography only plays a role in this process though; it doesn't work alone. The responsibility of my job is a little easier to handle with that mindset: you are part of a team, adding to evidence and the dissemination of information. I will do my utmost to bring these images and the information to the world and that obviously motivates me, but it doesn't allow me to become overwhelmed by thinking everything is on my shoulders alone.

For me, photographers are not distinct from journalists. Photographers go into war as a journalist as well as a photographer and on the whole they are very smart and often much more clued in than a lot of correspondents because they are often involved on a much deeper level than a lot of the journalists sitting back interviewing commanders in their headquarters. It reaches the point where, as a photographer, you come back from the front and the correspondents are sitting in the hotel and they say, 'What happened?' and you are caught in this difficult position: these guys were not really there but, on the other hand, it is important that the information gets out. In fact, there are a very small number of correspondents who go to the front with us that are jokingly referred to in the field as honorary photographers.

Basically, each conflict produces another generation of war photographers and war correspondents. All of us in my age group came from the wars in Yugoslavia. Working today in war photography there is maybe anywhere from twelve to twenty photographers and we see each other wherever we go around the world, although there are people who show up for one conflict here or there. There is a real bonding amongst us. Yet I have seen things start to change over the last couple of conflicts. In Afghanistan there were fewer of the group than you would have expected because people had got married, had children, or their values had changed. The group of photojournalists that started in the Gulf War and Yugoslavia are starting to disappear. In the last conflict in Iraq in 2003 we began to have a crossover of the different generations and there now seems to be a new group of hungry and motivated photojournalists to continue the work.

*Ron Haviv*

## The increasing danger in the job

At the beginning of every conflict there is some sort of grace period given to journalists by each of the sides involved but in each conflict that grace period gets shorter. At the beginning, every side wants you to tell their story but two weeks into the conflict, when they don't like everything on television and in the newspapers, they hate you; all your protection is gone. For the first few months in Croatia all our cars were plastered 'TV' and it was very helpful but, in retrospect, what Chris Morris and I would do was stupid. A number of times we drove up to one front line and asked them to stop fighting so we could drive down the street to the other side – otherwise it would take us six hours to drive what should be a five-minute drive – and they would! By the beginning of the war in Bosnia there was absolutely no way we would ever do something like that.

In terms of overall numbers, it is the cameramen and photographers who are often in the most danger but more so the photographers. A cameraman's lenses are just so much more powerful and the quality demanded from TV cameras, as opposed to the quality demanded of photographers, is very different. TV is a quick thirty seconds to two minutes of footage and quite often whatever the cameramen shoot gets shown. There is a much higher bar for photographers. The nature of a successful still image requires that we get closer and work a situation more so as to photograph as many variations as possible. All in all, the photographer often stays the longest and puts him- or herself at greater risk as a result.

But competition and the idea of getting the scoop exists less with photographers than with other parts of the media. This is primarily because we have to go into the most dangerous places and most of us don't like to do that alone.

If you get hurt you want to make sure somebody is there to take care of you and you want somebody that you respect and work well with to use each other's strengths to get the story. So you usually travel in groups of maybe three, but usually two. Quite often you will have a *Time* and a *Newsweek* photographer travelling together, or an AP and Reuters photographer together. The bosses back home say they don't want that to happen because they are in competition with each other but the photographers don't care. These are our friends, we trust them, we do good work together, and the objective is for the image to be seen by as many people as possible – just having one magazine or two magazines publishing the image is not going to do it. Photographing the event is much bigger than the actual mechanics of working, so we work together for safety and we share information.

## FACING DEATH

In 1994, during the war in Bosnia, a group of us went to cover what was happening in the siege of a UN safe haven called Bihac. But it was very difficult to get access so we were left just driving around Serb territory trying to find sympathetic commanders who would allow us to take photographs. We were pulled over by Serb Special Forces soldiers, but that was sort of normal for the way the war was going – you would be arrested every couple of days by one side and you would be interrogated for a couple of hours and end up drinking and smoking with them. This time these guys were very angry and we really had no idea what we had done. They told us to follow them to a local police station and, like so many times before, we sat there waiting to be released. Six or seven hours later a soldier came to take us back to our hotel because we were being deported. So I left a note for a colleague saying what had happened to us and we drove off into the darkness with two of the Serbian Special Forces soldiers, not knowing where we were going. At this point I started to think that something was going to happen to us – maybe we would be executed.

After a few hours the car pulled into a courtyard and, handcuffed together, we were thrown onto the ground into a small shed. Then the door burst open and two soldiers doused us with cold water saying something like, 'This is to clean the Muslim smell off you.' Being November it was quite cold and now we were even colder. After a few hours they came back, took off our handcuffs, and led us into some sort of farmhouse. There were a number of soldiers and a commander sitting behind a desk who accused us of being spies for the Bosnian army. We were put back into the shed.

In the early morning the door burst open again and they dragged my colleague out. I heard a gunshot and then silence. I spent another hour or so alone and then the soldiers dragged me back into the room where the commander told me my colleague had been shot and if I didn't confess to being a spy the same would happen to me. It was probably the next day before they came back for me again. With a hood over my head and my hands tied behind my back they began to interrogate me. Somebody would ask what my mission was and I would say that I was a photographer and then I would be punched in the face. The question would be asked again. I would say I was a journalist – punch; then I would say I was a photographer – punch. I tried to change my answer. I was still hoping that there was a possibility that this was basically just intimidation and there was still a way of surviving. After being punched in the face and the body for a while (I kind of lost track of time), they threw me back into the shed.

I started thinking about how when I had heard the gunshot I hadn't heard a body fall. I also wondered why they had taken the hood back. Maybe my colleague was still alive and they were actually bluffing. A few hours later I heard what I thought was my colleague screaming so I was hopeful that it was him and that things weren't going to be as drastic as they appeared.

While this was happening, the colleague I had left a note for, before we had been taken by the soldiers, had contacted *Newsweek* and my agency at the time, Saba. They began working hard on the diplomatic channels trying to create as much pressure as possible on the local Serbian government to find us. The US and French governments and the Russian government, which was acting as the messenger to the Serbian government, put a lot of pressure on very quickly. I think within thirty-six hours the message got down to this unit that they had to release us. It took about another day or so but finally we were handed over to some Federal Security Service guy on the border of Croatia and Serbia.

## Fear

When I am covering conflict, it is important for me to always acknowledge that I am scared 99.9 per cent of the time and to be able to use that fear as a survival mechanism. However, I can't allow it to take over and disable me from being able to move and think and take care of myself. I never want to be so fearful that I am paralysed. Actually, I am more fearful of *that* happening because that would be the most dangerous situation. Luckily, so far I have been able to work through it but there have been times when I have stayed in the room and not gone out because I felt like it wasn't the day to be out there – sometimes I would have that anticipation of what the day was going to be like. You have to learn how to recognise those feelings within yourself, not to the point of being overly superstitious, but just to be in touch with your inner feelings and use your judgment based on them.

Fear is never used against people in a macho sort of way. Everybody I work alongside is very respectful of people's feelings and fears. For example, when travelling around there might be a place where somebody wants to cross a street where there are snipers and somebody else doesn't want to. In those situations if people are scared then people are scared; it is respected. I am always amazed when people say that they are not scared. How can you be in these situations and not be scared? If you are in a war zone and all of a sudden you don't feel scared then it is definitely time to leave. Your value of life and death has changed. You have gone too far and you need to get out. Chris and I used to do that. We would return to New York and after a while we would be watching the news and we would say, 'It's still happening. We need to go back.' Sometimes it was easier to go back to the Balkans than it was to leave.

## THE IMAGE

I disagree with the cliché that the camera gives you protection. It brings you closer to the scene; everything is magnified as the faces fill the frames. But you don't walk through these areas with a camera to your face 100 per cent of the time. Maybe you have the camera up to your eye ten per cent of the time and the rest of the time you're looking at things everybody else is. So your camera is not going to offer you the emotional protection that you need to continue working. I have what I think of as a thin membrane that I use to protect my emotions while I am working, in order to keep going, to not be overwhelmed.

It is not always possible to take an image of war or famine that can differentiate that particular war or famine from any other, but that is the power. Take Yugoslavia for example: I took a picture in 1991 that I took *every* year. That is the point. That is the power. Why are we still seeing these same pictures over and over again? 'Hello, didn't you say when you saw this picture five years ago that you were going to stop this war and now here it is again?' Wouldn't it be great not to see these pictures any more? The strength is in the *repetition*.

I don't think that Western audiences should turn away from graphic images of war. They need to face the situations head-on and it is wrong for the media to say that people don't want to see images of war. The world is too small and too interconnected for people to turn away and it is our responsibility as journalists to help make sure they don't. One way to be successful is to make your photograph as visually interesting as possible in order to draw the audience in. I try to convey information about what is happening but do it in a way that provides an emotional connection between the viewer and the picture.

When you break it down it can sound quite harsh and unfeeling, but you are using light, composition and colour to make an image and that is really what differentiates the great photographers from somebody who is just going off with a camera. But you can talk to other photographers who would say the exact opposite: 'Well, if you make a real effort controlling the aesthetics you are making it about the aesthetics and art and you are diminishing the reality of the image.' But I find photographs like that incredibly uninteresting and I have no interest in the information. It loses it for me. We have had endless arguments amongst ourselves about it but it comes down to personal choice. I like to think that my photographs can exist as evidence *and* encourage the audience to make an emotional connection to the picture at the same time.

When people look at my work and they comment that my images look like pretty war pictures, or pretty photographs of something horrible, that is along the lines of what I want. I want you to be able to look at the image without having to turn the page but still understand the severity of what you are looking at. It is walking that fine line between seducing the viewer and conveying the information. I am still trying to do it and it is often very hard.

At the same time, American editors say my photos are too brutal for the American audience. After a while I accepted that the photographs I was taking in Yugoslavia would never be published in America but that *Paris Match* would publish them in France or *Stern* in Germany. Choosing different images for different publications became part of the workflow. Yet I don't know if what the American editors say is true, that the American public don't want to see graphic images (which goes along the same lines that all Americans aren't interested in foreign stories). There is some weird disconnect between the advertisers, who are the ones making the decisions, and the editors. My experience, from giving lectures around America, is that people who buy soap – the people the advertisers want – come up to me and say, 'How come we haven't seen these pictures before? We are really interested.' Who is making the decision on what the taste of the American public is?

## INDUSTRY CHANGES

My hope is that one of the main benefits of 9/11 is that the American people will realise that when they make a decision, vote for somebody, or when their president speaks about

Yemen or other foreign places, they won't say that is so far away that it doesn't affect them. They will know that it does. The media plays a role in this change as a main educator and that, for me, is the true hope of the future of photojournalism. Then photography will be given a second life because for freelancers like myself the job is definitely getting more difficult. There is less work, less money to support us and, if the major news organisations are not concerned with stories that are covered by freelance photographers, eventually those stories will disappear. Being able to choose where we want to go and getting support from news associations is becoming a way of the past for the freelance photographer: our world is disappearing.

News associations today are not sending their contract photographers out to some of the most dangerous or obscure places in the world. Instead they are relying more on stringers to supply their photographs because they have less responsibility toward them. So increasingly that means that where there are no stringers there are no pictures and lots of places are not being covered. Also, the news agencies are not taking responsibility for the people that do provide their product. Employers have all these different technicalities in relation to work agreements now. In many conflicts, some magazines used to employ a photographer on a day rate (on assignment), which meant that the magazine took full responsibility for your safety and paid your expenses. In order to get around that responsibility, some magazines now refuse to give day rates. Instead they give you a 'guarantee' that they will look at your photos. So, let's say the day rate is $500 (which hasn't changed more than $50 or $100 since the seventies): they would give you $3500 for the guarantee to look at your photos for the week, which means that they are paying you the same as if you were on assignment, but by giving you a 'guarantee' they are not actually employing you and therefore don't take any responsibility in case you get hurt.

In addition, the agencies are moving to own the content of photographers' work by either hiring photographers as staff, or by buying the rights to your photos. You used to be able to sell your picture for $50 or $100 everywhere. Now there are fewer places to sell the images to and so the photographer, who needs money will sell the rights to all of his or her work for the day for $100 and then the agency will own the rights to those images which means the photographer cannot resell their images. As big agencies are trying to control and, in my view, eventually own the images that are produced for them, I think that as photographers we have lost an intrinsic thing and we are definitely at a crossroads in terms of the way that we work with the agencies. A lot more people are taking staff jobs and not worrying about whether they own their images and some are signing work-for-hire contracts. Others are starting to realise that they need to be more aggressive in their fight for their rights and for the ownership of their images.

In the sixties, when photo agencies like Gamma, Sygma and later Sipa were started, they were meant to be beneficial for photographers – help them, protect them. By the nineties this had completely switched around: the agencies became bigger than the photographers. Being part of an agency is exemplified by what we did at VII Photo Agency. It was just a group of friends getting together and throwing some stuff up into the air and it developed into this agency that is pretty valuable in terms of photographers taking charge of their own lives and own careers. We all know each other, have all been friends, and we each have a real role in decisions, so the beauty of it is that both the mistakes and the right moves are all our responsibility. In the beginning it was easier but now we are starting to deal with more of the realities of running a business. But we are all learning and progressing, and so far we have been succeeding quite well in a normal business way. I look at VII more as a motivator than a pressure.

## READJUSTING TO 'NORMAL' LIFE

It took me quite a while to learn how to readjust to 'normal' civilisation after coming out of a war zone, and I damaged personal relationships. Eventually it became easier to readjust and I am getting better at it. I think that the misnomer is 'normal': what is a 'normal' life? To be a photojournalist, not just a war photojournalist, is a way of life; it is not a nine-to-five job, it is part of you. I work twenty hours on the job and then I come back and read the newspapers, surf the Internet, watch CNN – research for the next job. It is so intertwined in my life that there really is no separation. On the other hand, there is also the recognition that there should be a separation. I understand that I need to be able to survive, and I want to survive in 'normal' life because I don't want to live continuously in a war zone. Understanding how to reconcile those feelings and survive in both of those worlds enables me to go back and forth, but they are never really separate – it is all *my* normal way of life.

By doing this work, you get the feeling that life is incredibly fragile and can end any moment. So you have more respect for life; it is definitely a privilege to be alive. If I stopped and thought about what my experiences have given me, the answer would be the benefit of taking myself above the somewhat mundane type of normal life that one can have when back in the 'real' world. But to be honest with you, after a month or so back in New York you can easily forget that, but the fragility of life does hit you again when you are back in the field.

In terms of talking about what happens out in the field, it is very difficult to talk to people who haven't been there. We photojournalists are such a small group that we bond together and often can only really talk about our experiences amongst ourselves. If other people in our group are having problems, then we try to help each other out.

## UNDERSTANDING BRUTALITY

I don't think that I have found a way of totally explaining the brutality of humans but I have a theory that fear is a huge motivating factor. People involved in war use the feelings of fear that something will happen to me; fear that my family is going to be killed; fear that 'you are going to take my land and I won't be able to feed my family, so I need to protect my land and I am going to kill you and your family before you kill my family'. Although I am not a parent I can understand that somebody would do almost anything to protect their child, and even if the threat is not real it is very easy for people to rationalise it. When you talk with the combatants from either side of a conflict it is amazing to learn the historical reasons of why they are doing what they are doing. There is no question that those stories from the past and stories of fear are used to incite the masses; in Yugoslavia fear was manipulated and enhanced through propaganda by the politicians. Each side always fell back on 'they are coming to get you so get them first'. Neighbour turned on neighbour because they were driven into this frenzied state of fear. The United States' policy of first strike is completely derived from fear. It seems that we are moving into a spiralling cycle of fear and reprisal with no end.

But I don't think that fear is 100 per cent of the explanation for why we can be so brutal towards each other. I still think that to a large extent there are people who will take advantage of certain situations, who will be brutal and use whatever they can to achieve their goals. Essentially, I think that humanity is a tribal society and people can use that tribal mentality for good or for evil.

I don't think our work will have the effect of changing humankind. It will take generations of people like myself working to start to effect a change in the way people think. But in terms of photography making a difference and affecting the situation on the ground, our work does have influence. I am sure I have done things to change someone's life for the better. I think that my colleagues and I have definitely helped stop wars and saved lives. You say to yourself, 'Well, I was only able to help out that *one* family or that *one* person,' but that is enough for me right there. If I can save one life through my work or over my lifetime as a photographer, that is amazing. But hopefully I can do more than save just one person.

CHAPTER 11

# AHMED JADALLAH

## BIOGRAPHY

REUTERS PHOTOGRAPHER Ahmed Jadallah was born in the Jabalya refugee camp in the Gaza Strip, Palestine, and has lived and worked there all his life. On 6 March 2003, while working with Reuters cameraman Shams Odeh, both Odeh and he were hit by Israeli tank fire. Odeh, with a broken foot, and Ahmed, severely wounded in both legs, continued to shoot footage and photos after they were injured.

Ahmed was initially taken to al-Shifa hospital in Gaza but pressure on the Israeli authorities by Reuters saw him being moved to a hospital in Jerusalem and later to a London hospital. This interview was recorded in September 2003, six months after the shooting and three weeks after his last operation. In total, he has had five operations. At the time of the interview he still had one leg in plaster and was living in Reuters' accommodation in London.

In May 2002 he was named Photojournalist of the Year in

the Arab Journalism Awards in Dubai for his coverage of the Israeli-Palestinian conflict but was unable to attend the ceremony due to an Israeli travel ban. When Ahmed was transferred to the hospital in Jerusalem in March 2003 after being shot it was the first time he had been allowed to leave Gaza. In February 2004 he won the prestigious World Press Photo of the Year Award (Spot News) for the photo he took after that shooting. (At the time of writing it is unclear whether or not the Israelis will allow him to leave the country to accept the award.)

Ahmed is now living back in Gaza with his wife and three small children.

* * *

## Story

I want to describe the day of my injury. I have seen a lot of things in my life and very sad things in Gaza but that day was a special day for me. I was doing my job: I was going to work with my friend from Reuters to cover a big Israeli incursion into Jabalya, the biggest refugee camp in the Gaza Strip and the West Bank, and I was not expecting for one minute that I would get injured. The Israelis had destroyed three houses, one or two people had been killed, and we heard that they were starting to pull out. I went there to see what was going on, to see the damage.

There was a building on fire and the fire workers were trying to put it out. I was taking pictures and talking to the people around me: civilians, medical staff and fire workers. Suddenly something ... it is hard to describe when the bomb came to us ... everything was in silence for one second, two seconds. I look around and I see people dying slowly in front of me. People standing and then falling down and they are dying, lying on the ground, dying. All I see is dead people, and smoke, and some people in the background running away. It is really hard, you know, to see people dying in front of you and I was feeling that I was also dying. A big hole opened in the ground and I could not stand so I was falling down into this hole.

Then I woke up after one minute, two minutes . . . I cannot believe what I did. The first thing I thought of was my colleague Yannis Behrakis, a Reuters photographer from Greece, who had continued to take pictures of himself after he had been injured in Africa.* My legs had been broken, an artery had been severed, I was bleeding badly, I thought I was dying, and I could not move, but I did my job and I took pictures of the dead people beside me. After that I started asking for help and people came but the Israelis were shooting at us again. For ten minutes I could not reach an ambulance or any car to take me to the hospital because of the shooting, the chaos, the people dying. I was thinking about my family then, the best of the life I had known, because I really thought I was dying.

After they put me in an ambulance I went into a coma but I was waking sometimes – for me it was like a dream. A colleague and friend of mine, Jose Ribeiro, who was chief photographer for Reuters in Portugal and had been coming to help me in Gaza, was there and he told me that as soon as I woke up my father, my mother, everybody was around me but I didn't ask about anyone or how I was going to be; the only thing I asked was whether he had moved my pictures on the wire to London. I don't remember if I said this or not but they told me I did. That I took photos when I thought I was

* **Author's note:** Yannis Behrakis, a photographer for Reuters, escaped an ambush in Sierra Leone in 2000 that killed journalist Kurt Schork and cameraman Miguel Gil Moreno.

dying shows you how I like my job, how it is in my blood, even if it costs me my life.

## Why photography?

My family, my father, my mother are refugees from Palestine, from a village called Para, which is now in Israel. In 1948 my father and his family were kicked out of their home and fled to the Gaza Strip. I was born and grew up in the Jabalya refugee camp in Gaza, Palestine.*

I had always liked photography and after finishing my secondary school it was my dream to study journalism. At the beginning, though, I could not succeed. I got a scholarship and was supposed to go to America to study but because the Israelis would not allow me to travel it was cancelled so instead I studied science in Gaza. But I really wanted to be a photographer, a journalist, and I started working in the media. At the beginning I was a stringer for one of the local newspapers and then I worked with CBS television for three months as a cameraman. There was an office for Reuters in Gaza Strip so in 1992 I visited this office and spoke to the correspondent at the time who contacted the chief photographer of Jerusalem, Jim Hollander. I started working with Reuters then and am still shooting for them today in Gaza.

Actually, I took one course in photography at the beginning of my career but then I started to learn from the people who came from outside Gaza. I have a lot of friends from outside

---

*\*Author's note:* Jabalya camp, situated in northern Gaza, was established in 1948 by the 35,000 Palestinian refugees who had fled their villages in Southern Palestine. The refugees were eventually supplied with cement block shelters with asbestos roofs by the United Nations. Like most refugee camps, it is generally lacking basic infrastructure and consists of a labyrinth of tiny alleyways and tightly packed small houses. The current population is over 100,000 persons in an area of 1.4 square kilometres.

who I translated for in the Gaza Strip. I showed them around and if something was happening I would tell them and in return they taught me how to be a photographer. So I really learnt from photographer friends, especially two friends: Alexandra Avakian who is an American, and Alfred Zadah who is an Iranian-Armenian. These friends gave me the benefit of all their experience – more than fifteen or twenty years of photography in one year – and they taught me how to be a photographer. I learnt quickly because of their help but I would not have succeeded if I didn't love photography.

## Shooting the image

When I make an image I am trying to get strong and clear pictures to convey what is going on exactly – to tell the truth. It has to be accurate and unbiased – just the truth.

For me, I feel like I can just cover what I see because most of the time everything is reality. If I cover a house being destroyed, what bias could there be in covering it? It is a destroyed house; the Israelis said, 'We will destroy it,' and they did . . . It is the same if I cover the killing of a man or woman, or an Israeli army incursion. I am living in an area where there are a lot of things going on and I am publishing the reality of what is going on so it is clear for everyone who sees it. There is no need to be biased: telling the truth is enough. So the most important thing in my job is to tell the truth and to show the people of the world about this occupation of my people.

I believe that we are all the same, everybody has a family, and people of the world should be concerned that it could just as well be one of their sons or one of their small brothers suffering in the same situation. For me, I don't have any power, only the hope that there is change and only the ability to try my best as a journalist, as a photographer, to show what is going on.

But the job can be hard and while sometimes I keep working and taking photos, other times I stop taking pictures because maybe some people don't want me to take a photo: a mother being helped, or someone being killed, or some old people who just don't want to be photographed. So I feel for them. I cannot be stupid and just be concerned only about the pictures. No. I should be concerned about the lives of the people also. If I want to see that my pictures don't hurt someone or cause someone a problem, I would think about it and not take the photograph.

At one point I was working in one of the neighbourhoods in Gaza City, which was being targeted by the Israelis' warplanes looking for just one Hamas leader. During this offensive they killed fifteen Palestinians, including nine children, one of which was an eight-month-old baby. I was taking pictures of this when I found the baby's body between the rubble. I could not take the photo because I started to cry when I saw this. I was wondering what was it she had done to die like this between the rubble. Her problem was only that she was born in Gaza. It is not fair. I could not stop myself crying because I have three children and I thought about my children. My family doesn't live far away; it is only one kilometre between this accident and my house so this could be happening in my area, happening to my kids, to my baby. That is how I thought about it. But then I thought, 'I should tell the world about this, about what is happening here. It would be worse if you don't show this to the world. It is good to show this to the people. Maybe some people can make some change one day.' So I took the photo. But when I went home I lay down on the bed with my kids and held them and for maybe two or three nights I could not stop myself from crying when I thought about it. This is the hard thing in our job; we should be like machines but we are human beings and as people we care about everything... the suffering of so many people.

## SOME ARE GOOD AND SOME ARE BAD

Sometimes, just being there as a photographer can help. For example, if an Israeli soldier wants to arrest someone and then they see a photographer or journalist, sometimes they might stop beating him. So we might stop something bad from happening just by being there. But other times, bad things have happened to me just because I am a photographer. One day an Israeli settler attacked me with his gun and tried to beat me with it to prevent me from taking pictures. I was beaten many times by Israeli soldiers during the first Intifada that began in Jabalya in December 1987 and sometimes they confiscated my films.

But with the Israeli soldiers there are levels of behaviour; it is different from soldier to soldier, from officer to officer. Some of them are nice; some of them are very bad. Always when a new group of soldiers comes into Gaza you face difficulties, you find problems, but you can get to know them. We can talk lightly and after that there can be some kind of like... they understand, we understand... a kind of not quite communication but they do not behave like they did at the beginning. It is the same thing with people everywhere – the Palestinian side, Israeli side, Arab side – some are good and some are bad.

## TARGETING THE MEDIA

I think that the Israelis are deliberately targeting the media now. I will give you my example. There was no reason why they targeted me that day I was hit by tank fire. In broad daylight I was standing with a man and some ambulance people, and there was a dead woman, and they targeted us. Why? I can tell you that at the time there was no gunman where we were standing – no gunman, only civilians. On the other side of the street there was a gunman but he was more than 100 metres away from us and they didn't target him, they targeted us, the civilians on the other side of the street. I don't understand it. I will leave the answer to this up to everybody.

Also, more than thirty journalists and photographers have been killed in the last two years in different areas. The day in Baghdad when the US hit the Palestine Hotel, Abu Dhabi TV and Al-Jazeera, they said they were accidents! You can make one mistake during a day but how is it possible to make three mistakes in one day, in even less than half an hour with three main offices in three different areas? It is a good question to ask.

Mazen Dana, who was a Palestinian cameraman also working for Reuters, was shot dead by the American troops in Iraq a few weeks ago. He was my best friend. When I heard the news I wished that I had died and he was not dead. He was filming the Abu Ghraib jail in front of the Americans for some time before they shot him. It is very amazing. He had been injured in Palestine nine or ten times; he had been beaten *many* times; been arrested *many* times; he was a hero for all the Palestinian journalists; but, you know, this is life – he was killed in Iraq, on another story. I felt it was like a bomb had gone off when I heard the news of his death; it was bad.

Our job in the media is looking for problems but now some people don't like us because we like to tell the truth and some people do not like the truth. Those people don't want peace.

## Leaving Gaza

I had two brothers killed by the Israelis, one in 1994 and one in 1988. Although I wanted to get out, I was not allowed to leave the Gaza Strip for a long time. Never was I allowed to freely move between Palestine and Israel, never: not in war, not in vacation, never. Yet my name, through my photos, was travelling the world every day. Reuters was using the photos everywhere but my body was stuck in Gaza for a long time because without any reason the Israelis had my name on a list of people who were not allowed to leave. I spoke with them many times and sent many letters but I realised that always they were saying it was for security reasons, which I didn't believe. 'If you have anything on me,' I said to them, 'take me to court, judge me.'

So I was always hoping to be out of Gaza; it was my dream to get out with my family, to see the world, but I was not allowed to leave. Then, the first time I got out of Gaza, it was not my dream. My dream was to go with my family on vacation to see Reuters' major office in London but I feel sad that the first time, after more than twenty years, I got out of Gaza by being on a stretcher. Three months from hospital to hospital was not my dream of how I would leave Gaza.

When I was first shot my big boss from London Reuters, Steve, came quickly to Gaza with my chief in Jerusalem, Reinhard Krause. They stayed in Gaza for five days visiting me in the hospital and visiting my family. After I was moved to a Jerusalem hospital, the Israelis refused to give a permit to my brothers, my father and my mother to come and visit me in Jerusalem. I don't know why. They allowed my wife, but not every day and only during specific times of the day. She could only come from 10am and she had to leave at 5pm. She could not stay overnight with me and sometimes she was stopped for hours at the checkpoints. She would leave Gaza at six in the morning and she only entered Israel at ten. At the time I needed somebody. I could not move to feed myself, to treat myself, but this is the life of the Palestinian.

So mostly I was alone in hospital in Jerusalem and in that time you need friends to be with the family so it was important to me that every day Steve and Reinhard went to my house to stay with my wife, my kids, my father, my mother and my brothers, and at the same time came to visit me in hospital in Jerusalem. During this time they were trying to arrange to get me out and they succeeded. If Reuters had not arranged to get a permit from Israel to get out of the country I would not be in London now. Reuters has paid for everything; they have been really very, very good to me. I am very happy with them.

Recently I went back to visit my family in Gaza and was then able to return again to London. I hope this ability to move in and out of Gaza and Israel will continue because I can't see any reason to stop me. I was very happy that I went back to visit the family for one month. Thousands of friends came to my house, thousands – I am not kidding when I say thousands. For a whole month everybody had just one minute, two minutes, to sit and then they had to go because of the crowd. People in Gaza like me. I talk to the kids, the old men, the old women – I never looked down on them. When I saw some old women sitting outside drinking tea I would stop my car and sit with them, ten minutes of talking and drinking tea with them would make them happy and then I would go. If I saw kids who needed help – maybe they were walking to school – even though I wouldn't have enough room for everybody I would drive them, like five, six people in my car to the school. I don't know if I should say this or not but when I went out to cover some houses being destroyed I would take money with me so I could give it to the mothers or the fathers without anybody seeing, just something simple to help them to continue for a week. Also, when I see a guy being killed I know what that means to the father, to the mother, so I speak to the people when they cry. And they know me; they remember that I also lost two brothers and that I have two brothers that are still alive and it gives them some cause to continue.

## STAYING SANE IN GAZA

I have been covering Gaza for twenty years. I don't think any person could continue like this without going crazy because what I see most of the time is only violence. There is nothing much else happening. So why don't I go crazy? First of all, I like the life – the photography. Secondly, I have a lot of friends who are psychology doctors and I see how they treat people and I learn from them how not to become intensively down. I take two days off – Saturday and Sunday every week and I close my phone down; I don't listen to any news; I spend Saturday at home with the family without changing any clothes; I do nothing. I have a fish tank at my home so I spend one hour just looking at this. It is relaxing. And I have some music to stop the pressures. We don't have enough parks in Gaza but still I take my kids to the small park and play with them. Sunday, I take the family to the beach, whether it is breakfast or lunch, and we sit in the sand and I play with my kids. And sometimes I stay in a hotel in Gaza in front of the beach for a week, ten days. I close my phone down and all I see from my window is the beach. I imagine to myself that I am now in Lebanon, I am now in America, in Egypt, and I forget that I am in Gaza. I feel that I am on vacation, somewhere different. I am not crazy yet so I have succeeded and I can continue to work.

I think about the first time I will have to stand in front of a tank again, once I recover from my injury, and I am not looking forward to it. But I have to continue my work, to cover what is happening. But it is sometimes really too hard. I wish for this war to be stopped one day so I can just take pictures of nice things, of peaceful things, of people with normal lives. I want to shoot something nice.

## ENDING WAR

Human rights are what are important for me in my work but they are especially important for kids everywhere. I see a lot of bad things happen to the Palestinian kids. They should not be involved in this: they should be out of all this violence. It really concerns me very much because the kids in Gaza could lose their house, their father, their family; it is not fair and I hope to see the Palestinian kids live as other kids in the world live their lives. If you compared how many Palestinian children suffer with how many Israeli children suffer you would see that Palestinian children suffer much more and in greater numbers than Israeli children. But especially after my injury I don't believe that any child should be suffering. I know what it means when you get injured. So I am talking about the same concerns for the Israeli children because they should not be caught up in the same issues either. They should have peace also.

Everybody in Palestine has hopes and dreams that we can have a life like other people have lives, like other people's kids have lives, but our life in Gaza is under occupation so it is not like others: it is scary and it is wrong. I would also like to see some future for my kids. I want to find them a good

Eddie Adams' Pulitzer Prize-winning image of South Vietnamese police chief Nguyen Ngoc Loan executing a bound Vietcong prisoner in front of journalists in the streets of Saigon on 1 February 1968. Although the photo became an iconic anti-war image, Adams said that his photo had been misinterpreted because he felt Loan was a hero, justified in killing his captive who had been caught murdering civilians. Adams believes his photo destroyed Loan's life.

A vulture looms over a starving child in Ayod, Southern Sudan, during the famine in March 1993. When the photo was featured on the cover of *Time* magazine it resulted in massive aid being shipped to the famine victims. The photographer, Kevin Carter, shooed the vulture away but left the child who was apparently only about 100 metres from a feeding station. Shortly after winning the Pulitzer Prize for this photo, Kevin Carter committed suicide.

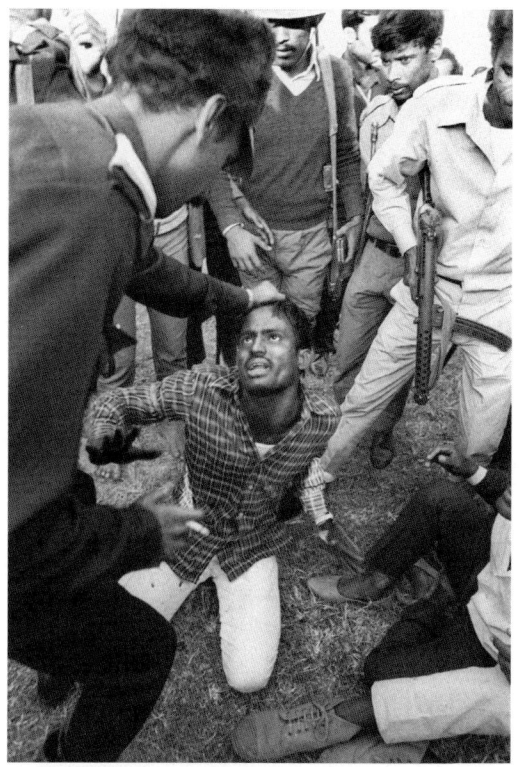

In Bangladesh during a 'victory' rally in a stadium in 1971 after the war involving Bengal's independence from Pakistan, Penny Tweedie took this photo of a captive before she and some other journalists and photographers left the stadium in protest, believing that their presence was inciting an execution. Two photographers that stayed later won the Pulitzer Prize for their images of the execution.

Photographer Susan Meiselas was in El Salvador in December 1980 to document the exhumation of the bodies of four nuns from the American Maryknoll Order who had been kidnapped, raped and executed by five members of the Salvadoran National Guardsmen. These women were four of approximately 75,000 people killed in El Salvador by death squads during the vicious civil war.

In Soweto township, South Africa, in September 1990, ANC supporters attacked and set alight Lindsaye Tshabalala, a defenceless man incorrectly identified as an enemy Inkatha. The photographer, Greg Marinovich, was unable to stop the killing frenzy. Later, Marinovich said he would not testify against the killers, explaining that he was only able to get his images out to the world because he was accepted by people as a journalist, not as a police informer.

In the Bosnian town of Bijeljina in May 1992 members of the Serbian warlord Arkan's Tiger militia dragged a middle-aged man and his wife, together with another woman, out on to the street and executed them. Although photographer Ron Haviv was warned not to take photos by the soldiers he was accompanying, he was determined that he would never again witness an execution without documenting it, as had happened early on in his career.

On the same occasion, Ron Haviv captured this image as a Serbian soldier pushed the young Muslim man to his knees. The man raised his hands and made a plea to Haviv to save his life. Despite Haviv's entreaties on his behalf, the militia took him away. Shortly after that, he was thrown out of a window and landed at Haviv's feet, only to be taken again into the building by the militiamen. Haviv believes he was probably killed.

Haviv aims to capture confronting images that people can look at without having to turn the page but still be able to understand the severity of what they are viewing. This image shows Bosnian and Croatian prisoners of war in the Serb-run Trnopolje camp in Bosnia in August 1992. All sides of the Bosnian conflict ran prison camps where many people lost their lives. Several commanders of these camps have been indicted for war crimes.

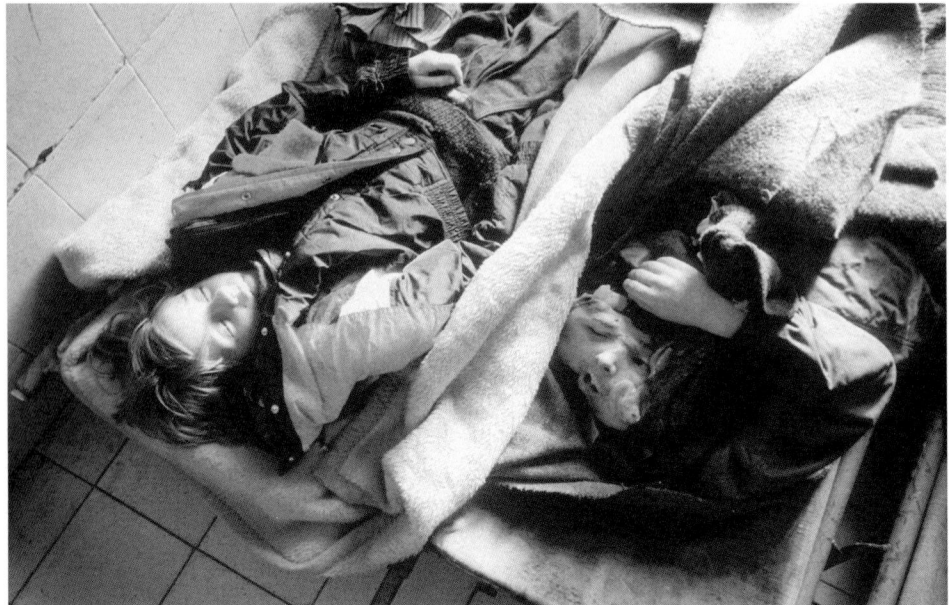

Christopher Morris photographed these corpses of children who had been killed playing in a Sarajevo park during the siege of the city by Serbian forces in early February 1994. When their father and grandfather came to identify them they found the mortician had placed one of the children's faces on upside down. Morris had been documenting the siege of the city for over 40 days straight and felt on the verge of an emotional breakdown but stayed to continue documenting the plight of the civilians.

A starving man moves towards an emergency feeding station during the famine in the Sudan in 1993. As noted by the photographer, James Nachtwey, in Sudan 'as in Somalia, the denial of food was used as a weapon of mass destruction, and vast numbers of people were subjected to slow death by starvation and disease'.

Glenn Middleton took this photo in the camps in Goma. 'It was scenes like this,' he said, 'that woke us each morning; the dead were laid out for collection. Unidentified and unwanted. A grim reminder to anyone deciding to return to Rwanda at this time that only death would greet you there.'

Ahmed Jadallah took this photo of the aftermath of a March 2003 Israeli tank attack in Jabalya refugee camp in the Gaza Strip while lying on the ground after having both his legs broken and an artery severed in the attack. Jadallah says there were no gunmen in the vicinity when they were targeted, only civilians. In 2004 he won the World Press Photo of the Year Award (Spot News) for this image.

A little girl severely injured by an allied bomb attack in Basra, Iraq, on 22 March 2003. In the Western press her damaged feet were cropped out of the photo because of perceived Western 'sensitivities' to the graphic nature of the image. In the poor world the photo was shown in its entirety.

home where they can stay, a good education, and a good life, which is hard to find in Gaza. I need this violence to stop one day and to have peace for our children like other children in the world have.

The people, the politicians who make all this war, I don't think are people. Believe me. War, whether the politicians are right or wrong, is an ugly word, an ugly thing. Nobody likes the war. Never ever should someone you love be killed in war. If these people who make the war thought for one second that one of their sons would be injured, if they really thought about the pain of *any* injured boy or girl, they would not make war. I am not just talking about the Palestinian and Israeli governments; I am talking about everybody – the militants on both sides also. Nobody likes the war; nobody likes to be beaten; nobody wants to be killed. That is what I see and know from my experience of both my people and the Israeli people.

When I was in the Israeli hospital in Jerusalem for two weeks I was with Israeli people. Some of them were settlers, some weren't settlers, and some of them were soldiers, but we could get on and live there in the hospital together. The conclusion of all of this for me is that if we could live together in the hospital we could live together outside in the world. In the end, we are all human beings and, in the end, everybody can live with each other.

Some people cannot see that though, because of their interests in money and power and things like that. But as a human being I challenge the average person in America that they could live side by side with the people in Iraq. The people who live in Israel – and I am talking about civilians, not politicians – could live with the Palestinians in Gaza and the West Bank, and they have. There were some Jewish Israelis at my wedding in Gaza. An Israeli friend used to come and eat at our house; we would eat in their houses, sleep in their houses. Israelis were coming to our market in Gaza to shop, our people were working in Israel, but now nobody talks. Israeli friends of mine cannot come to see me; I cannot go to see them. I don't know what is going on with the world. We should live within peace. All of us are human, all of us have lives, all of us have families, we have interests, we have children, we have land, so why fight each other for nothing?

I believe in God, you know. I believed in him before I was injured but I believe more strongly now after I was injured because that day there was only one thing that helped me, and that was God. Fourteen Palestinians around me were killed, some of them with their heads blown off, and only I survived. Somebody came and picked me from the middle of this. If you want to look at it in a rational way, I should have been killed. So I believe in God, in a kind god who helped me. But I also believe in something else, and the power of believing in that something – not necessarily religion but human rights – means I continue because I hope one day not to see anyone, from any side, from any part of the world, suffer from war for even one night. Yes, I hope one day to stop this violence, to have peace, for children everywhere to have peace. War, in whatever place war happens, always finishes with peace. The solution is not war; the solution is peace. Always.

# CHAPTER 12

# DONATELLA LORCH

## Biography

ALWAYS IN LOVE WITH the north-west frontier of Pakistan and Afghanistan, in 1987 Donatella Lorch was a relief worker in Pakistan for the International Rescue Committee. In 1988 she began her career as a *New York Times* stringer in Afghanistan and in 1989 smuggled herself into the country dressed as an Afghani woman to report on the Mujaheddin underground during the Soviet occupation. In 1991 she covered the Gulf War from the press pool in Riyadh. Donatella then moved to *The New York Times* in 1993 where she was East Africa bureau chief and covered the civil wars and famines in Sudan, Burundi, Zaire and Somalia, and the genocide in Rwanda. In 1996 she reported on the war in Kosovo as well as on Israel, Iraq and Asia for NBC TV. She worked for *Newsweek* in Washington from 1999 until early 2004 when she became the Director of the Knight International Press Fellowships for the International Centre for Journalists.

Donatella has two Masters degrees in international relations and journalism, and middle-eastern cultures. In 1996 she won the Outstanding Reporting on Refugee Issues from the Women's Commission on Refugee Women and Children, and in 2002 was awarded an Alicia Patterson Fellowship to write a book on refugees in the US.

In her own words Donatella is now 'happily ensconced in DC suburbia', after recently marrying a man with three children.

\* \* \*

# Story

Sometimes the images you remember don't have anything to do with war. I spent nine weeks in Baghdad in 1998. I love the Iraqis; they had a horrendous, vicious, evil government under Saddam yet they are amazing people. I will always remember I had this wonderful driver who would open up and talk to me when there was no one else in the car. He told me stories about when he was a soldier in the Gulf War and was sent into Kuwait City. His unit had been stuck there for about a week and a half without any food so he and his buddies just went AWOL and walked back to Baghdad, living off vegetables that they found in farms here and there. I asked him why he wasn't arrested when he got back and he smiled at me as if I didn't understand history and said, 'They were busy looking after the Shiites.'

After he entrusted me with his story, I felt an amazing feeling of warmth and closeness. In this situation, more than anything, you feel like you understand. Even the government minder – the government spy – was wonderful and charming. He desperately wanted English books to read. But trying to explain this relationship to someone back home was complicated. They would go, 'What, and you trusted him?' We didn't trust him; we enjoyed each other's company. He was doing his job and I was doing mine. There isn't a hell of a lot to spy on us about. Where else would I meet a guy as interesting and as warm as this and work with him for nine weeks?

And so that story sort of defined how we can often . . . well, not misunderstand the story, but here is a country that people like me should've really hated because we are Americans. It had this evil dictator, Saddam Hussein, but this Iraqi ex-soldier took me under his wing, was protective of me, and told me these great stories about how he fought on the other side of the war. Boy, was it a human story he told me.

We spent years out of contact. I had no idea what happened to him except that he found occasional employment whenever colleagues of mine went through Baghdad. I thought of him often as the war drums began over Iraq. That time around I didn't go to Iraq but got married instead, smack in the middle of the American 'invasion' (not the best of times considering many of my friends were embedded with the US military or sitting in Baghdad and obviously couldn't attend the wedding). A few weeks after I returned from my honeymoon I received a wedding present from my Iraqi friend. It was a beautiful filigree silver bracelet, hand carried from Baghdad by a colleague of mine. I was awed and humbled by this message of friendship. How could he think of me and my happiness when he was no doubt deeply worried about his and his family's safety and their economic ability to survive? It is moments like these that make all those miserable times on the road and endless weeks away from home worthwhile. I have often wondered whether I could ever match such generosity of spirit.

My whole working life has been a string of these stories.

They are the things I want to remember more than what it was like to be shot at or what it was like to watch people being killed in Rwanda. I would rather talk about the great moments where you open the door to something else – such an amazing feeling.

## Reporting war

In my job I don't think that we actually go out to be war correspondents. In a way, we go out to record people's lives. I never really knew as a child what I was good at and even at forty I don't know what I want to do for the rest of my life. But I think my mother gave me a great sense of curiosity and adventure. From the time I was little I fantasised about being a war reporter – I always thought that it was a pity that I arrived in this world after Vietnam. Why couldn't I have lived at the time of Michael Herr and met Sean Flynn?*

Every reporter covers things differently. I look at my colleagues to see how they cover the same story and I say, 'Well, he saw it that way, I saw it this way.' You can't be good at all types of journalism and I am the first person to say that I am not a good investigative reporter. I didn't want to work behind a desk. This work allowed me to do what I have figured out I am better at, which is getting to know people, getting them to talk to me, telling me their stories. I don't know how to go into a library and dig through four thousand million pages of tax returns to find the kernel that I am looking for, but I am good at getting people to open up. My ex-boyfriend used to say that when I was on a plane ride that lasted longer than thirty-five minutes I would come back with

***Author's note**: Michael Herr was a journalist who covered the Vietnam War for *Esquire* magazine and wrote the best-selling book on the Vietnam War *Dispatches*. Sean Flynn was the journalist son of actor Errol Flynn who died covering the war in Vietnam.

the home phone number and the email of whoever was sitting next to me. He used to find that creepy but I am fascinated by people. I like people – unless I am in a really bad mood.

What amazes and perplexes me and keeps drawing me back is trying to figure out what makes people tick. I think that not knowing what questions to ask next but wanting to explore different things is what makes a good journalist. For example, in the case of post-genocide Rwanda, after you did all the traditional, standard, post-genocide stories of the fighting, the mass graves and the retaliatory killings and revenge, you then had to start figuring out where the story was. I remember a Sunday morning in the hotel in Kigali trying to convince my colleague Alex that we really needed to go to church. He said, 'I don't want to go to church!' And I said, 'Not for the reason of going to church but it is obvious that there are certain factors here: many people were killed in churches, many priests were involved in the killings, now all these people are getting married – it is all about reaffirming the fact that you are alive. As someone who was raised Catholic I want to know what that guy is saying on the pulpit – how the priest can explain what happened!' Alex had never thought of it that way. As it turned out, I had to drag him to the story and I think it was one of the stories he was most satisfied with in Rwanda.

Media organisations have very strict rules of behaviour. The NBC policy booklet is a folder that is four inches thick. No one really reads it but it covers everything from how you can't give bribes to cross borders to every little possible thing you could imagine. The *New York Times* has very strict rules about journalistic behaviour, even down to gift-receiving.

Do you break rules? Yes. You run checkpoints and you smuggle yourself into a city but it is easier in the third world. If you did that in Guantanamo Bay in Cuba, the Americans would most probably drag you off to jail. You try not to break the rules of the country, and you certainly don't break the rules of a country on purpose, but if it is a question of survival and a question of following the rules completely . . . well . . .

People always say it was so hard to do war and I think, well, you should try doing crime in New York! I covered crime in New York for the *New York Times* and spending day after day doing that was in a way more emotion-churning for me than my time in Afghanistan. I will always remember one February 11 I went to this druggy neighbourhood in the Bronx with Dith Pran, the photographer from the Cambodian killing fields. A fifteen-year-old girl had been killed by her sixteen-year-old brother at their seventeen-year-old sister's birthday party. When the mother let us into the apartment, she had been drinking all night long. The apartment was empty of furniture, windows broken, it was cold, and they were so poor they didn't even have a refrigerator. It was one of those incredibly poor black families; you know, standard three generations of black women raising kids. The girl had borrowed eggs and butter from the neighbours to make this cake and there were half-eaten pieces all over the apartment. She wanted to be a dentist when she grew up because her teeth hurt all the time. The mother just broke down in my arms sobbing and Pran didn't take a single picture. On the way out I turned on the radio and John Lennon's 'Imagine' was playing. Pran said, 'I would rather live in a rice paddy in Cambodia than live as they did.' That was one of the stories that really stuck with me. That was hard.

## WRITING THE STORY

It is complex to explain what my missions are. When you are on assignment the mission is to do the best story I can, break the most news I can, figure out whether I can find myself a niche that four hundred million other reporters are not all tapping into – a big challenge these days. On my more cynical days my mission is to survive my editors.

You have so many editors willing to cut your story so why would any journalist want to censor their own story? I have written stories describing what it is like walking over hundreds of corpses. I remember describing a wild pig eating the corpse of a child and it got in the paper. I remember describing people having their heads blown off. It is how you write it. When I did television I remember one of the executive producers saying, 'Oh, we can't show that on morning television because people are eating their morning cereal,' so they did the censoring for me. The main problem with American journalism and network television is that so much of it is infotainment. American television is not the BBC. It is not ITN. It is a very different situation in America so you write whatever you see and what you hear, then you have to fight with your editor just to get the story in. Some days you will get lots of space and some days you won't. If you write for a weekly magazine you will get very little space, unless it is a huge, massive story. A good portion of what I wrote when I was with *Newsweek* never saw the light of day. It can be immensely frustrating.

Basically, I don't write for an audience. I write with the thought: 'If one person picks this up, will they want to keep on reading?' The usual test for me if I pick up the *New Yorker* is: can I read past the first page? If I can read past the first page, boy, that is a damn good writer. Most of the time I say, 'Next article,' and then I read the cartoons. It has to be really good writing to hold my attention because I am just so overwhelmed by everything that has to be read. How much time do we have to read something in the newspaper, magazines, listen to the radio, go to work, read books and watch TV? So to succeed in this industry what you have to be able to do is see a really horrific scene and then describe it in a way the person wants to read it. Sometimes it works and sometimes it doesn't; sometimes it is easy and sometimes I struggle endlessly.

What inspires me is breaking a story, telling it better than others. It is a definite high being able to help people through a story I write: walking down dirt alleys in refugee camps and little kids dragging me off to their tents so Grandma can kiss me; becoming friends with American doctors who were so intensely involved and believed in what they were doing. One of my producers used to say, 'Dony, don't play God.' But another producer said, 'Why not if it works!' I also think the wildness and exoticness of the job inspires me but there are often heavy amounts of boredom. I remember being stuck in Afghanistan for two weeks in the middle of summer. It was hot, not much shade, and I counted the cups of sweet green tea I was drinking per day. I had not even brought books to read. I had nothing to do and I had to learn to sit with myself. It was really hard but I sort of figured out how to do it.

## BECOMING INVOLVED

I constantly feel inadequate. I always compare and contrast what we leave behind when we leave a place. I always come out minus a sweater, minus a rain jacket, because I've given them away, but it is not like you are going to make any difference. Making a difference is about creating jobs, giving health care, giving a future. But I do try to help in any way I can. I have given a lot of my money to street kids for food. I have helped a lot of individual families that I have met and I helped a little kid get cancer treatment – that was when my producer said I was playing God. I used the media to do it: we filmed the story of this boy for NBC and a whole bunch of viewers wanted to help. I helped the women who had been raped in a small village in Kosovo because they welcomed me into their lives and they trusted me. In another case, when the refugees crossed the border into Albania they used to hand out these small pieces of paper with 'call a relative here, call a relative there' so their family knew where they were and I used to go back and call the relatives. Refugees usually always ask you for help but, as a journalist, sometimes it is very frustrating because you can't do anything. We might stand on a dirt road in Tanzania and watch 250,000 refugees walk past us. We are always part of the haves, not the have-nots. People say that our ability to walk in and out of people's suffering is what makes the job easier but it is what makes the job hard.

The overwhelming thing about starving children is that when someone is starving you don't give them candy, you don't give them food, because it turns their whole system inside out and you could hurt them more than help them; that's the first thing that people who work in the feeding kitchens tell you. There was an incident where a woman who worked for World Food Program (WFP) who was still breastfeeding her second kid took a woman's baby and she breastfed the baby. The big issue was whether she should have done it? Médecins Sans Frontières said that if she had been working for them they would have fired her. There are all these different issues involved. Here is a baby that is starving and it hasn't had rich milk ever in its life and the WFP woman was going to leave on a plane and you had all the other starving mothers ganging up on the woman who had had her starving child breastfed. You can sometimes forget that you might do more damage than good when you're trying to help.

## Fear

I once took an SAS course in combat first aid and I remember all the medics asking, 'What is the first thing that you do when you arrive on the scene and there are broken limbs and blood splattered everywhere and they are shooting at you?' Everyone came up with all these different theories but the first thing to remember is 'don't panic' and you tell yourself over and over again: 'I have just got to focus on the physical things around me: where am I, where am I going, what is happening?' You don't want to think about what is going on in your body. That is a very handy little thing to remember. You know that feeling when you are driving down the road and you put the brakes on just in time to miss an accident and for a moment your heart is beating really fast? OK, just multiply that twenty or thirty times and that is fear. I have had incredible fear. Once, when I was under a tank attack in a bunker I sang songs to myself under my breath. It calmed me down. You focus on the moment and figure out how to get out of it, think of other things, take deep breaths, and you remain *calm*.

In Afghanistan we came under rocket attack and it was my mother's birthday. I felt like it was such a shitty thing to do to die on my mother's birthday. I don't want to die on her birthday and I was angry with myself so I made all these little deals with God (I always make these little deals with God): 'Not on her birthday. You can do it tomorrow but not on her birthday.' I am very sensitive so I don't want to die on Christmas Day either because it will ruin it for everyone I know forever.

## Burnout

Working in TV burnt me out. I walked out of television because I felt that I had lost touch with reality. I would wake up in hotel rooms and not know where I was sometimes – well, that is standard, but I didn't have time to *feel* any more. And I know from my friends at the BBC that it is the same thing for them. In TV they work you to the bone in an inhumane way on a breaking story. They will work you twenty hours a day – not that print people don't work twenty hours a day but it is a very different type of pressure and tension. In television you have got to write your script, edit it, find the feed point and get to it while you have a window to feed your film. You are being pulled right and left, top to bottom, and it is utterly exhausting and not just physically but emotionally. Now I don't have to dread the call that tells me, 'Do you mind leaving at 3 o'clock in the morning?' I came to hate that. I got to the point where I guess I was probably suffering from burnout. I just didn't want to get on another plane. I didn't want to be told what the story was by an editor who knew nothing about a story.

You realise you are traumatised only when you move from the place where you see all this stuff and get beamed down to your house in Europe or Australia, into the first world, where everything is hunky-dory and no one has heard of the country you have been to and no one wants to know. It really didn't hit us until we left. I went from Somalia to Nairobi, from Rwanda to Nairobi, where I had to cope with getting carjacked, getting shot at, figuring out how to bribe the telephone people in Kenya so they would stop cutting my lines – you know, your average day there. How we lived was almost like a lesser extension of what we had seen – it was a version of a struggle for survival.

I got terribly sick after a trip to Africa. I had hepatitis, all these joint problems, arthritis all over my body, and nobody could figure out what I was suffering from. All they could tell me was that my auto-immune system had attacked my body. Ultimately, I think I was completely, utterly stressed out and my body did not like the antibiotics I was taking. You are sick because if you are doing a short assignment for a month or a few weeks you are running on no sleep and then you finish and everything sort of crashes. You get your tonsillitis, your dysentery. Especially during the Rwandan genocide, everyone just kept getting sick with one thing after the next. I had a really bad case of cerebral malaria and that whacked me. A lot of other people had hepatitis, some had TB. In one year in Africa, five of my friends were killed and a few got shot.

When I came back to the States after Rwanda I didn't know what was wrong with me. The *New York Times* was starting to require that you were debriefed by this psychiatrist with so many acronyms after her name that I can't even remember what her name was. I remember spending forty-five minutes with her and she didn't even know where Rwanda was. I thought, 'What in the world am I doing here?' I mean, I was never going to tell her stuff that I told my buddies. I wasn't going to tell her how I felt. I wasn't really sure how I felt. I always thought that I was in control to a certain extent, but I knew certain things like my temper had gotten much shorter and I felt very lost and that feeling would only go away when I went back to Africa. I didn't want to come back home to America. I missed my friends and the freedom of Africa terribly. I didn't really know what was affecting me at all because I knew nothing about PTSD. There are times still when I wonder about the days when I get really horrendous nightmares.

I always thought this was only happening to me and that my buddies from my days in Africa didn't go through the same degree of trauma. I thought this was maybe because I wasn't married and I didn't have a husband and kids. About two years after I left Africa I was talking to a friend who used to cover Africa for *Time* magazine and he was telling me he had a really tough time when he came back to his life in America, a real struggle with depression, with sadness, and yet he is married with kids. I don't know why he brought it up – men don't usually bring it up; I think it was something that I had written. I would be curious to know how the men deal with trauma, especially married men. I have another friend who disappears, doesn't answer his phone for a bunch of days at a time, and drinks a lot when he comes back from assignments. Another friend stays in bed for two or three days. I have talked to her about it, not directly, but I said, 'Do you think of it as a figment of something else? Have you thought about going to see someone to talk about it?' And she is like: 'I am perfectly strong. I don't need to do that because I know it passes after a few days,' and yet I know she struggles with depression.

Although photojournalist Ron Haviv and I knew each other for quite a while, before he mentioned some of his experiences in Bosnia and even when he did I had to draw them out of him; you can spend hours talking to him about anything and everything. And photojournalist Greg Marinovich is an interesting guy. I like Greg a lot. He has a good heart. He will talk to you about the depression he experienced after he was shot and severely wounded in April 1994 by a UN peacekeeper's bullet while covering the township violence in Thokoza, South Africa. He had a tough time coming out of that and I don't blame him. His close friend Ken Oosterbroek was killed in the same incident. I couldn't begin to fathom what Greg went through. I worked with him on his first assignment after his recovery and it was nine months after the genocide in Rwanda so we covered a story about children of rape – just to cheer him up!

I remember after my friend Dan Eldon* died I was very upset while talking to my then boyfriend and his line to me was, 'Get on with it.' Oh, I railed about Dan's death. There was disbelief and I cried about it for ages. I don't know whether fear came from losing my friends; fear that it could have been me; fear that it happened to people that were very close to me, that did the same thing that I did; fear that it was just around the corner for me. But for years now I have had a very intense fear of losing people I am very close to. I don't mean losing in terms of dying; I mean separating myself. Goodbyes from my family have always been hard when I have gone for long trips but more so after Dan died. This fear usually messes up my personal relationships.

## Getting a life

I travelled ninety per cent of my last year at NBC, and my friends in the business were the only people I travelled with. None of my friends at home ever wanted to make plans with me when I came back home because I couldn't make plans; I couldn't even make vacation plans. My personal life was non-existent. You know, all these guys can go back to their wives and kids who are waiting for them. I used to have a few single male friends up until very recently and now they have a wife; the wife doesn't work, she just raises the child and when she gets too bored she goes back home to where she is from, and

---

* **Author's note:** Eldon was a young freelance photographer working for Reuters. On 12 July 1993 he and three other journalists went to cover the aftermath of an American bombing raid in Mogadishu, Somalia, in which over sixty civilians were killed. The enraged crowd took out their anger on the journalists who were stoned and shot dead. Lorch had spent the previous night with them laughing and joking on the roof of their hotel but had chosen to take a flight home to Nairobi rather than continuing to cover events in Mogadishu.

isn't life lovely? And whenever they have an argument they call me up to complain and say, 'Well, I can't leave her, you know, what would I do? It would be lonely.' Men can never be alone for longer than thirty minutes. It's hard for women in my profession to maintain a relationship at home.

I eventually chose to go to Washington because I wanted to get a life. I'm not sure if you ever know when the right time is to stop or whether you know that when you *did* stop it was the right time. I look at some of my friends and I think they should stop: they are burnt out. Are my women friends fucked up? Are they going to be these bitter women who have never had children, who will live alone because they never wanted to say no to an assignment? I know a few of those. All they do is get together and complain that they don't have a life. I think that they made the choice and they have got to put up with it. I liked the work but I didn't want to become that sort of person and I was sick and tired of listening to women like these. I wanted to have friends in other professions.

Would I have been happier to have gotten married at twenty-two and raised a family, never having done what I did? No, I think it probably would have driven me nuts. This work takes you away from the daily, boring commutes to work and trips to the mall. You don't have to pay your bills when you are out there travelling and you don't have to worry about the electricity or the rent. You put everything on hold. All the million and one little chicken peckings of your life go on hold when you go out in the field; all you do is focus on the story. It is a wonderful feeling of liberation and freedom. The truth is I miss it terribly. When my friends call me up and say, 'Hi, I'm calling you from Bethlehem and I am watching the tanks roll in,' I am like, 'OK, take a deep breath, Dony; you don't have to be there.' I am really happy to be living at home but there are days that I wish I were elsewhere. I still miss the life I used to have but not as constantly.

## WOMEN IN THE PROFESSION

My greatest inspiration in journalism has been women in the business, women like Deborah Amos (correspondent for the ABC News, New York, and for National Public Radio) whom I met as a cub reporter while covering war in Afghanistan. They taught me by example and through their friendship, and they made it obvious to me that I too have to give back. It is because I have met such amazing women that I am frustrated and disgusted with those who brag about sleeping their way into assignments. When I was in the field, my hope and aim was to be respected by my male counterparts. Not necesssarily liked but respected. Sleeping with them was not the best technique for gaining their respect. But I didn't and I don't. Hey, we've all had our shares of relationships on the road but the thought of sleeping with someone who can advance my career gives me the creeps. I have had a lot of men flirt with me – you know, the 'Why don't you come away with me and we will see what jobs you can get?' type of thing.

I always remember one of the female press people for a relief agency in Goma, Zaire [Congo], who got all the guys to cover her press briefings (there was so much competition between the relief agencies to get the reporters' attention). She wore this one-piece, sort of glued-on black outfit without a panty- or bra-line anywhere. It was like 'wow' in the middle of a cholera epidemic! Yes, use your femininity but I am against the sort of thing she was doing. Does using your femininity mean that you are going to be wearing your fishnet stockings when you get on board your helicopter gunship? No. You can use your femininity even if you are in filthy jeans and jacket with a woollen hat on your head and haven't washed in two weeks. I always carry perfume and lipstick with me wherever I go because when I am really gross and dirty I think that putting on perfume and lipstick makes me feel better. I also think that it helps at checkpoints. So I have used my femininity in terms of trying to turn on the charm. My male buddies always like travelling with me because I always get them through checkpoints – as a woman you are not as threatening as a man.

The day that Kuwait City fell during the Gulf War I drove into the city with four or five guys in my car. We were all with the media pool in Riyadh initially and then everyone just gunned it because the minute Kuwait City fell the pool fell apart and we were on our own. We got lost on the first night because the wind from the oil fires blew in our direction, so we couldn't even see in front of the car. We didn't have a map of the city and we ended up in Kuwait City Equestrian Club for the night. Of course, the next day we had no food and water and so we drove downtown and it was totally destroyed. We went to the American embassy and there were some American soldiers there. They didn't know who we were and we didn't want to threaten them so we pulled up a couple of hundred yards away. One of my colleagues decided that I should walk up to the soldiers, bat my eyelashes and get water and food. So I chatted with the guys and yes, we got water and food. Would they have given it to the guys? Probably, but my colleagues thought that a woman was less threatening.

There are some women in the business who have been amazingly good friends to me and as a result of that I have tried to help out younger women, too. Deborah Amos is an example of this. Her courage, her gumption and her damn good reporting inspired. In my eyes, she's one of the best out there.

I worked alongside Corinne Dufka (correspondent and photojournalist for Reuters who joined Human Rights Watch in 1999 and won a Macarthur Genius Award in 2002) and I am in awe of her fearlessness, her courage. And Jennifer Parmelee, who was with the *Washington Post* in Africa, was a great buddy of mine. Yes, we could be catty and mean but we were really friends and, boy, did we have a better time than the guys. They liked to hang with us. We were better company than their male colleagues.

## WITHIN THE PROFESSION

Among foreign correspondents overseas there is a lot of camaraderie but not among American reporters in the States. You have to form a group but, once you form it, it is not like everyone is everyone else's buddy. You form distinct groups of four, five or six, and sometimes you interweave with other groups, but basically that is your little survival group and sometimes it is only for one story, sometimes for several stories. While you have your little survival group, you also have those reporters that you don't get along with at all.

Bravery is talked about within the profession but I don't know much about bravery. How do you define bravery? I don't think the guys who always take the greatest risks – the cowboys – are brave. In Africa we all knew who the cowboys were because you were all stuck together in the same hotel. We would hang out with them in the evening, but I didn't travel with the cowboys. I talked to them a lot, I asked them about the stories they were working on, we socialised, but that was it.

The things that give you status within the industry are varied. Breaking a story is definitely a major status symbol that makes you recognised. I think a well-written story also wins huge praise, even though sometimes it might be grudging praise. Messing up a story is another way of getting noticed – obviously not in a good way – as is self-promotion. I can't tell you the number of emails that went around about the story filed recently by an American journalist who was trying to get into Ramallah and kept being turned back by the Israelis. His story was all about him. Who gives a damn that he couldn't get in! What also makes you noticed in the profession is if you earn five million dollars a year. Christiane Amanpour from CNN earns at least three . . . I have lost track of her millions; the figure keeps on going up every year. A lot of journalism right now has become identified in terms of its 'celebrities' and I think that there is this sense among reporters that the public looks at foreign correspondents only as Christiane. There is only one Christiane, not because she runs into the middle of danger, but because there is only one television reporter covering foreign news who is so well known and so well paid. She is a very good reporter but she is not the world of reporting.

## LESSONS FROM THE JOB

My experiences have coloured my world in the sense that I look at teenagers in America and I feel that they live these wonderful, middle-class, coddled lives and I always think that if I had a teenager I would like him or her to see how three-quarters of the world lives. And as I look at my friends and my siblings I feel like I want to shake them a bit into reality. I get frustrated and short-tempered with people who don't understand how the rest of the world works, especially in the case of Israel and the American involvement, but I do not have intense political discussions with people because I think that arguing doesn't get any of us anywhere. So many people say about the Palestinians, 'I don't understand how they can blow themselves up.' I know why they are doing it. You just have to put yourself into their shoes when you look at those pictures of the bulldozers going through Jenin and see the oppression. You have lived in a damn refugee camp for your entire life. Are you supposed to like the Israelis after all this? If I had the chance to talk to any of these Palestinian suicide bombers I think I would have found them bitter, idealistic, and torn apart emotionally, but were they evil? Is what they did horrible? Yes, killing innocent people is absolutely horrendous, but are they evil people? I don't know; I can't answer that. I can tell you that a lot of the Hutu killers I met are evil people. So how can I differentiate between those two situations? I don't know.

I think it is society that creates that kind of evil and I think you have to differentiate between the levels of evil that were unleashed. In Rwanda there were those who believed that to gain power they had to obliterate a whole race. That is hard for me to fathom. I grew up in a nice little liberal American household. It is hard to explain what went on in Rwanda but my anger about it stems from the way the West ignored it. That is what really pisses me off. After Rwanda I thought that humankind was truly evil and I wanted to figure out how they could be so evil. Now I don't think people are evil; I think people have an evil side. That evil side is either built up or kept down by society, by events around them. So I think I have grown to understand a bit more about the extremes of hatred and pain. One thing that this job has taught me is the incredible complexity of human emotions and of my own emotions: I have such amazing love, strength, and hatred myself. That is how my job colours my life. I am also very grateful for what I have. Not that I wouldn't want more but, hey, that sort of sentiment is all about being an American, isn't it? Wanting more, wanting bigger cars, bigger everything . . .

This job that I did for however many years is a privilege, an honour, and I think the minute that people in my profession lose track of that we become too cocky. There are many cocky people out there who think that they are hot shit because they are a war correspondent. They forget that it is an incredible privilege and a responsibility. We have a responsibility towards others, in terms of not making ourselves seem larger than life, not boasting about what we do. The privilege is the ability to move between worlds: to be able to live and work and write from refugee camps or massacre sites in a humane, understanding, gentle way, as opposed to the standard 'Is there anyone here who has been raped and speaks English?', which, by the way, we all think at times. We know so much about so many different worlds while most people live in just one world. To enter other people's worlds and gain access to their feelings is like you are handed this incredible, fragile thing.

A lot of people think that I am exotic because of what I have done, but I am not. But, you know, the grass is always greener on the other side.

CHAPTER 13

# SUSAN MEISELAS

## Biography

AFTER COMPLETING HER first degree in anthropology and a Masters degree in visual education at Harvard, Susan Meiselas taught photography to teachers and children in the Bronx. She began covering war in Nicaragua and El Salvador in the late seventies and became a member of the prestigious Magnum photo agency in 1976. In El Salvador she photographed the uncovering of the graves of the Maryknoll nuns and the massacre in the town of El Mozote, both of which led to questioning and investigations into Washington's relationship with Salvadoran right-wing death squads during that country's violent twelve-year civil war.

After spending a decade in Central America as a freelance photographer, Susan's work with the Kurds in Northern Iraq in 1992 led her to spend six years working on a visual history of Kurdistan which included an interactive web site www.akakurdistan.com and the book *Kurdistan: In the Shadow of History* (Random House, 1997).

She has directed and co-produced two films, *Living at Risk* and *Pictures from a Revolution* with her partner Richard P. Rogers and Alfred Guizzetti and has assisted in the publication of books for Salvadoran and Chilean photographers. Susan is the author of *Nicaragua* (Pantheon Books, 1981); *Carnival Strippers* (Distributed Art Publishers, reprint, 2004); *Pandora's Box* (Trebruk Publishing, 2002); *Encounters with the Dani* (Steidl, 2003); and is editor of *Chile* (W.W. Norton & Company, 1990). She is also the recipient of a number of awards including the Overseas Press Club's Robert Capa Gold Medal Award in 1979 for Outstanding Courage and Reporting; the Photojournalist of the Year Award from the American Society of Media Photographers in 1982, and the Leica Award for Excellence in the same year – all for her work in Central America. In 1984 Susan received a Photographer's Fellowship from the National Endowment of the Arts and a Macarthur Fellowship in 1992, which enabled her to continue her work in Kurdistan. In 1994 she received the Hasselblad Photography Prize for Exceptional Photographic Achievement.

Susan lives in New York.

\* \* \*

## Story

In a way, El Mozote\* is still a big story but it is a complicated story for me. It is certainly an example of being completely

---

\* **Author's note:** On 11 December 1981, with the Reagan administration supporting the right-wing government in El Salvador, an American-trained unit of the Salvadoran army, the Atlacatl Battalion, massacred over 800 civilians from the village of El Mozote. The villagers were deliberately

absorbed into the history of a particular place and taking probably the greatest risk I was capable of at the time.

What resonates for me about that story is that the civil war that was happening in El Salvador led both Ray Bonner and me to feel that the most important thing to understand in the country at that time was the peasant life under the guerrillas inside Morazan, the northern district of El Salvador whose access had been cut off by the Salvadoran military. Government troops had launched an offensive three weeks earlier, but nobody really knew anything about what was going on there. Because it was so remote and entering was difficult it took some time for us to organise a network of contacts to get into the area and, just before we were to go, there was a broadcast from Radio Venceremos, the Salvadoran guerrilla radio, reporting a massacre on the outskirts of the village of El Mozote in Morazan. Of course, hearing about the massacre made it even more important to get there but that wasn't the only reason for our trip.

I remember the journey past the refugee camps, walking all night across the border with Honduras, but I can't remember how it was that we exactly came upon El Mozote.

and systematically executed in groups, with the men tortured and then executed first, followed by the execution of the women and finally, locked in the convent, the children were machine-gunned to death. At least 131 children under the age of twelve were killed, with the average age being six years. In January, Susan Meiselas and Ray Bonner had come upon El Mozote. Ray Bonner and Alma Guillermoprieto first published news of the massacre on 27 January 1982 in the *New York Times* and the *Washington Post* respectively. An investigation into what happened in El Mozote began in 1989 by the Human Rights Office of the Archbishop of San Salvador and continued in 1992 under the auspices of the United Nations. The subsequent report was published in April 1993. For further information, see United Nations Report of the UN Truth Commission on El Salvador, S/2550 1 April 1993, http://www.derechos.org/nizkor/salvador/informes/truth.html and Mark Danner, *The Massacre at El Mozote: A Parable of the Cold War* (Vintage Books, New York, 1994).

What is so vivid to me now is that we had no sense of the scale of what we were seeing. We walked into this tiny village and clearly everybody had fled very abruptly. There were beans on the floor that had been cooking, pots turned over. We walked around the plaza and it was hard to figure out what had happened or to see more than the total destruction of a community. We saw a few burnt bones under the collapsed tiled roofs and we could smell the tremendous stench of death but there was only one group of fourteen bodies decomposing on the side of a cornfield that was visible. At the time we didn't know anything more than what we were seeing. A week later, one of the survivors, Rufina Amaya, told Ray and I that over a thousand people had been killed but by then it was too dangerous to return to investigate any further.

For me, El Mozote is still a kind of bewitching remembrance of the sense that we had come upon something terrible that clearly had happened but we were not sure exactly how, so we began by desperately trying to collect testimony. My pictures showed only fragments, not enough to prove anything, yet they showed something had in fact taken place. At the time of the discovery of El Mozote we had a tremendous sense of its significance. We felt: 'This is it. We have evidence!' We didn't doubt that there had indeed been a massacre, although the US and Salvadoran governments denied it had happened. But it never occurred to me that our evidence was not enough to stop US military aid to El Salvador or that my pictures wouldn't hold the weight of what they needed to stand up against.

Within that year, the pictures were shown to the US Congress and presented in Geneva to the Human Rights Commission. You can imagine the kind of debate that occurred around that time. But it was not until ten years later when Mark Danner (a staff writer at the *New Yorker*) went back to El Mozote and did a thorough investigation that the American-trained Atlacatl Battalion was implicated and it was not until after the peace process in Salvador in 1991 that the United Nations Truth Commission authorised an Argentinean forensic team to begin the exhumation that proved the massacre had taken place. I am not sure what the final count of victims is now; they are still digging for the bones.

I think that in a way this is a story that brought me right to the centre of probably the most critical moment in my career as a journalist – being put on the line and challenged for what I had seen. Ray, who wrote for the *New York Times*, and Alma Guillermoprieto, who wrote for the *Washington Post* (and also had been to the village), were challenged directly with the *Wall Street Journal* suggesting that Ray and Alma were sympathetic to the guerrillas and that was why they reported what had happened in El Mozote. My pictures were just passed over because they weren't sufficient to really prove any 'facts'. The writers took the heat more so than I.

Twenty years later, when they exhumed the graves of those killed in the massacre, it surprised me that the people who were fighting in and around El Mozote for nearly ten years didn't come back to honour the dead when they were reburied. What kind of a loss is that community still living with that is not really photographable? I can make a photograph of people carrying small coffins of bones to be reburied, but I can't really make a picture of that hollow place of their loss now.

So El Mozote and all that happened around it is a kind of strange circle for me. On one hand, I made strong images of people brutally killed in that massacre but, on the other hand, what picture can I make that carries the weight of what that massacre means now to people? I made an image but it does not carry what I am still living with, this thing that so touched me. As a photographer you can only make pictures of things that are there before you. You can't always make images of loss and of all that you feel.

## Choosing where you need to be

When I first went to Nicaragua I had no idea about real war and I didn't choose to go to war. I became interested in that place, the war evolved around me, and I stayed with it. I followed the popular insurrection to then cover the coup in El Salvador. There I watched people move from legitimate public protest – something I myself had done ten years earlier over the Vietnam War – to being mowed down in the street and then going underground or becoming guerrillas in the mountains. I wanted to understand how people get to the place that they take positions that they care enough about to protest and then feel the necessity to take up arms. So I chose to stay through the eighties in Central America and then Latin America rather than move across the globe – like many people who worked alongside me did – because of the nature of those wars and the possibility that one could come to know those particular histories and people. I like getting to know things more deeply but always the concern I have is: 'What am I contributing by landing in this place that I know nothing about?' By staying longer, or revisiting a place, you build an understanding and, for me, it has just felt like the right choice. I felt in some strange way that as an American I belonged in Central and Latin America.

People tend to go to the centre of where the news is because they think that it is where they can be most effective but sometimes you can make the judgment to go in totally the opposite direction. Just because you do, though, doesn't mean that you can bring the story you're working on to life, and when you don't it really makes you wonder why you are taking the risks. In other words, it is not so surprising that people take the risk to get the return of front-page news because that is obviously feeding their careers and their egos. It is much harder as a professional to go to places that aren't in central focus and sustain your belief that they are important. The last war Ray Bonner and I covered together was in Nagorno-Karabakh and I think we both had this feeling of: 'What are we doing here?' We were taking tremendous risks to cover a place that nobody really wanted to know more about but that *we* were driven to find out about.

## CHALLENGES

The challenge in doing this work is staying curious enough to want to place yourself in unfamiliar settings that force you to interact in unpredictable ways. How does one continuously want to do that? Ultimately, you have to just pack your bag and get on the plane and take the chance. You also have to totally trust your intuition and have a willingness to gamble. I like something about the unpredictable unfolding of life and this job satisfies that.

But how do you avoid the state where things start to look or feel as though you have seen them before? How do people who are covering the Israeli/Palestinian conflict stay caring about each and every one of those deaths? After so many years of Intifada, how do you still feel that each of those deaths is important to cover? 'Does one more picture of this matter? Is anyone taking any notice?' as the war photographer Don McCullin asked. You need to stay outside of that kind of jadedness, that morass.

Also, while lots of times the camera can make you feel invisible, and that it even protects you, it is absolutely an

Susan Meiselas

illusion of: 'It isn't happening to me, it is happening to them.' So as a journalist there may eventually be a sense of horror that you progress to from all that you have witnessed, a place where you can't imagine anything greater than what you've already seen, and therefore your own life seems less important. I don't think that I have come to that place, except perhaps as a viewer, as a reader, but not as a photographer.

We need to think about how we interpret the world. The InterPress News Service was a third-world news service with limited resources. In the mid-eighties they developed a network of regional reporters who tried to report on their own countries from within, and they hoped to interface with the newspapers of the first world so that readers would learn about how these countries saw themselves. But unfortunately our Western culture is too dominant and the *New York Times* and other similar media outlets didn't seem to value what those reporters had to say. I think first-world journalists need to consider how we can get out of that construct and how that might change things.

## MAKING THE IMAGE AND ENGAGING THE AUDIENCE

Making an image is a very intuitive process: whatever you understand is going on in that moment you try to frame with a tension between the formal qualities of the photograph and the content. Sometimes you get it and sometimes you don't. There are obviously pictures one feels proud of. Probably the most important from my point of view historically were those of the El Mozote massacre and the discovery of the Maryknoll nuns\*. There are other kinds of pictures that I remember, not

---

\* **Author's note:** On 2 December 1980 five Salvadoran national guardsmen abducted, tortured, raped and then killed four American Maryknoll nuns who were missionaries in El Salvador: Ita Ford, Maura Clarke, Dorothy

because of what is imaged, but because they were capturing something that I was feeling. I also think of photographs that weren't taken at a certain moment because to do so involved crossing a line.

I remember once when I wanted to photograph the bringing home of a young boy who had been wounded. In that particular instance there wasn't the time to have the family understand who I was, what I was doing, why I would want those images, or why they might be important. It is a very subtle thing and I self-censored in that situation and didn't take the photo. I have to feel that people want a picture made, but that line between the pursuit of information and exploitation is so thin. I think other people in the profession can sometimes work in opposition to that and get the photo – steal the image almost.

There are also some photographs that I still am stunned by. For example, a photograph by Harry Mattison* shows members of the Salvadoran army holding trophies of hacked arms and legs and bodies. Part of the question that image raises is what do you do as a photographer in that situation? Another is whether or not you judge the photographers who

Kazel and Jean Donovan. Two days later, Susan Meiselas and John Hoagland searched the back roads and were the first to discover the place where the nuns' bodies were buried in shallow graves.

Although five soldiers were found guilty by a Salvadoran court and sentenced to thirty years jail, twenty years later the families of the nuns filed a civil lawsuit against the former Salvadoran defence minister José Guillermo García and former national guard director Carlos Eugenio Vides Casanova (both retired and living in Florida). The suit claimed that command responsibility meant that they were ultimately responsible for the deaths. They were acquitted by a federal court jury.

The twelve-year civil war in El Salvador is said to have claimed 75,000 lives.

* **Author's note:** Harry Mattison is a photojournalist who worked in Central America for *Time* magazine and published with Meiselas, *El Salvador: Work of Thirty Photographers*.

have made a choice to capture such an image. You only know what you can live with and I think that is the bottom line. To this day, I don't know if I could have made that photograph; people performing for a camera is a very dangerous zone for me. But I have made difficult images that I felt had to be made if they depicted the horror of what I had seen. My picture of the body on the landscape from Nicaragua is graphic, and yes, the Maryknoll nuns came out of the ground with their underwear wrapped around their ankles and it was horrible the way they were dragged out of the earth, but I felt that I had to make that image for readers to come to terms with the reality it depicted.

The problem is not that there are not enough people out there collecting and witnessing but how we in the profession can find ways to reconsider this process of bridging the world at home with what we as photographers are witnessing so readers can make real connections and become involved. There seem to be fewer and fewer options and opportunities to tell stories in magazines these days and I guess this is a real disappointment, but it has led me to find other mediums within which to work: documentary films, books and, more recently, multimedia formats. So while the still pictures have power, it has never been just an image alone that carries enough of the meaning for me. Sometimes there are stories that still pictures don't capture sufficiently. So I think you need to build your own environment for images if you are really going to have any kind of impact. All these mediums are different though: different audiences, different kinds of afterlife. Understanding the breadth of that terrain is important: where does the work belong, where does it start, and what will it evolve into?

## KURDISTAN AND DOCUMENTING HISTORY

I had been reading about what had happened to the Kurds just before the Gulf War started, and decided to go into Kurdistan in Northern Iraq as a freelance photographer. The fact that no magazines were interested in my photographs is what led me to a very different kind of storytelling project in Kurdistan and eventually the creation of the Kurdistan web site. The feeling and belief that I had in the seventies and the eighties, particularly documenting massacres and abuses, was that the act of documenting, of making the image, was enough but then the Kurdistan War began to let me see what documenting could mean in a way that the working news could not.

The Kurds had fled, they came back, were resettled, and as far as the world was concerned the story was over, but I didn't even know what the story was. My own pictures were only a small part of a bigger story that somehow had to be told. I wondered how many travellers to Kurdistan had shaped events by their witnessing through their photographs and I thought about how all of those images were now dispersed. I was interested in the imagemakers who had come before me and how much they had affected other people's journeys, like a pebble that changes everything when it is thrown in the water and the ripples flow out. Sometimes we in the media think the important pebble is having a front-page story but I am now more interested in the stories around that first story and how photographers can perhaps be more creative in the ways we engage an audience.

So, for me, being a photographer is not a job that ends with making the picture. You need to find ways to bring people closer so that they can relate to what is going on in the world. I don't know the simple answer but I don't think it is necessarily going to be only getting people to read newspapers and magazines. I think we need to give readers a broader framework in which to conceptualise and in which they can view other lives so that they feel the immediacy of what is happening to those people. If we can do that then we are creating an environment where readers and viewers connect to people in a completely new way. The Kurdistan web site went beyond just viewing images. For over six years now through the web site there is an exchange going on between people talking about what has and what should happen to the Kurds.

So rather than just saying, 'We know the public don't know and don't want to know,' there has to be a way in which the media bring readers into the 'wanting to know' about other people and places. I am not saying that I have answers to this challenge yet but it is a sort of quest for me.

Probably though, what has been a deeper experience for me ultimately, whatever these twenty-five years have been, is seeing how a community reconstitutes and re-knows itself through this gathering process, through acknowledging other people's ways of seeing them, and seeing themselves through how others have seen them. This collecting of visual history that I have been focusing on now has given me more of a sense of contribution than any single image I've made.

I don't feel I began to think about history until I was pulled into the insurrection of Nicaragua and now it has come to be something that I think more and more about: a place in time and my crossing the path of that place at a particular time. Photographing the Maryknoll nuns began with a sense of outrage but I am now seeing the longer-term effects of my work and understanding how much it takes to actually do something tangible from the initial act of witnessing. In a strange way I get more pleasure now knowing that twenty years after their death, Bill Ford, the brother of one of the Maryknoll nuns, brought a civil suit against the generals who were in power then and held responsible for creating the conditions that led to their assassination. My few pictures were a small part of that case. Recording and just being part of that cycle of history becomes important to me.

But I don't go into these settings with a sense of what I am trying to get from them. I don't set that kind of an objective. I guess I think of myself as being fluid; I am just trying to assimilate in a way and I hope to leave a place with some sense, through pictures, that can render what I have experienced. After my return home it sometimes takes me time to know what I can do with them. So getting the work on to a front page is one level, but in a longer time frame I am always thinking about what will be enduring. What have I taken? What have I given? What kind of a relationship do I want with my own material or my own past? I guess I want to feel close to it. I want the feeling of my story connecting to other people's stories.

## BALANCING

The hardest thing in doing this work is the balancing between recognising your own needs and acknowledging where other people have their needs. You are always balancing and that could be anything from food and water, health issues, or shelter, and of course you do sometimes feel guilty. But the costs for us journalists are not as great as they are for the people who live in the places we cover. Things were pretty hairy at times in El Salvador but the fact that I knew I could always get out and recoup is a significant difference and a privilege that separates us. And you do get out because you understand that you need to preserve a functioning capability and balance. The people who didn't get out in time burnt out.

Those who cared a lot about me didn't think I was good at looking after myself. Maybe I am more thoughtful about it now, maybe I understand it better now; it is always hard to gauge whether I am looking after myself well but unfortunately you can only depend on your own judgment. When family and friends read about the places I go to, it sounds so horrific that it is extremely difficult for them. People who care the most about you want to protect you and don't want you to expose yourself to danger as you choose to do in this job, and that becomes complicated. How can you reassure them when, in fact, you can't guarantee that you are going to be OK? So they need to be able to care enough to let you go and then trust your judgment in each situation.

A specific example for me was when my father heard on a radio that I had been blown up by a landmine in El Salvador. Somehow the news had travelled so fast via radio that it reached him before I was able to make a phone call. That was really painful for him – especially because there wasn't any news beyond that fact – so in his mind he had played out the entire scenario. My father has been remarkable. Understanding what was propelling me he would encourage me, and at the same time not become overly protective or let me know that I was a kind of burden for him to be preoccupied with. That is a real gift from him. It is hard to be in a dangerous place and at the same time feel responsible to the people who care the most about me.

Most of the time that I was in Central America I felt dominated completely by men: it was a male world and I was learning the rules from them. I had wonderful alliances, partnerships and pals, but there are different issues for men and women because of traditional gender roles. The man is supposed to go out and hunt and so the men in the field that I know, for the most part, don't maintain their home lives – their wives do. Yet for me to have a home life, which I felt that I needed, I had to be able to create it and value it, and that is challenging. I had to consider to what extent I saw my life, my community, as the people in the field I was working with – a world that shifts constantly from one site to another? Or to what extent I wanted to have another kind of community: family and home life? I don't know about other women in the profession but I know how hard it was for me to maintain a personal life. I felt it was real work, tremendous work, but I chose it because it was important to me.

Even though I am saying that I think there is this difference with men who had women raising their children and a nurtured environment to come home to, in some ways my partner, Dick, played that role for me, but he found it very difficult, extremely difficult. He hated that I left, but at the same time he wanted to support me, and so I had to confront the pain it was causing him. Dick and I knew each other for thirty years, a long, long period, and sometimes I would go for two weeks and come back five-and-a-half months later. That was pretty tough stuff to endure in the relationship and have enough of a relationship to piece back together again. There were years that we weren't together at all because I was covering and consumed with Central America and that demanded a life on the road. It was challenging for both of us and it was kind of amazing what we achieved. But it was always negotiated in some way. I think that most male colleagues that I have worked with don't negotiate, they declare. They do what they want to do and their women most often are willing to accommodate, or adapt.

Negotiating the difficult decision about having children while working in the field under danger is not going to change for women. I always thought that I was going to have children. So what happened? I got caught in a history that was racing before me, I grabbed on and went with it and suddenly children become so secondary to the passions of becoming part of history. Of course, there is a cost to that but I wouldn't reject everything from the time I made that choice. I value that period of my life too much. The biggest difference when you go back to these gender issues is that men don't have to make that particular choice within specific time frames. I don't know many men who say, 'I have a child; I can't take this kind of risk any more.'

## MAGNUM, CAMARADERIE AND COMMUNITY

There is definitely a hierarchy among photographers, though there are different kinds of layers. There is the hierarchy that has to do with contracts, assignments and prominence in print. Then there is the hierarchy that has got to do with how well you might be known within the museum culture, the educational context or by the general public. There are also the people who think how gutsy, how daring, and how much you have been out there is what is important. I felt like I was probably seen one way when I was on that kind of cutting edge and very few people understood when I chose to pursue the project I did in Kurdistan. Also there are people who melt into the background as they work and there are people who are very involved in celebrating who they are in the process of doing what they do. It just comes down to personal style in the end but I think that I am happiest if I am not noticed. In the field I believe it is about the people I am photographing, not about me. Too often it becomes about the people reporting on their subjects.

There are photographers who have benefited or been

buoyed by the institutions they work for. Certain news or photo agencies become one's community in some cases and I feel that way with Magnum. It is a little harbour, a point of reference. If you think about who's inside Magnum as an artistic community with tremendous range it is kind of an amazing thing to be part of, such a diverse and dynamic community. It is an inherited family that you mix with but there are some uncles and aunts that you like better than others. Perhaps the common culture in Magnum is how people commit to bringing their work together as books or exhibits with the emphasis not just given to the pictures from a particular place at a moment in time that might be on a front page, but with coherence and vision about what will last in time.

I think one of the hardest things about this profession is its competitiveness. It is continuous. The people who tend to work together are the ones who figure out that they are not competing, but they are still conditioned to think competitively. There are many nasty stories in the field of how people cut other people out. On the other hand, the camaraderie and bonding that takes place is a very powerful part of the dynamic that makes it possible to survive those critical times. But I think that it is a loss for many of us that the camaraderie in the field doesn't always translate to the home front. Maybe we will have a drink together every once in a while and there have been a couple of encounters with old reporters coming together for somebody's fiftieth birthday but it is different to meeting with other friends from home for their fiftieth birthdays. Taking the time to celebrate a fiftieth birthday is a kind of process of acknowledgment, which doesn't often happen within the profession because there is a denial of self in this work; you know, the work is so important that one's life is sometimes considered secondary. For some reason, sustaining continuity with the community one finds in the field when one is home is often difficult, if not impossible, but at the same time sharing the field experience with one's partner is also difficult. You separate parts of your life in this profession.

I sometimes hate being part of what some people call the media circus, which I occasionally feel is a very arrogant culture. I know I am part of it, but I also feel different than it, and I can't always resolve those feelings. I can easily be in a sort of no-man's land, wondering where do I belong in it. But that does not mean hating the job. I still think it's a privilege.

## Working with emotions

There was the question in the eighties of whether I should be on a contract and work only for one magazine. I have to say it was a deal I didn't take when it was offered by *Time* because I was afraid that I would be placed somewhere I didn't have any particular feelings for or connection to. I knew I would perform perfectly fine, and I would make images, but how would that feed me in some other sense? I can't take photographs easily that I don't care anything about and I would rather not do the work if I don't feel there is a connection. I don't mind that connection is costly; I would rather live with that cost.

I think that my emotion comes with this connection that I seek and feel I need – to have some meaning in the place that I am. Some people think that I can't function because I am emotional. I find that construct a difficult one because, for me, the fact that I am emotional means I seek a different kind of connection that deepens my relationship to a place. I don't think that it means that I can't still record what I am seeing because under fire I am very calm and I am very cool-headed. Yes, there has to be interest in the actual fighting, otherwise you can't cover it but I was always trying to go beyond the war front per se to see the integration of the community in and around that war front. Often I would be told that I was too involved in Central America. Too involved from whose perspective and for what? I may be involved in a community but I know we are always outsiders. But I often have said that I think of myself as inside as an outsider can be.

Definitely after El Salvador I suffered post-traumatic stress disorder – being blown up by a mine in 1981 was a huge thing. I think that mines are different from crossfire or even bombing. The way you work is to wander into places not knowing where you are going but being curious about almost everything. Mines come out of nowhere. It deeply undermined my ability to work and it took me about a year to get back into the field. I lost my friend, South African journalist Ian Mates, who was driving the car – he died within twenty-four hours. John Hoagland, who worked for *Newsweek* was in the back seat and was injured slightly, as I was with shrapnel. It was miraculous that I didn't lose my eye. It was also terrible to be flown out of El Salvador having invested quite a lot of time there, feeling I was part of what was evolving and not wanting to miss anything. As soon as I got airlifted out, I felt the accumulation of what I had been doing and realised I was pretty shaken by it.

I don't remember how long it was before I got myself back and mobilised but I still remember who called me when I was hospitalised and who took time to see me. It is very interesting who in the end understands what it means to be there for someone – sadly, it's fairly rare amongst this professional community. That is partly why my personal community has become so important. Maybe I needed that experience back in the eighties to know that I couldn't invest fully in that work community because they were just not going to be there. I found that they were not very good at caring and it has taken me a long time to learn how to do it for myself, to create other kinds of community that buffer that loss. It is just horrifying about how 'unthere' they were, how quickly people just moved on to other places.

At times I do go towards my fear. I sometimes know that I feel fearful and I look at it saying, 'I know this is about fear. I have to deal with the fact that I have the fear.' I become fearful of the fear and so I try to see myself facing that fear and try to look at it in a cold way. It doesn't mean that it always works, and it is not to say that there aren't times that fear can't be paralysing, but that goes back to somehow accepting that that is where you are. It is all about those moments when you recognise this is how you are feeling and it is OK to be feeling it, even if it is not what other people are feeling.

John Hoagland was killed in a crossfire within a year of that ambush we survived together. I so clearly remember this group of photographers all distraught and in disbelief that John had been killed. You know, it seemed impossible because he had been through a lot; he knew the country well; he had committed to being there in a real way and people trusted his judgment. I remember we spent a lot of time talking through the night after he died and the next morning everybody got up and went back out on the road – the road being symbolic of just being out there and the randomness of what could happen. I didn't go; I didn't feel that I was ready to go out there. It wasn't specific; it wasn't that there was a firefight – I wasn't avoiding something that was tangible. It was just that sense that I hadn't let go of what had happened to John and I wasn't ready to go back out there. That is one of the things that you have to learn: to trust yourself completely.

\* \* \*

*Bearing Witness*

I describe my life during that period in Central and Latin America as crossing the river and getting caught in the current. The main work was just going downstream, avoiding the rocks and not completely crashing, just trying to get to the other side. And now I know I am on the other side of the river and I am very aware of what that river is and the ecstasy of the river. But I went a long way away from other people and any sense of whatever else was important. I am now in a place where I don't quite know what the next terrain will be. It is hard when you are in that zone but there is some sense that you have to live it, trust it, and hope that it is going to take you somewhere that you have been searching for.

If my life were to end tomorrow, what would I be most remembered for? Those images of the witnessing, or the act of witnessing, as a kind of model for other people to think about, to link other people to regional communities and to try to strengthen those communities by supporting them. To include other photographers' work in such an effort is a hard thing for some people in this profession to do, but it made complete sense to me in the eighties to be working on collective projects, whether in Chile or in El Salvador with Salvadoran photographers as well as first-worlders all bringing their work together. So I guess I have chosen to place myself on that border between cultures and, although I am not sure where it is leading me, it seems to have become the place that I am, and perhaps the only place for me to be, right now.

## CHAPTER 14

# GLENN MIDDLETON

## BIOGRAPHY

Born in Zimbabwe, Glenn Middleton grew up in South Africa under the apartheid regime. After finishing compulsory military service in 1983, Glenn worked for a number of local media outlets in Johannesburg before becoming a freelance cameraman in 1988. In 1991 he joined the Johannesburg bureau of the BBC. In April 1993 he was shot when police opened fire on a crowd of demonstrators outside the Protea Police Station in Soweto.

Glenn has covered social issues and conflict throughout Africa, Europe and the Middle East, including the fall of the Berlin Wall and the most recent conflicts in Africa, the former Yugoslavia, Afghanistan and Iraq where he moved with the US marines and was one of the first to film the occupation of Saddam's hometown of Tikrit in Northern Iraq.

On special assignments for the BBC, Glenn has exposed child witches in the Democratic Republic of Congo, the illegal diamond trade in Angola and warlords in Sierra Leone. He has worked on a number of highly acclaimed BBC documentaries including *A Journey into Darkness*, which examined the genocide in Rwanda and won the Royal Television Society of Journalists Award for best foreign documentary in 1994, and *The Dying Game*, a documentary about AIDS in Africa which was nominated for an Emmy. In 2003 he was an individual finalist for the Rory Peck Award for Hard News for his work in Africa, Egypt and Iraq in 2002 and 2003. His nomination noted that 'Middleton's portfolio contains powerful and disturbing images of some of the world's major ongoing issues. As he records famine in Angola, AIDS in Botswana, housing shortages in South Africa, child soldiers in Liberia, his own involvement is evident.'

Glenn is married, has three children (triplets) and lives in Johannesburg.

\* \* \*

## STORY

BBC correspondent George Alagiah and I were in Rwanda in 1994 covering the genocide. We were driving down towards the Zairian border in a big four-wheel drive and it was pouring with rain. We were going down a hill on a really winding road when we came upon a guy on a bicycle. He had a little kid on the seat behind him. I told our driver to back off because I didn't want this guy on the bike to feel that he had to speed up, but as I watched him I could almost sense that he was already out of control, picking up more and more speed as he was going down the hill. Each bend that we came to we could see that he had to go out wider, picking up momentum and becoming more out of control. He was going to hurt himself; he was going to go off the cliff; he was going to crash into the side of the mountain or into another car, or whatever, but sooner or later this guy was going to have a wipe-out.

Eventually, on the last bend, the poor guy lost it and went off the road, crashing into the storm drain – big cement boulders, rocks, all sorts of things. It almost happened in slow motion for me. I felt so helpless. The poor little kid on the back who was just holding on behind his dad didn't even know what was coming; we just saw them flying through the air. We got out of the car and ran up to the scene of the accident, expecting to see them injured, blood all over the place. I was imagining loading them into the back of our car and taking them off to the hospital. By the time we got there the man was picking his son up off the ground. He saw me running and he got scared. He must have thought, 'What is happening here? Am I in trouble because I had this accident? This white man is going to come and shout at me.' I could see real fear in his face when he saw me and all I wanted to do was offer my assistance in whatever way I could. I tried to help him pick up his baby and he pushed my hand away.

What really affected me was that there was no crying. This poor guy and his little kid weren't showing their pain. They had just had an enormous accident off the side of the cliff into a big cement bolder and they were physically hurt. They showed no pain and they didn't want my help. I think that the usual thing for a little kid to do when he has had a horrible accident like this is to burst into tears and scream and shout, but there was no emotion. That really, really affected me.

That, for me, is what happens on such a large scale around our continent: people in pain cannot express their hurt; there is never any crying. I think that so many Africans have suffered so much in their lives. Life must be such an uphill battle that this guy just thought, 'Oh well, it is not serious. We can still walk. Let's just get up, fix the bicycle and keep going.' He was probably going down to the local markets to work, or get some food, or something, but the fact that there was no emotion . . . What has become of his life that he cannot show emotion? And even that poor little boy, what has become of him? What has he had to experience in life that he cannot show emotion? It can happen to a whole nation, and it does. Try to imagine the trauma that the people of Rwanda have experienced with the genocide. Their lives are so hard.

When a human being cannot show emotions what do we do to change that?

# GETTING STARTED

I was fortunate enough as a kid to find out that I had a talent as a photographer. Then, during my national service which most young white fellows had to do in South Africa in the early eighties, I fell off my horse and got infected hepatitis. When I returned to my unit I was unable to continue with the duties of a soldier so I opened up a little photographic unit and, if there was any event involving the army, I was basically there as the assigned photographer.

I cleared out of the army in 1982, at the height of some of the worst situations in the country. Fortunately, I hadn't been close to the violence as a soldier as so many of my colleagues had who were either sent to the border regions or into townships to protect the residents, or do whatever they did – basically terrorise a lot of people in the townships. When I left the army I had a reasonably good portfolio and I got a job with the *Rand Daily Mail* in Johannesburg, which allowed me to get into the townships and really try to show the public what was actually going on there. But we were under extreme restrictions from the authorities and quite often our offices were raided by security police. Eventually, the newspaper was closed down and I got a job as a cameraman at the local government broadcaster.

Although this was video work, it was quite an easy transition for me but I only lasted two years with them because my pictures were almost always edited even though I risked my life going into the townships, quite often undercover. We were so blinded to what was actually going on by the press block in South Africa. I think that foreigners saw a lot more of what was happening than the South Africans did. Knowing what I had actually seen and experienced in the townships – the police corruption, the brutality and the pain and suffering – I found it really frustrating that these things weren't being shown. In the evenings I would say to my friends or family, 'Come and watch this stuff that I did today – it is really interesting. You have got to see what is happening out there,'; they would switch on the telly and it just wouldn't be the same. It wouldn't be the same place; it wasn't the same day. Because it was heavily edited, it seemed so foreign to me even though I had just filmed the images.

If you worked for the local media your pictures weren't going to get anywhere so I soon realised the direction that I needed to go. I resigned and went freelance. I started doing work for the foreign networks and eventually I got a contract with the BBC where we work much closer as a team and I can assist more in the scripting and editing. The correspondent sits right next to me during the edit and some of the time they will say, 'You show me the best pictures that you have filmed and I will write to the pictures.' So in one respect I am sort of dictating a bit as to what is going to be written because I'm showing the strongest possible images that I have and the correspondent is saying, 'OK. I can write to that.'

I now cover the entire African continent for the BBC and

often bigger stories beyond our borders. Because Africa is such a difficult and dangerous patch to work, if there are other regions in the world where there is conflict the BBC has a policy of deploying their most experienced crews – they don't send in a journalist or a cameraperson who is not familiar with a war zone. More and more now they tend to pull us out of Africa to cover the more dangerous conflicts around the world.

But it is only when you're doing the job that you actually start to find out whether your inner self can handle it. Only when you are experiencing the hardship of covering a war zone do you really come to terms with the importance of the job, of being in such a strong position to expose a story. You ask yourself questions: 'Am I able to go past someone who is starving – begging for food, water? Am I able to go into a refugee camp with a bottle of mineral water, and maybe some food in my backpack, and do my job properly where women and children are dying of starvation? Am I able to break away from it all and separate myself from the story?' In this line of work if you get cut up about a story, or personally involved, you are not going to cope. You need to ask yourself all those questions about the quality of life that *you* have because it is only a matter of time before what you see at work is going to start affecting you and, when it does, that is when you make the biggest decision of whether or not you can continue doing the work.

## COPING MECHANISMS

I am very aware of all the stress that one can gather in these sorts of jobs so very quickly in my career I learnt to build a large barrier between my personal and professional life so that I don't get too affected by what I am doing while I am working. I learnt to do that because I did start becoming personally involved and taking the baggage home with me. With that barrier I am protected from what is going on around me, although I am recording all those images onto tape. Now I am able to go into a situation, switch off, and do the story as best I can. I don't have to take on that baggage. I think that as soon as you start getting personally involved in the pain and violence it is going to destroy you.

But, equally, those protective barriers can be broken down. The release for me is seeing my story being broadcast. That is another little mental coping mechanism that I have. As soon as I see that the story is going out, I believe that I've helped in some way. I have gone out there, done my job as best as I can, the story goes out on the telly, people see it and, regardless of what they think or say or do afterwards, my feeling is that I have helped as much as I can. That barrier disappears and I feel almost a relief. I release the trauma that I have experienced with the story because it is painful to hang on to that. So, mentally I build up the barrier and then I break it down. I have to do that in order to be able to continue doing this job that I love.

It is a lot easier talking to people who can relate to what you are feeling so I might have an hour's conversation about the experiences with my colleagues on the story to debrief. But you will very seldom see one colleague just going to another colleague and saying, 'Listen, I think you really should take a break. You need time out.' That doesn't happen; at least I don't think that it happens enough, purely because it is a cut-throat industry with a lot of egos so once you have let the cat out of the bag that you are having problems coping, people are going to start talking about you. It is a nasty thing, but I think you would be cast out of the loop very quickly.

Often people start relying on booze and drugs to cope. You often find little groups of people getting together and it is always the same guys and girls in one corner of the bar getting shit-faced. Colleagues of mine have committed suicide. I say colleagues not friends because if I sensed that a really close friend was suffering or had a problem coping with the trauma of the job I might feel that I had the right to discuss it with them, but I think that those sorts of things should be done professionally.

When I am out in the field as a cameraman in a war zone or a refugee camp, I am almost like a machine. I've separated myself from things that are going to affect me mentally. I go out there, get the pictures that I need, and then I try and break away from it. I go back to my hotel room and I leave the refugees in the refugee camp. I think about all the good things in my life: my family, the next holiday, the next fishing trip. I try to imagine what my family is doing at home. I speak to my kids and my wife and I start becoming a dad again, a husband again. So I almost have two separate lives and I must be able to distinguish between the two.

What really helps me a lot is when I come back from a story I like to overnight somewhere before I get back to Johannesburg. Just that downtime mentally will allow me to become the normal Glenn Middleton again. I get a lot of mixed feelings about the stories and I want some time to myself before going home. There are a lot of unanswered questions I need to ask myself: 'Did I go about it correctly? Have I done the right thing here?' But what the downtime really allows me to do is to just become a normal person again.

Quite often, when I get back home, I know that I have brought back some trauma. My body is telling me I need to discuss it. I get quite tearful and I need to ask myself why. And suddenly it will pop up and I will talk about it. Even just thinking about it will help me. I do a lot of thinking, but my body does talk to me. It will tell me something is not right and I need to get rid of it. So I will go fishing. When I am fishing I can be by myself, or I can have a mate with me, and we might not necessarily talk to each other for an hour but I think, 'Life is not so bad any more.' Or my wife, Tracey, will know if something is worrying me and will ask me questions, hoping that I will open up and talk about my worries. She knows the best thing for me is to talk about it.

It is especially difficult for Tracey when I leave for work, though. She might be thinking I'm on the front line but I could be in a hot bubble bath. I worry when I go out onto the front line, I worry when we are trying to get an interview with a warlord, or some child soldier has stopped me at a roadblock, but I am not worried when I am in the pub with my mates having a couple of beers, or when I am having a bubble bath watching the telly in my hotel room. But Tracey doesn't know what I am doing or where I am so for Tracey it is a twenty-four hour worry when I am away.

If I am in a war zone she won't watch the telly. I often phone up and say, 'My darling, we are going to have a two-and-a-half-minute piece on the telly in half an hour; if you are there, switch on.' And she might very well do it, but for her it brings the reality of what I am doing a little bit closer to home. So she also has to build up a barrier to protect herself, a defence mechanism to not get involved with the story. It is bad enough *me* coming home with a lot of baggage; we don't need two people at home affected by the same story. So I think for her the easiest way to deal with what I do is the less she knows about it the better. She has said to me that if I ever want to discuss anything with her I can. I don't usually discuss with her what I have done and she doesn't always ask unless she feels something is worrying me or I need to unburden. Quite often she will hear about something I've experienced from a friend that I've spoken to. That's the way she prefers it. I'm happy with that.

I watch the news bulletins every day to see what stories are breaking, where things are moving, because it gives me a chance to say, 'Well, I will probably be going there next.' But there are times where I don't want to see a telly. I just need time out. Again, I think that is a form of protection when I am feeling overloaded on the job. But I have so many mixed feelings. I fight with my emotions a lot of the time. It will be really small things that will tick me off and I know I shouldn't be around my wife and my family because I am not myself. Something has annoyed me, or affected me, and I am not the real me. I don't want them to see me like that: to be shouting and screaming at my kids because something unrelated to their lives has upset me. So I disappear until I know that I can be a normal person again. I am becoming better and better at doing that.

I have lost a lot of friendships over the years because I think it is quite difficult for friends to understand what I do. They have such normal family lives and jobs. They don't really know what I am doing most of the time and it is quite difficult to answer their questions directly because all the stories that I do are for the international viewer and a lot of my friends watch the local station. When friends phone up and I say, 'Sorry guys, I can't do that fishing trip with you chaps this weekend because I am going to a war zone', they don't necessarily understand. I have had to disappoint them so many times. Most of them think that I am crazy. Why would I want to go to a war zone? Why do I leave my family at home? The answer is because it is what I do. I get a huge amount of satisfaction out of what I do. I don't want to think of the day that I am going to have to give it all up.

I always knew that I wanted to be a dad, to have kids that

I could bring up and love. I have another life at home as a husband and a father. I am a father, I am a husband, and those things are very important to me. They make me realise that I have another life apart from work, and you need that other life; you need that balance in this job.

## ENGAGING THE VIEWER

There is so much pain and suffering that goes on around the African continent that I feel it has become a duty for me to go into refugee camps, war zones, whatever it might be, to experience all sorts of things. And I hope that what I experience, what I record, will change opinion, politics, people's minds and people's perceptions about Africa in particular. It is only recently I have become a parent and in the last five years you would probably notice that on all my rushes I concentrate more on filming kids, babies, mums. I try to capture the sounds and images that make viewers sit up and say, 'Hey, I can relate to that. My kid does that,' and thereby make them realise that these people are human beings. I try to capture the viewer's imagination with images that they can relate to and that will bring them closer to the telly. I want them to turn up the volume. It is a real challenge because at the end of the day I don't think people care enough.

Sure, I will get a piece on the news bulletin and maybe people will give donations to their local NGO but for the man sitting in his living room, what is he going to do to make a difference? At the end of the day this guy has got his house, his job, his car, his dog, his cat; he has got a life and he is protecting that little life from anything that might threaten it. He almost discards things that are happening around him because he doesn't want those things to affect him. It is so easy for a viewer to switch channels when another refugee camp pops up, or another warlord or rebel leader in Africa who is in the process of destroying his country – 'Well, we see that all the time. It was on the telly last week. It is going to be on telly again next week.' Television has exposed all these problems around the continent and the images often don't affect people any more. We have become so hardened to the difficulties of our own human race that it has almost become the situation now that only the strongest survive. 'If you show weakness, that is your problem; it has nothing to do with me. If, because of where you live, or what you do, or the colour of your skin, or the language that you speak, you have a more difficult time, well, that is your problem. Why should it affect my life?' These perceptions must change.

## GIVING SOMETHING BACK

I am a white South African and we are not very proud of our history. Quite often you will find white South Africans saying, 'Oh well, I never voted in the old apartheid system . . . I didn't want to go into the army.' In the end, the reality is that we are white South Africans and our history is very difficult to come to terms with because of the atrocities that happened under our apartheid system. I still don't believe that white South Africans really understand the pain and suffering that was inflicted on the blacks. What I think is that I can make a difference by going out and exposing issues, and through our profession we can make a difference, make South Africa a better place for all.

There is a sense of responsibility for me to do what I do. It is what I can give back to humanity. Some guys do the job because of the adrenaline, purely and simply. There are a couple of adrenaline junkies out there and they just do the work because they think it is cool to be shot at, cool to be in an environment where people are dying and suffering. For me, it is a way I can pay back society.

I did a story in the Congo a couple of years ago about a so-called prophet. Basically he was looking after children who were mainly homeless. Unfortunately, for some of these kids, their own parents claimed that they had been bewitched so they had abandoned them. It could have been because of something very simple that happened in the home like the fridge breaking down, or not enough rain that season. In a situation like this the parents get suspicious and all someone like this 'prophet' has to say is, 'Well, maybe your children have been bewitched.' So, the parents offloaded their kids at this compound at a cost and this chap supposedly tried to get rid of the witchcraft. He believed in himself so much that he didn't mind us walking around his compound and filming while he was going through these exorcisms. There were some horrific incidents where the parents would want to see their kids, but prior to the visit the people working with the 'prophet' would insert foreign objects into the children and then make them drink a potion so that when the parents came they would see their kids vomiting up live fish, nuts and bolts. The parents would pay again for the prophet to do another month's work on their 'bewitched' kids. I was so excited about the fact that we were going to expose this guy – we were going to show the world what was going on in there and they were going to put a stop to it, and that is exactly what happened! It went out on air and this guy's whole operation was closed down.

When I saw that particular story released I was so relieved for all those little kids. I knew that I had helped them. Something like that really, really touches my heart. I love getting feedback about things that I do. When you know that your colleagues, your friends, your family and the public are appreciative of what you do, that gives you more inspiration to go back and do it again. I think if you don't get the rewards, if you don't get the feedback, the 'hero-grams', it would be very difficult. Sometimes you would have to think, 'Well, why am I doing this?' Any recognition is good.

I really enjoy what I do. I love my work. I meet a lot of very interesting people and also very horrible people, but what inspires me most about my job is that I can record things as they happen – history in the making – and I can go back to a country, or a story, and see that things have changed: the people's lives have improved.

## Covering conflicts

I remember the days when I used to do freelance camera work – I was a lot younger and a lot braver. You have got to fight your way into the industry because there are a lot of people out there wanting to do the same sort of work and unfortunately it leads you down that road where you have to be braver, take more risks than the next guy. If there is a war zone, the BBC sometimes pays news agencies to get the pictures. So Reuters or AP go to the front line and the BBC pays these news agencies a lot of money every year because they are on the front line. The freelance cameramen or stringers are the ones that have to be even more competitive than the broadcast cameramen. They have got to be braver, and younger. I think that inevitably, if you are a stringer or a freelancer, you have really got to put your neck out there to make a difference because if you don't you aren't going to get the work.

Ultimately though, the BBC will leave it up to the individual correspondent or the cameraperson it employs to make the final decision as to whether or not a situation is too dangerous. In fact, recently I got a call from a producer saying, 'If we were to get official accreditation, would you be keen to go to Zimbabwe with me?' I said no. There have been horrible stories in the media stating that people working for the BBC and foreign correspondents covering the elections are actually spies working for the British government. I am not prepared to take risks in a situation where I am going to be a target. Send me to Afghanistan again, into Angola, fine, but I don't want to go to Zimbabwe – not while we are banned from going there. Also, Tracey said to me she didn't want me to go to Zimbabwe and I have to take her opinions very seriously. She has never, ever said to me I don't want you to go to Rwanda or Liberia or Sierra Leone or any of the other war zones but she said I don't want you to go to Zimbabwe, and I can understand her concerns. Therefore, saying no was easy because maybe I feel confident enough that it is not going to affect my career in any way. If it does, so be it.

People like myself who do the camera work and the editing, people we call shoot-editors, almost edit the piece while we are filming. We get to a stage where we know that we have enough to do the story and at that point we pack up and go. I am very disciplined and I can say, 'Guys, let's go,' especially if there are bullets flying. There is no hanging about to see what happens next. You need to be able to judge when you should leave and that comes with experience. Because a lot of journalists have been killed over the years – and the BBC has lost a few – I think it is probably in line with their agreement with the insurance companies to send correspondents on hostile-environment courses where ex-British marines teach you the dangers of operating as a journalist in a war zone. Though the reality is, as I was once told by a soldier, cameramen like myself have much more front-line experience in wars than most marines in the British army.

I think that where I am quite fortunate is that I go back to the same stories and I get to know a particular faction, a particular tribe. It is what I have done for fourteen or fifteen years now. When London gives me the green light to go into a story, even though it might be a year later, I can prepare myself for it. I have memories of the past so I build up an image of what to expect and normally I am right. But, in saying that, I always have to prepare myself for the worst because things can change on a daily basis in a war zone. You can go to the front line and the people involved are your friends, they love the camera, but then you go back in the afternoon and it might be a completely different scenario – the people are no longer so willing to be filmed and they're no longer your friends. You can feel it, and that comes with experience. Some of the signs are quite obvious like, 'Why are we the only car driving down this road?' But, in the end, you don't really know if you are in the wrong area until a bad situation is upon you. Sometimes you miss the most obvious things and afterwards you say, 'Well, that was really dumb. Why did we do that?'

I always have this fear of failing, this constant fear of what if I don't have a job in a week, or in a month's time? I have the huge responsibility of supporting my family and I know that regardless of what happens in my family life – even now the triplets have come along – I am going to have to continue doing what I am doing for the BBC. What has changed is my awareness that I am in a conflict area. I can smell the danger. I get scared. I start sweating. I just know that this is not right. But so often, in my situation, I find myself doing stupid things. In a split second you just get taken away from reality and that is where accidents happen. It is a type of craziness; it is addictive. You know you don't want to go down that road, but you are going down that road anyway. I would hate to say that in a dangerous situation like this I had forgotten about who I am because I wouldn't want that to be the case, but you do get caught up in the moment and it all seems unrealistic until you get back to the editing and you see you actually did do something very risky. It scares me. But I do those things less and less now because every time I say to myself, 'What was that about? What did you do that for? Have you absolutely lost it?' You build up a subconscious awareness so that the next time you are in that same environment you don't repeat the same mistakes.

It doesn't become easier going into a war zone. This job is becoming more difficult for me to do because I understand the dangers more and more. I keep reminding myself that people die in this profession. People die! And I keep saying to myself, 'Why am I here? Why do I keep going into a war zone? I don't have to be here.' It is a good thing for me to be scared and understand the fear. I am not afraid to announce it because it will make me even more cautious than I was a week ago. The older I get and the more experience I have and the more wars I see, the more I come to realise that one day I am going to become a statistic. I am not meant to be there. So I get in and out of there fast. I think that for someone who can't relate to that, who doesn't understand the dangers of being on the front line when the bullets are flying, their number is up. If you don't understand that, be careful – you are in the wrong business.

I hope that one day I will be able to say, 'I'm out of here.' I can't say when, but I see it definitely happening. Yet it is so difficult to imagine doing something else. I am absolutely addicted to my work. I am addicted to the action. I am addicted to the fear. I love it. I love my job. I think that there are always these conflicting fears and concerns and worries that make me continue doing it and there is that love/hate relationship. It is very difficult to say that I am going to stop next week or next month. I think that something is going to have to happen in order for me to say, 'Enough is enough.' Something is going to have to really change my mind.

# CHAPTER 15

# CHRISTOPHER MORRIS

## Biography

CHRISTOPHER MORRIS BEGAN HIS career in the back offices of the photo agency Black Star and worked his way up to become an elite member of the agency. In 2001 he left to become a founding member of the newly formed Photo Agency VII along with Ron Haviv. Today Chris is contracted to *Time* magazine and in his career of more than two decades he has covered over nineteen conflicts in places such as Central America, the former Soviet Union, the Middle East and Africa to become one of the world's top conflict photographers. Until recently he was dismissive of those who choose not to go to the front lines of the most dangerous conflicts but with the birth of his first child he made the decision to quit the dangerous craft of war photography. Changing direction is usually a difficult choice for any photographer but it is particularly hard, he says, when covering war is what people expect you to do and what they pay you for.

He is the recipient of numerous photographic awards including the Robert Capa Gold Medal Award and the Olivier Rebbot Award from the Overseas Press Club for his work in Yugoslavia, the Magazine Photographer of the Year Award in 1992, the Infinity Photojournalist Award from the International Center of Photography in 1992, and a number of World Press Photo Awards. His images are featured extensively in a number of books including Peter Howes' *Shooting Under Fire: The World of the War Photographer* (Artisan, New York, 2002); Giorgio Baravalle's (ed) *Rethink: Causes and Consequences of September 11* (de.MO, New York, 2003); and Photo Agency VII's *WAR* (de.MO, New York, 2004).

He is married with two children and lives in Tampa, Florida, in the United States.

\* \* \*

# STORY

Sarajevo: height of the siege of the city by the Serbs in February 1994, deep winter, and I had already been there for over forty days straight. Every day six dead, ten dead, eighteen dead; it just went on and on and on: shelling, sniping, shelling, sniping. I got a call that there were six kids playing in the snow who had been killed by shelling: four girls, two boys, something like that. My friend Enrico and I went out there but the bodies had just been removed. All that was there was bloody snow. So we went into the morgue and took a few pictures.

These little kids were dressed in their little ski outfits. They had their little gloves on; they were all very, very pretty and what I noticed – the horror of it – was one of the older girls, she was maybe six or seven, was missing her face. When I say missing her face, the shrapnel had removed the front part of her face and you could look down at her hair and her little clothes but you could see the back of her head inside the skull. There was nothing inside.

When we went back in the morning the father and grandfather came in to identify the bodies. The mortician had put her face back on but it was upside down and the father saw this and he clutched his children and wept. It was one of the most horrific scenes that I saw. The same images I saw, they saw, but this image was their kids. It was a family. And this was just from some piece of metal falling out of the sky and onto the kids playing in the snow. It happened daily there and the West basically did nothing. It did nothing at the beginning of the war. It was just that whole outlook on the world: whatever . . .

You don't deal with that; you can't. I don't really feel it if I meet a soldier who becomes my friend and a round comes and hits him and he dies. I don't weep over him dying. He died because he was a gunman. His lot in life was to fight, even if it is not right, even if he is a good guy or a bad guy. But when it comes to *children* and *women* . . .

Later that night, after I saw the children in the mortuary, I heard Clinton being asked in a briefing about what he was going to do about Sarajevo. He said, 'There is no humanitarian crisis in Sarajevo. The people aren't starving to death. There is nothing that needs to be done' – something like that. I could not believe it. I lost it. I called my office and demanded to speak to the managing editor at *Time* and because I knew people in Washington, to get in touch with them to tell them what I had just seen. I was so upset and distraught that my editors told me to leave Sarajevo.

So how do you know when to leave? When you are on the verge of an emotional breakdown. But that next day after the kids were killed in the snow I was driving out of Sarajevo and one of the big market blasts occurred. I turned around and went right back in.

## MAKING A NAME IN WAR PHOTOGRAPHY

Early on I knew I wanted to be a photojournalist and to me the ultimate in photojournalism was to be a war photographer. I liked to travel to the most exotic places but doing travel photography didn't really excite me. War photography was exciting initially, and frightening, yes. You would get the adrenaline rush. It is very fulfilling.

But photojournalism is a very selfish business for the photographer. I know maybe Jim Nachtwey won't appreciate this comment, or Ron Haviv, or the other photographers, but to me it is almost like if you want to win awards and do really well quickly in photojournalism, you become a war photographer. That is where the most amazing pictures are to be made because that is where life and death collide. Two people are trying to kill each other and, as a photojournalist, you are trying to put yourself right in the middle to document it and if you can do it well you get a lot of recognition for it really fast; there are a lot of motivations from awards and things like that. Certainly, it happened to me. My career was like 'boom' overnight. Just by doing war photography, everybody knew who I was. They open up *Time* or *Newsweek* and they see these photos and it is like, 'Wow, who is that?' And then two weeks later and again some other war: 'Wow, who's that?' With Ron, that recognition only took one or two trips; he did really well.

There are always young people that you see on stories who want to become war photographers and they always try to latch on because the best way to do it is to latch on to somebody with experience. A lot of people are shunned, meaning they are not let into a certain group or clique of photographers, because of their personality, their traits. It is a real bonding thing. You have to kind of feel a person out if you are going to let someone in. I have let people ride with me and taken them under my wing, and after a day or two I don't want to be with them any more.

Covering wars worldwide you are looking at maybe ten to twenty photographers, max, who do it. That excludes the local photographers from each country, the ones who work for the wires. I am talking about the ones that come and go. It is a small group. In America you are looking at four or five, France four or five, Germany two or three, and then there are a few Dutch and there are some Brits, so it totals out at around twenty people at any given time. We are all very, very competitive but we are all very close and we are all friends.

It is very strange that there is this stereotype that we are drug addicts and alcoholics because one thing I have noticed is that there is not a lot of drug use. It doesn't really exist and I have not encountered a lot of alcoholism either. Ron doesn't really drink, I don't drink, Jim doesn't drink, Patrick Chauvel doesn't really drink, Luc Delahaye doesn't drink. There is a fringe, but that is a minority where there might be some drug use, but it is not rampant – it is not an issue.

## Getting the image

I was looking at the footage from Ramallah when the Israelis laid siege to the city in 2002 trying to judge how I would have attempted to get the image. It is as if you gamble – the bulldozers are going in and they are knocking down buildings, the troops are out, and your instinct is to stay put, but you say, 'Fuck it,' and you just run. It is like you take a gamble: are the

Israelis going to shoot me? Or you are in a position with ten to fifteen photographers and you notice that at that building way down the road there is a big engagement so you all decide to go. You hook up in groups and you start to go, building to building to building, and by the time you get there you are down to two or three. People start to drop back as the danger increases. That kind of risk-taking behaviour does give a photographer status but it is very personal. You just figure it out as you go. It is like the guy who runs for the touchdown where everybody looks and says, 'Wow!' When you have the photos and you haven't been shot it feels good. You come back and everyone says you are a nut, you are crazy, you shouldn't do that, you could have been killed, but if the pictures are good and you are alive . . . !

Photographers I know, especially some of the Europeans, are very fatalistic: 'Well, if death is meant for me it is meant for me, but it is never going to happen.' But it is so easy for it to happen. So easy to make a fatal mistake and you don't even have to make the fatal mistake yourself. It could be the driver you are relying on, it could be a soldier, it could be a bandit. It is absolutely out of your control. When I used to leave home I would pack up my apartment as if I might not come back. I used to like tidying it up a little bit. You close the door on your apartment and lock it and think maybe I am not going to come back. Yugoslavia, Chechnya, some of the Africa stories, hard core, really hard core, but I really enjoyed it at the time. Well, I was young; I was in my late twenties, early thirties. Back then I was not afraid. I had no fear.

## Fear

I learnt early on in my career that the moment of fear in your toes – the moment you feel it – you squash it immediately because if you don't it is like a tidal wave. It will just consume you. You just have to use all those internal psychological things: peer pressure; looking beyond what the image might be; not thinking; thinking of something beautiful, somebody you are in love with. There are mental ways you can do it. But you do have to squash the fear immediately because I saw people get hurt and killed succumbing to fear. With fear, people don't know how to react: they don't see; they make stupid mistakes. Fear is a paralysing drug. It is really controlling.

There are numerous incidents where I have felt fear and it was not necessarily always in combat. It is where I might have been dragged out of a building; dragged out of a car; thrown into a ditch with a gun put in my face and they are going to kill me. It's where I feel, 'Right, now I am going to die.' It's like in the movies. You think the guy should get up and run; he should do something because he is going to die. What is he going to do? You see people in movies not showing fear and while that is not real, in another way it is real because while it is happening you are mentally trying to judge how he is going to react if I start to do this or that.

I do look differently now on the photographers who did not want to cover war. They were afraid and it is OK to be afraid. During the Gulf War in 1991, the US military picked four photographers that they would allow to go as far forward as they wanted to go. They put two with the army and two with the marines. I picked the marines. We drew straws but David Turnley for US News got one of the best draws. He was to be deployed with the army and his mission was to be dropped behind enemy lines by helicopter – not on the second helicopter but on the first helicopter with no armour, no support, and left there in Iraq. That was the mission. To me, that is like a prize: you want that. It is like Robert Capa in the Normandy invasion. They are only giving the opportunity to four photographers so when you get the opportunity you take it. But when David was briefed on what he was going to do he instead went back in the rear where he got the best picture of the war: that helicopter photo of the GI distraught when he discovers his best friend is in one of the body-bags next to him.

The Turnley brothers (Peter and David) aren't considered war photographers because, in my view, they never covered wars: they covered refugees and aftermaths of wars. It used to really make some of us photographers bitter back then because they seemed to have this image that they were these great war photographers, but we didn't believe they were. But now I can look back and I can understand. I shouldn't judge them on that because they didn't want to be war photographers and now I don't want to be a war photographer either. I think that they had a lot of pressure on them because of their reputations. I just didn't like the fact that they came back and were portrayed as war photographers.

It was kind of like a letdown after the Gulf War. I had put myself as far forward as I could go – the tip of the spear with the marines – but the Iraqis didn't fight, they were captured. Then I broke up with my first wife and it was hard. I was in a daze and I just didn't know what I was going to do so I said, 'Well, fuck it. I am going to go off and I am going to cover war like I have never covered a war before.' I went to Yugoslavia and I thought, 'Now, here is a war.' Unlike in the Gulf War, in the first six months there was complete access to anywhere and to any group so I decided that I was going to go all out. I took Ron Haviv with me and we survived. But later in the war, because both sides understood that the press wasn't helping them, they locked out all the media. By the time of the Bosnian War we couldn't go to the front lines. It was very, very difficult to do our job.

## Burnout

You can't take a certain type of photo without it damaging you. Early on in the eighties I was *in love* with photography. I would get back from a story and I had this ritual: get all the materials, sit down with a light table, maybe have a drink – a cognac or something – and search out the jewels. Pick out the twenty best images. I used to *love* to do that. But then at one point – and it started with the Croatian War – I would come back to New York and I would put down the images and it would cause me to have a breakdown. I would just start weeping uncontrollably. I would look at the images and it was like the people I had photographed were tugging on my soul. From that point on I stopped editing my work for almost twelve years. I still have not gone back through any of my returns from all those wars except for Chechnya, which I recently did just to put some stuff on the Photo Agency VII web site. I relied on the editors of *Time* and the editors at my agency at Black Star to do the edit. I wouldn't look at them at all. So for me I shut it out but for Jim Nachtwey it has been different. Jim kept that tight, rigid control on his work, his love of his photography. I lost the love of my photography. So by about '94, or '95 I really burnt out on it. It was like a treadmill: it was a job, it became a career and now how do I get off? I can't get off; what else am I going to do? They are not going to use me for anything else.

When my first daughter was around two years old I was in Chechnya and had some really close calls. I came out and when they wanted me to go back in I said, 'I won't.' Those Chechnyan photos were the hardest to take because of my daughter. It was like I was gambling with my life and maybe the outcome was I was not going to go home to her. That was the moment that I really let *Time* know that I didn't want to do this any more. 'Find me something else.' It is sad when you are seen as a war photographer and that is what people want to pay you to do and that is what you have to do to pay the mortgage.

Sure I would take those risks when I had just my wife to worry about, because my wife knew what I did before we married. But that is what I meant when I said photojournalism is a selfish business: selfish to your mother, your parents, your sisters, your cousins, your wife, your girlfriend; it is just very selfish. 'You stay back here; I am going to go off and maybe I am going to come home, maybe I am not, and I will leave you this mess of a life – all the bills, all the debt and all the pain.' The only thing that was ever going to turn it around for me was my daughter, but even when she was a little baby I didn't experience that feeling. It didn't happen until she started talking and she could hold on to my pants and say, 'Daddy, Daddy, don't go to work.'

## THE UNPUBLISHED IMAGE

I was amazed at the horror of what weapons do to victims, to children, to women. I had seen a few dead people but I hadn't really encountered shelling and bombing from planes or what shrapnel does to people until the late eighties in Afghanistan. The only victims I saw were fighters so it was easier for me back then. It wasn't until much later, working in Panama and then working in Yugoslavia, that I really saw the civilian end of it: the death of children, women, innocent people. It is a real mind game emotionally to photograph a scene of death that has been inflicted by weapons.

As a photojournalist, there are lots of photographs that you desperately want shown but you know that no one will publish them. The magazines won't publish them because of advertising space and the outrage that they would receive. It is a very sanitised version of war we see in the media. Even in the World Trade Center disaster you didn't see any of the victims splayed out on the sidewalk. How many images of victims have we seen from the World Trade Center? There are none in this society but if it is Rwanda – if it is Rwandans being slaughtered – that's all right, we can show it. I recently saw a photograph – I can't believe *Paris Match* ran it – of the severed head of one of the suicide bombers in Israel. I couldn't believe that *Paris Match* ran it but now I can show some people. It is a very shocking photo but that is the kind of stuff that you see as a photojournalist and it is the type of photograph that never gets published. The US media would never run that, never, ever.

Early on in Sarajevo I went out to photograph shells landing and there was this car that had just gotten hit and was on fire. I saw there were two guys in the car and I went around to the driver's side to take a picture. The side of the car was full of holes from the shrapnel and I looked up and there was a head. The body had been severed and the head was sitting in the door staring at me with its eyes open. I freaked out. I ran because I was thinking, 'It is going to happen to me. If I stand here, another shell is going to come in,' because they just drop one in the mortar tube and then they reload and drop another. They don't usually change the angle and so all you can think is, 'Here comes another one.'

I regretted later not taking the picture because I used to take photos like that mainly to shock my editors back home – 'Look what is happening here! A child without a head in his little school outfit!' – but they were not going to run them. For instance, during the war in Somalia, the US killed hundreds of Somalis by firing into buildings trying to get the warlord Aidid before the 'Black Hawk Down' incident, but there are no photographs of that. If it is written about it is one thing to say twenty-eight people were killed in a building, or a suicide bomber kills so many people, but there are really no images of it. You might see some sheets covering bodies but everything is very sanitised in our society. That is the part of the industry that bothers me.

## Dealing with trauma

Early on, when you are young, you encounter something very horrific and very shocking and you tend to put a pretty instant shield up because it is like you were almost preparing for it and all of a sudden, finally, you have faced it. You don't want to have that emotional breakdown so early in your career. So I think the younger journalists tend to be a bit stronger. But today there are certain stories that I know if I try to relive them they can almost cause me to have a breakdown because they are so shocking. You are dealing with humans at their worst. Most of those stories I try to keep tucked away at the back of my mind.

I am curious at what point and over what types of incidents this has happened for my colleagues. It is ironic because we don't talk about the issues involved in what we do. It is very strange that we don't. We don't talk about the emotional toll that our job plays on us. You spend a lot of time riding around in cars together but I have never talked about those things with Ron and I have never talked about them with Jim. I have an Italian friend, Enrico, and we are close and have talked about these issues a little bit but it is more about laughter and fun – a lot of black humour, a lot. Talking about the emotional toll is depressing and you don't want to be with somebody who is . . . you don't want to talk, trust me. So we keep a lot of stuff built up inside us.

I have covered around nineteen conflicts and in those conflicts I have seen a lot. Some conflicts are longer than others, like the Croatian War, the Bosnian War, or Chechnya. You don't go once for two weeks and that is it. You spend maybe four or six months working in a place or longer – five years in Yugoslavia. So you see a lot but there really is nobody to talk to. The only ones who would understand are people that have done it. Until you have smelt it, felt it, been there, it isn't real. If you want to get some kind of useful feedback, there really is nobody to talk to.

Sometimes you see things and sometimes you are close to death and you hurt and cry, but because you are maybe deep in Chechnya, or Rwanda, or Liberia, you just can't hop in a taxi and leave. So the best people to be with are people that can make you laugh. At least, *I* like to work with people that make me laugh. Patrick Chauvel, Luc Delahaye, Jim . . . well, you don't really laugh with Jim because he is quite serious about what he is doing; he has a light side about him but when he is working he is not that light but you have a good time with him anyway. You have dinner, you talk about your close calls but you don't talk about the war. It is too depressing. It is too frightening.

You also definitely don't go back and tell your editors. You basically just want them to publish the photos and that is your real motivation: you want to get this stuff out. It is not so much that you won't get the next job because if you are already doing the work you know you are going to get the next job. Without calling my editors, I could turn around and get on the next plane to Israel and they wouldn't mind. They trust the ones that are really good at the job. They want you there but no editor would ever, ever say you have to go to a war zone. Never. It is the photographer who convinces the editor; the editor is usually saying, 'I don't really want you to go. We'll pick up some pictures from somebody else.' They have that hidden burden of bearing that responsibility, the corporate financial responsibility, if you are maimed or wounded or killed or kidnapped.

## The role of photojournalism

There is no real place for photojournalists any more. Photojournalism has turned into a Walmart or a Kmart of photography. Photography is not looked upon as this grand thing and I didn't want to be part of the Walmart general-type of photographer. I wanted to be thought of on a higher level and that is why I moved to VII. I know the members of VII quite well. We are like a family. It took a lot for me to pull away from Black Star because, for me, that was like a family; that was where I started. I was not, and am not, in the business for financial reasons. I would never really push my work and try to sell it. I shot my stuff for *Time* and I was happy to do it but I reached the point also where my work was not being seen and I wanted to do some books, I wanted to do some exhibits, and I wanted people to go in and look at my work. I knew if I was with the photographers at VII people would look at my work. I don't think that we at VII will ever be more than ten or twelve photographers. There are already ten of us so we have almost reached our limit.

## Compassion fatigue

I used to be a news junkie – absolutely, one thousand per cent, full time. I used to go to sleep with the news, wake up with it, always have it on. Now I don't watch TV. I don't watch the news any more at all. When I first moved to Florida from New York in the mid-nineties I was still a news junkie and I was amazed at society, how most people didn't even know where any of the places in the news were. How could you be like that? But, now that I am out there and I have kind of got out of the business, I understand why they don't watch it. Why would they? Why would you want to come home and turn on your TV at dinnertime and watch horrific things? Following the news every day does something physically inside of you, to your health and your faith. Why should people put themselves through that? I know journalists need to report it but I now understand why people don't want to watch it.

I have noticed what happens to me if I watch something, or look at that photograph in *Paris Match* of the suicide bomber's head, or read some horrific story; it does something to you inside. I almost feel like you have got to say a prayer before you open up Jim Nachtwey's book *Inferno\**. I find there is so much evil that comes out of it. I told Jim, 'I need some voodoo candles to light to keep safe.' It is a very heavy book. Do you think your mind can go through that book, the whole book, in one sitting?

I am sorry but I think there is no hope for humanity. I don't find there is any hope. There is no hope for the Palestinians, there is no hope for Africa . . . well, you can hope for them but there will always be war. It is human nature. The Palestinians and the Israelis signed peace agreements in Israel back in 1993 and conflict in Yugoslavia is ending but war always comes back. In Israel, the Palestinians have been really pushed to the edge. I don't agree with what they do; it is horrific. If they were doing it to army bases and places like

---

\* **Author's note:** *Inferno* is a large format, black-and-white photographic book with over 400 photos. In the words of Nachtwey, it 'represents a personal journey through the dark reaches of the last decade'. James Nachtwey, *Inferno* (Phaidon Press Inc, London, 1999).

that I really could understand it because I have worked a lot in Israel and seen how the Israelis treat the Palestinians. But they are just going in and killing civilians. Totally insane! And a war happened in Lower Manhattan – the World Trade Center. There is always going to be a war and one day, somewhere, in some way, some nuclear thing is going to happen and you never know when it will come home and bite us, bite the Western world.

As I've said, the job is very selfish, very personal, almost like you are doing it for yourself and the secondary stuff is you are to inform and shock society about what is going on in the world. But nothing has ever changed. It has just never changed. OK, NATO finally bombed the Serbs but it took four or five years. Go to Sarajevo and look at the cemetery, look at the soccer field and all the dead. You have to be there taking the photos, because if the photos didn't exist NATO would never have bombed the Serbs, but the photos didn't help the Rwandans. The way to make a change in society is if you take the world leaders to the war. For instance, during the Bosnian War if you had taken Chelsea Clinton and strapped her to a street pole in Sarajevo or made her go fetch water in Sarajevo under siege realising that maybe she was going to come back, maybe she was not, that would have resulted in change. If you had taken the then UN Secretary-General Boutros-Ghali's wife and daughter and made them live in Sarajevo for a week, that would have made change. But, of course, that is not going to happen; leaders are not stupid, they are not going to go there and risk their lives or those of *their* loved-ones.

What I am getting at is that photojournalism doesn't really help. Yes, it helps keep wars more contained, but it doesn't stop them. Yes, there is a place for photojournalism, there is a reason to do it, but you should not go out there and say, 'This is going to change something.' I don't think the photojournalist's job is to try to change society; it is just to inform.

**Author's note:** After this interview, Chris returned to covering war embedded with the front-line 3rd Brigade of the US army's 3rd Infantry Division during the war in Iraq.

## CHAPTER 16

# DAVID RIEFF

### BIOGRAPHY

BORN IN BOSTON IN THE United States, David Rieff is a freelance author who has worked as an editor, program director and professor of creative writing. He has been a fellow at the World Policy Institute, the New York Institute for the Humanities at New York University, a member of the Council on Foreign Relations and board member of the Arms Division of Human Rights Watch and the Central Eurasia Project of the Open Society Institute.

David was an author rather than a reporter and never intended to cover war. By the beginning of the nineties he had written three books about non-white immigrants to the United States and in 1992 had a contract to write another book, this time focusing on immigrants to Western Europe, and he moved to Berlin. After watching the war in Bosnia on TV every night, David decided to go there to do just one story. In the end, he stayed to cover the break-up of the Balkans and then moved on to Rwanda. As David says, he was 'hijacked by the Bosnian War'. Rather than covering the fighting, David focuses on refugee issues and the humanitarian effects of war and, as such, spends a lot of his time with aid workers.

David has covered conflict in Bosnia, Kosovo, Rwanda, Congo, Sudan, Liberia, Central Asia and Afghanistan and has written five books: *Slaughterhouse: Bosnia and the Failure of the West* (Simon and Schuster, New York, 1996); *The Exile: Cuba In the Heart of Miami* (Vintage, London, 1993); *Los Angeles: Capital of the Third World* (Touchstone Books, New York, reprint 1992); *Going to Miami: Exiles, Tourists, and Refugees in the New America* (University Press of Florida, Florida, reprint 2000); and *A Bed for the Night: Humanitarianism in Crisis* (Simon and Schuster, New York, 2002). He co-edited *Crimes of War: What the Public Should Know* (W. W. Norton and Co, New York, 1999) with Roy Gutman. He is also a contributing writer to the *New York Times* magazine.

David is single and lives in New York.

* * *

## Story

I don't know if this is a story exactly. I don't forget anything so I am not sure there is one thing that sticks with me or is the sort of emblematic moment of my career but in Goma (Democratic Republic of Congo), in the cholera time in the late summer of '94, I used to drive down the roads in the camps. The camps were cities bigger than most real cities – a million people in them. You would drive down the road and there would be all these people, and it was Africa, and it was a refugee camp. I have been in hundreds of refugee camps all over the world and there are always people milling about. There are people sitting there with their bundles on the side of the road; there are people lying down; there are people doing pretty much everything visibly. You would drive down the road with someone from a UN agency to do an errand and half an hour later you would come back and there would be fifty bodies that hadn't been there earlier along that same kilometre of road. Later in the day you would go and there would be those fifty bodies and fifty bodies from 700 other places in the camp, being buried in mass graves covered with lime.

This was a level of dying that was hard to comprehend. I have seen lots of people die but it was very much like the apocalypse and I never, ever understood it. It was like seeing the horror of the world pushed right up to your face.

The photographer Gilles Peress likes to say that there are two ways to tell a story: on your feet with the living or on your knees with the dead. One does try to be on one's knees with the dead but this was dying beyond dying. I couldn't understand it. It was like being on some crazy promontory looking down into hell. Life seemed different to me after that.

I think it was purely because of the numbers of people and the way it seemed as if people were completely stripped of identity simply by the amount that were dying. Even aid workers failed the triage test because in emergencies like that they are forced to use the public-health model, the triage model, and they have to abandon so many of the dying. I didn't know what to do with that situation and maybe the fact that I didn't know what to do with it sticks with me in a way as a kind of emblem of what it is really all about. And also as a reproach and as a reminder that no matter how good you are, how hard you try, you are not going to come more than halfway there in describing what you are seeing.

I didn't know how to tell that story. I think that failure is maybe what stays with me because it rendered me completely impotent as a writer, as a professional, as a human being and if I couldn't do the job then what was I doing there?

## Why cover war?

I started doing war coverage properly in Bosnia in 1992. I was much older than a lot of the people who were there, and I had had another life. I was never a reporter; I was always a magazine writer, a book writer, and to some extent a political activist, although a very reluctant activist. Principally I was interested in the humanitarian stuff. I came to wars because humanitarian crises largely take place in war and if you are going to do the job of covering these crises properly you have to be there.

I lived in Sarajevo for a great chunk of the war in Bosnia, and also with the Serbs in the north early in the war. I wrote some of the earlier stories, although not the earliest by any means – Ed Vulliamy from the *Observer* and Roy Gutman were the first and the most heroic in terms of what they did and what they risked. But I was in northern Bosnia at a bad time in the summer of 1992 and I sort of changed profession. After working as a magazine writer and as someone who wrote about immigration I became a writer about humanitarian issues, humanitarian relief, the dilemmas of relief.

I am interested in war because it is war. War is the norm in human history. Either you have got to be turned on by it in some way, or in some way not mind – or maybe both. I think I am more the latter. It was also easier for me to deal with it because I had actually travelled a great deal in the poor world as a sort of wandering kid and I had written a lot about immigration so those worlds were quite comfortable to me. There is nothing strange to me about turning up in Kigali, or Jakarta, or Rwanda, and I guess it gets easier with experience.

But, for me, Bosnia wasn't just a story; it was a cause. I really thought this war marked the revival of fascism in Europe. I started with watching the Serb front-line forces as they were cleansing the north. They were exhibitionistic in those days but later they clamped down and the media were all eventually made *persona non grata*. By 1994 they turned us all out and it was quite hard to operate. I really thought it was our Spanish Civil War; this is where the West really should be making a stand to fight this new kind of fascism: the revival of the ethnic state. But Bosnia went on to show that all these lessons of the past century were totally unlearnt. The phrase 'never again' turned out to mean 'never again would Germans kill Jews in the 1940s'. Nothing has changed.

## HUMANITARIANISM AND HUMAN RIGHTS

I deeply admire humanitarian organisations and I think that in a world that is largely a slaughterhouse the people who do this work and help strangers are the last of the 'just' – to use the Jewish image – so I am happy in their company. But what I like about humanitarian action is what humanitarians themselves least like about it, which is its limitations, its modesty. For me, that is the part that makes moral sense. I think charity in and of itself, and solidarity in and of itself, make moral sense to me because they don't pretend that the world is a better place than it is. It is this wonderful phrase of an International Committee of the Red Cross (ICRC) official: 'Humanitarian action is trying to bring a measure of humanity, always insufficient, into situations that shouldn't exist.' That seems to me a realistic, moral act whereas the Kofi Annans of this world who think that humanitarian action can be part of some holistic solution to everything are just engaging in wishful thinking. I think the notion of human rights is a waste of hope and the phrase 'international community' is wishful thinking. All this stuff over the past fifty years is self-flattering, liberal nonsense; that we are all living in a different world, in the rule of law, would be nice but it is not true. There has been no revolution of moral concern. There are just a lot of people who want consoling mythologies about how things are really going to work out. They are like children asking for fairytales. That is why we, in the West, love the concept of human rights because it is a new fantasy; it is salvation. I don't need this hope. Maybe my readers need it and maybe the reason I am such a controversial writer is because I don't believe there is much hope. All of life ends in death in the light of eternity.

I don't think that it is natural to care about people 5000 or 300 miles away. It might be natural to care about your neighbour because you know your neighbour, but I don't see why the death of a stranger should matter to an ordinary person. I think it is amazing if people are moved even some of the time. I really think that it is a utopian illusion to imagine that we can care about strangers the way we care about people we know. I am amazed that we can do it at all and so I consider any degree of compassion to be marvellous. I am very pleased when it works and I obviously try to elicit those feelings in my writing.

## COMPASSION

For me, there are wars and experiences where I feel some connection and there are some places that just drive me crazy, where I feel compassion less. I think everybody has moments in which they are better and moments in which they are worse. Even Jim Nachtwey, who comes as close to being 'Mr Compassion' as it gets, has his ups and downs. Maybe not in the work he publishes in books, but if you look at his pictures there are things where obviously he hasn't made that deep connection; he is just going through the motions. I deeply admire him, don't get me wrong; he and Gilles Peress and Sabastiao Salgado are for me the three guys who are in their prime doing fantastic work. So I couldn't be a bigger fan but he has his moments of compassion fatigue too, whatever he says. We all do. I think it is an occupational hazard. The danger is not when you experience compassion fatigue intermittently but when you become cynical and you go from being a decent person to being some clone of Evelyn Waugh. Then it is time to hang it up.

Often with what I am writing about, I don't know what the solution is. When people say that ordinary people can change things, to me that supposes a fact not in evidence: that we know the correct thing to do. Sometimes we do, as in Rwanda, but other times we absolutely don't. Just saying we care, or we are sorry, or it pains us to see people suffering, does not mean anyone knows what to do without making it worse. This is an important point because I think that most of the time we don't know what to do. If that is true, then compassion becomes a very different emotion.

I think that there is an ideology in some people's work that the victim is always good and innocent but I don't believe that to be true. I think victims are often – not always – but often, the wicked. I actually think that victim and victimiser are roles that in most historical crises are interchangeable. Read any history of conflict that is long enough and the last are first and the first are last, or the victims are the victimisers more than once.

To describe things in terms of the 'victimhood' of people is often to misunderstand the reality one is seeing at that moment. It would be like finding the German army retreating in Russia in 1943. I could have made a hundred pictures about the Waffen-SS, haunted, haggard and what would that have told you?

People like me go to a place and say, 'These people are suffering and their suffering imparts some special claim on us.' But what if their suffering is the direct result of their actions? Can you then go back and say they were brainwashed as children and go the full Alice Miller route of no one is responsible for anything? At that point you really have turned the world into a fairytale in which Slobodan Milosevic and Ariel Sharon are just a couple of big bad wolves and everybody else is just a victim.

## CONTROVERSIAL WRITINGS

A journalist's role is to puncture euphemisms and denounce the kind of thinking that is based on meaningless or obfuscatory language. I think writers and photographers should be as unconstructive as possible. I don't think that we should become servants of our hopes either. We are there to be critical, to tell the truth insofar as one can know it.

There is the old Jewish joke: two Jews, three political parties. I have a bit of that sense of the world myself. I think several contradictory things at once. Maybe if I had a more coherent view of the world I wouldn't be saying this stuff. There are certain positions I take because I think somebody has got to, and if I don't do it, who will? But I am not just arguing something for the sake of it. I often emphasise one side of what I think to provoke, but I would never stand for something that I didn't at least believe in to some extent. It is just that I often see the other point of view.

So I make judgments about things all the time because I am partly a pundit; I am all judgment, in a way. I am a very extreme guy. I am always out on some limb busy sawing off the branch as long as I am at it. I enjoy taking a controversial position but if I didn't feel passionate about something I wouldn't risk my neck. I don't know if I get people thinking with what I write. I hope so. Sometimes I just annoy people.

## WITNESSES IN WAR-CRIMES TRIBUNALS

I am hesitant to weigh in as I don't have strong feelings about this but I think we journalists should become witnesses in war-crimes cases. I don't see what the problem is. I know Roy Gutman from *Newsweek* is very reluctant to testify and Ed Vulliamy isn't; these are the two guys who first discovered these Serbian concentration camps in Bosnia. I don't see why you can't testify as a citizen who happened to be there rather than as a journalist. How can Roy edit and shape a book with me like *Crimes of War* in which he basically argues that we must use the laws of war, international humanitarian law, as a principal way of organising our reporting and then say that when it comes to actually participating fully in that legal project then it is off-limits? But look, I don't know. Both Roy Gutman and Robert Fisk (who also argues against becoming a witness) are great reporters and I would quarrel with them over this issue very reluctantly.

## FEAR

I have been fearful, we all have. As a journalist in the field, you have to stop it or you panic and then you are much more likely to get killed or get somebody else killed, which in a way is worse. If you can't stop it, you have to find a way to live with it. I have displaced a lot of fear onto flying on planes so I have become this white-knuckled flyer, which might seem ridiculous given the places I go. I remember thinking, 'Look, you have decided to do this work and you have just got to say it is OK to die.' That was incredibly calming although it doesn't work all the time.

Fear is a funny thing. It often happens after the fact. You will do something mildly intrepid and while you are doing it you are not actually very conscious of it, particularly if it is something you feel is really important. I once walked into one of the *genocidaire*'s camps in Rwanda to get an interview, which in retrospect was unbelievably dumb, and I wasn't conscious of being afraid. Afterwards, back in the hotel, I was shaking like a leaf. I stayed in bed for a day. Fear often comes after you've done something dangerous, when you realise what an idiot you have been.

Susan Meiselas and I were once together with a whole bunch of people in Tajikistan. We'd had a ghastly day seeing some awful things and we wanted to go back to the place we were staying. On the map it wasn't that far. We both were the most experienced people there and we should have known better than to travel at night. We crossed the line. We had a very, very bad encounter with some very stoned soldiers, which really could have ended with all of us getting shot. And I thought, 'Oh shit, you have got to watch out here.' If you are doing stupid things it is time to at least take a break because one of the deformations of the job is that it begins to seem normal. Instead of remembering you are an outsider, not a combatant, you end up walking through the minefield just thinking, 'Oh right, the minefield . . .' That is when it is time to come back home, write four profiles of Oprah Winfrey and just chill out for a while.

I am not good at looking after myself. I remember once I was with Gary Knight, a great photographer, in a place called Dobrinja during the siege of Sarajevo. If things were rough in

Sarajevo, things were five times rougher in Dobrinja. The Serbs were right up in front of us, fifty metres away, and we got stuck by a sniper and couldn't move – our car was about twenty metres away but it could have been on Mars. I remember thinking, 'I don't even ride the subways after midnight in New York City. What am I doing here? There is some guy with a gun on a hill over there trying to kill me. What is this?'

What is actually, in some ways, worse about fear is the anticipation. For instance, before I went to the West Bank a while ago I got out a flak jacket and dusted it off. I was taking things out and leaving them around. As long as that stupid flak jacket was sitting in front of me, I was going to be fantasising about terrible things, whereas once I got to Nablus, I was in Nablus. While I was at home, I was worrying about Nablus because Nablus was an unreal thing in my head. I didn't know what I would do in the West Bank. My plan was to hang out with one of the humanitarian agencies and live with them for a week and see what it was like. The fighting always comes to you. There is no need to go chase it. As Roy Gutman says, 'No unnecessary trips.' I actually think the anticipation of being in a bad situation is the worst fear.

## Why cover human tragedy?

I have no idea if other people in this profession feel the same way, but on the one hand I find that we make complete shambles of our family lives; we all have various degrees of PTSD; and we are all living in this kind of perpetual weird adolescence. There are a million things to be said about us that are justifiably negative and yet, on the other hand, if I didn't do this I don't know how I would live in this society. I don't know how I would justify my own privileges. It makes the pleasures of home in this corner of the world – and the pleasures are deep and serious and I love them – morally bearable. I don't think in terms of guilt but in terms of bearable and unbearable. I don't feel guilty because guilt to me feels like a sacrifice and I enjoy my work a lot; it is fun. In fact, it is not just fun, it is better than fun: it is an extraordinary privilege. I don't know what the price of it is. I am sure the bill is being paid in instalments, hire purchase and all that, but it is still a privilege.

I think we all feel that this job gives us the ultimate opportunity to watch humanity while knowing that what we are seeing is only part of the story: human beings behaving in extreme ways for both good and bad. There is so much generosity in these extreme situations as well as cruelty and horror.

I do think a lot about being afraid of boredom, particularly the boredom of daily life in the West. And so to probably put it less charitably toward all of us journalists there is a fascination in covering human tragedy that goes beyond morals. You get to try your hand, however unsatisfactorily, at telling a piece of the truth. What could be a bigger privilege? That's worth dying for.

Yet, as a journalist, you live with the fact that we all know so much more than we know how to say. It is not because we are being censored (although sometimes this happens), or worse still censoring ourselves (whether consciously or unconsciously) but I just think that we are trying to do something that is too much, that is overwhelming. How do you describe a genocide? Probably only a poet can do that properly. Sometimes I read certain kinds of poetry and I think, 'Oh yes, that is sort of closer to what is worth saying about this than anything I could ever say.' I just don't think that those of us who are prose writers of ordinary talent, which is what we all are, are up to it, are capable of doing justice to what we see. We do our best though.

## Camaraderie

The end of the workday is special because you are back with people who have had the same experience as you. I always liked that and I am not particularly gregarious. I like the world of the hotel or the house. I like its dedication, the stripped-down quality of it in the sense that you are there, you have got these hours between the time you stopped working and the time you start again. People are incredibly nice to each other, incredibly solicitous and look out for each other, even though on some level I suppose we are all competitors. I find the average behaviour of people so far above the way we all behave at home that that alone is an enticement to do this job.

There is a level of sharing that on one level is very homey stuff, not some grand thing that these people are your spiritual kin or anything like that. For instance, in Sarajevo there were very strict limits on what you could bring in when you came in on the UN or NATO planes. So you would have two bottles of Scotch and nobody ever dreamed of keeping it for themselves. People would come around the room and you would pour it out and at the end of the day it was all gone. That was just normal. If you had a packet of cigarettes – we all smoked in those days in Sarajevo; sometimes I think it was our profession – there was no question of hoarding. There was no question of not sharing. If someone needed a ride you gave them a ride if you had space in your vehicle. It was as simple as that. It wasn't a question of even thinking about it.

I remember once taking this terrible ferry to get to Kosovo

– hours and hours waiting in between the decks with people crushed in like a soccer stadium in the third world where everyone gets crushed to death. And sweat! I lost five pounds just waiting. Suddenly I see Gilles Peress, Joanne Mariner from Human Rights Watch, and Eric Stover from Physicians for Human Rights. They don't have a room but because of this bizarre coincidence of my mother living in the port of Bari in Italy she had made me a reservation. I am going to my cabin and they follow me. They don't have to say anything. It is not like I have to say, 'Oh, you can share the room.' It is assumed that my room is their room. It would never occur to them or me otherwise. It is not an issue; it is not an option; it is just the way this ecosystem works. It is a privilege to have access to that behaviour from others – and that behaviour *on your own part*. Maybe because it is so atrophied in other contexts. Maybe in a better world we would all live that way all the time but we don't, or I don't anyway, and I don't think that those three people probably do either.

There seemed to be camaraderie even among people who maybe didn't have all that much in common back home. It's not that real friendships weren't made; lots of people got together – not just erotically though some became couples in a longer lasting sense – but I don't know that it transports back to home in the sense that it influences the way you behave professionally at home. But the camaraderie certainly transports home in the sense that the people you lived with and have gone through this experience with are your brothers and sisters. On a certain level Ed Vulliamy can ask me for things and I can ask him for things that somebody I know from home could not. I feel we all have a different kind of claim on each other and maybe that is just the way that we got used to living together. Those of us who lived through these things know each other in a different way.

It is not necessarily that these are people you have the most profound conversations with, or if I were getting a divorce, or falling in love, or if I had some deep personal dilemma, that I would necessarily go to talk to. Nonetheless, there is a sort of claim, a special bond, and the ease of the claim is different to anything back at home. I feel that most of us feel that way but I don't think that anyone ever voices it. I don't think anyone ever has to.

I don't usually talk to anyone about what I have felt and seen – I am not much for that and my experience is that most people who don't do this work don't want to hear about it. You learn quickly that you really can't come home and talk about it. People may love you, care about you, worry like crazy about you, wish like crazy you wouldn't go back (and they tell you that once you are past a certain age that you are nuts to go back) but they don't want to hear about it. They tend to treat you like you have got some unbelievably risky sports obsession. So to the extent you talk about it at all it is only with people who do the same thing as you and those aren't necessarily your best friends. I hang around with all kinds of people so if it has been really rough I might want to be more among journalists or aid workers and sometimes you might end up getting drunk with somebody who has also been to a similar situation.

### 'The wings of madness'

You do change when you go to war. I don't know if you lose something. Maybe. The best image I can give in explanation is that we are all some version of the Greek myth of Persephone, the goddess who angers some god and is condemned to spend half the year in Hades and half the year on Earth. I think that is what we are all like. We all live in Hades part of the time. I feel like I am always on the verge of breaking down but that is what gives me my edge and I think the edge is the only place to be, in the sense that that is where the truth is. Anything else would be disrespectful of reality, which is so moving and terrible and horrendous. It is precisely because I am still able to walk around at some level without my skin on that gives what I do whatever merit it has – which obviously sometimes is not very much and sometimes, I flatter myself, is a reasonable amount.

As war journalists, we all live with two notions. One is the actual physical danger and as you leave your apartment each time you say, 'Will I see this again?' But no one is putting a gun to your head forcing you to do this job so if you didn't feel passionately about it you wouldn't do it. If I lived to be a hundred I could make a perfectly good living as a writer without seeing another war. The second notion is the moral Russian roulette, which I take more seriously. Every time I see another person die I wonder, 'What on earth are you playing at here with your own sanity? What are you doing?' because there are two dangers: firstly that you might come to treat what you are seeing as normal in the sense of a normal experience, and secondly, that if you do it long enough you become cynical. So I live worrying that I will become cynical and worrying that it will drive me crazy. I feel that I am navigating between the two and not sure which I am more headed toward. I don't necessarily think it is the cynical one that scares me the most; I am not sure I could become cynical about those things but I could easily see myself driven crazy by it.

Jim Nachtwey says that with every photo he becomes more sensitised. I don't know him personally but I know Gilles Peress really well and certainly Gilles has had his bouts, as we all have, with just being overwhelmed by what he has seen. Rwanda was like that for him. There is somewhere in Baudelaire's journals where he says, 'I feel the wind of the wings of madness.' I think that you feel that wind all the time but with god's grace the bird doesn't come into view. I also think that because you know how cynical things are, the wind of that bird touches your face. I guess what I think is that you keep trying to fight it off. You keep trying to do an honest job. So I don't worry about the edge but I worry about the falling over it because there is a moment when you go crazy. If I were ever to go to a shrink, which I would never do because I am really against them – I wish to keep whatever pathetic delusions of sanity I can muster to myself – he or she would probably have a field day. You know, six syndromes all named after me.

I think everything at once about this job: it is incredibly great and incredibly self-indulgent: we are all a bunch of shy egomaniacs and at the same time we are actually doing something that needs to be done and deserve at least a little credit for doing it.

You can't take yourself too seriously in this job; you have to take what you write or the pictures you make seriously but you shouldn't take yourself too seriously. I do insist there is a distinction.

I am a writer and I think that you do what you are good at. I understand some of these situations, or have some way of describing them, or analysing them, that has some value. And I think that I do it well and I would rather do that well than write profiles of Rupert Murdoch. I expect writing about war and humanitarian issues will always be part of my life. Beyond that I am a smart guy who is willing to get shot at. It seems to me that it is a pretty good use to make of my time in this world: to go and try to tell the truth so far as I can get at it and try to analyse it for people. A lot of what I do is not really reporting but analysis and that is enough: tell the truth as you see it; give voice to people who might not otherwise have it; be critical of everybody. I don't need to know more than that.

# CHAPTER 17

# SORIOUS SAMURA

## Biography

WITH A BACKGROUND IN theatre, Sorious Samura taught himself video work and as a freelancer began documenting the violence in his homeland of Sierra Leone. In January 1999 rebel forces entered the capital, Freetown, and with no international journalists left in the country Sorious' footage, which the West initially refused to show because of its graphic nature, won him international acclaim.

Sorious now works at Insight News Limited in London and has produced a number of award-winning documentaries on important African issues including *Cry Freetown* (1999), which covered the civil war in his country, and *Return to Freetown* (2002), which documented the use of child soldiers during the fighting and as victims of injustice. *Exodus from Africa* (2001) covered the migration of sub-Saharan Africans to Europe in search of a better future, while *Walking on Ashes* (2001) considered the political situation in Uganda to ask how

African people might escape the cycle of violence and decline that is all too common throughout the continent. During the making of these documentaries, Sorious escaped death in Sierra Leone, was attacked by immigrants in Morocco, and was jailed for being a spy in Liberia.

His documentaries have won numerous awards including the Rory Peck Award and the Mohammad Amin Award (he was the first person to win both) for *Cry Freetown* in 1999. Sorious won the 1999 CNN African Journalist of the Year Award, and in 2000 and again in 2001 *Cry Freetown* and then *Exodus from Africa* won the Best TV Documentary at the One World Media Awards. Both these documentaries also won Emmy Awards: *Cry Freetown* for Best Investigative Programme in 2001 and *Exodus from Africa* for best director in 2002. They have also won or been short-listed for numerous other awards. *Return to Freetown* won the Overseas Press Club Award in 2002.

Sorious is married and lives in England.

\* \* \*

## Story

One thing that will never go away and has been part of me since I shot the footage of the civil war\* in Sierra Leone in 1999

\***Author's note:** In 1961 Sierra Leone gained independence from the British only to see successive governments dominated by a small political elite who profited from the country's diamond wealth. In early 1991 the Revolutionary United Front (RUF) backed by President Charles Taylor of Liberia, launched an armed insurrection against the government. From 1991 to 1999 Sierra Leone was crushed by a bloody civil war.

The ousted military junta, the Armed Forces Revolutionary Council (AFRC), then became a second rebel faction in the civil war. In January 1999 the rebels attacked and took control of the capital, Freetown, only to retreat again from ECOMOG (the armed monitoring group set up by the Economic Community of West African States in 1990 after the bloody civil war in Liberia), which had by this time become one of the fighting factions.

was of a boy shot by peacekeepers in the opening of my documentary *Cry Freetown*. I wasn't sure at the time, and even now I am not sure, whether I should have continued filming, continued to bear witness, or whether I should have dropped the camera and just argued there and then for his life. Maybe I could have saved him; maybe not. Filming in hostile zones is very unpredictable for even the most experienced cameramen. I filmed that boy pleading first with the rebels and then with the peacekeepers and I captured every moment until they shot him. I filmed him dying and kicking until they put him on a wheelbarrow and took him to a grave.

I have seen other people being killed but that boy, his image, his voice ... The eyes are flashing through mine saying something like, 'You should have done something to save my life.' It is always there. But it must be said that as much as that haunts me even now I don't know whether I am being hard on myself. One thing I know though is that it is something I have to live with. People have said to me that I could have saved him but they don't understand the circumstances in which I was filming. I knew at the time there was nothing I could do to save people because I had seen a father plead with the peacekeepers to save the life of his own son and the father was the first person they shot. He said to them, 'This is my son. He is not a rebel. He has never done anything. What are you thinking?' One just walked behind him and

> In July 1999 all parties agreed to a regionally brokered cease-fire that included an amnesty for all parties. A few of the rebel leaders were drafted into the new administration of a country that is in ruins and whose economy has collapsed.
>
> One of the most brutal aspects of this conflict was the abduction and use of children as soldiers by the AFRC, the RUF, ECOMOG and the KAMAJORS, 'civil militias allied to the government forces', together with systematic severing of limbs by the rebels. It is estimated that approximately 50,000 people were killed, 100,000 mutilated and 500,000 people displaced in neighbouring countries during the civil war.

blew his head off. I saw that with my own two eyes. Things like these not only tell you about the level of madness but serve as a warning to anyone who intends to obstruct the men and women with guns. So those thoughts were in my head when filming the boy pleading for his life to the peacekeepers.

To some extent I have also questioned myself whether the camera pushed the peacekeeper to pull the trigger but I don't think so. I have seen rebels and the peacekeepers lining up people and shooting them even when the camera was not there. There was complete madness: these guys had lost the plot.

So all those questions have been with me and that boy has always been part of me, has always haunted me. I prayed to forget about the incident, to not even talk about it, but it has never gone and for me the boy's voice is like the voice of the innocents. I can remember exactly what he was saying. Sometimes when I talk or think about his murder he will be right there in front of me and I will think again that I should have saved him. Once I went home and played the tape and realised that his eyes were not looking at me. I don't know how I see them . . . Whenever that happens the next day I get up and I write something. And it gives me more reason to keep going because sometimes I think he is saying to me, 'You have got to continue representing us. You have got to continue telling our stories . . . the stories of the voiceless.'

I really don't like it that people keep asking if I need counselling. Almost everybody identifies me with these dramatic stories so I think the moment I start having counselling will be the end of my genuine representation of the real people whose story I'm dying to tell. But I have now started to understand that maybe something good has come of it. For me, that scene has become my African driving force. The message is 'don't stop now'. That is what he is saying to me. I have decided that he can't have died in vain and I will keep pushing because of that.

*Bearing Witness*

I would love to go to Nigeria to find the peacekeeper who shot the boy. Of course, what he did was bad but maybe he wasn't a bad man. Who am I to condemn? In the middle of what was going on, these guys also looked after my life. My film has been shown all over the world so the peacekeeper must have seen it himself. He looked into the eyes of the person he was killing. I would just love to know what he is going through and what is different for him now. I want to talk to him and understand whether I am going through half of what he is going through, or he is going through half of what I am going through. I want to know if he shares the same guilt as I, or if he is not human at all, just an evil guy.

Maybe, by meeting him, it would help me understand soldiers. Maybe through his answers I would be able to get some answers about why and how all this happens. If this man was going through what I am going through then perhaps I would not be so hard on myself – at least I only took the pictures; he pulled the trigger. I don't think any amount of answers will make the memory of the boy go away though.

Maybe my footage could give the children of these soldiers opportunities to question their dads about the work they do – taking innocent lives. I would love to sit a US general down who uses warheads and ask him to explain to his children what he does for a living and what the warheads he uses do to innocent people. Likewise, I would love to do the same thing with that Nigerian soldier. Get him to explain what the trigger that he pulled did to that child and that child's family.

## DOCUMENTING INJUSTICE

I think that almost every youngster who gets to mid-secondary school in Sierra Leone is bound to know that the newspapers are crap and the government station conveys propaganda. You start learning about corruption, injustice, in the classroom. We were not allowed to ask questions. Culturally, it is seen as a sign of disrespect if you ask your elders too many questions. If you asked too many questions in the classroom you were in trouble! When it comes to school exams even if you did well, the teachers would tell you to bring money, drinks, or even worse, 'your mum for your result'! If the male teachers saw your mum or perhaps your female relative as beautiful, they would straight away try to forge a relationship with her, and if you somehow didn't play a role in facilitating that, they would fail you or find other ways of making you pay. So, quickly your eyes were opened to corruption and injustice.

But I was fortunate enough to have a drama teacher (Dele Charley, blessed memory) who thought that he could use theatre to educate us. He formed a theatre group, which I joined when I was in the third form, and by the time I got to the fourth form I had joined his adult group, Tabule, outside the school. He was somebody I respected, somebody who stood for the truth. In Sierra Leone, theatre, at that time, played the role that journalism was supposed to play so this group was trying to educate society; it wasn't holding back on the things that were wrong. I was happy and quickly I started realising that somehow I was capable of standing up for people.

As soon as you form a theatre group in most parts of Africa, not just Sierra Leone, you are seen by the governments as opposing them. When I joined this theatre group it was like the defenceless, voiceless people around me started seeing me as some kind of hero because I would dare to go on stage and say things that some of them would want to say but couldn't. That started giving me some strength, a belief in myself. I learnt about responsibility, about caring for and standing up for all people. I think that if you become a strong figure in Africa everyone looks up to you.

When I left school I worked for The Lagoonda, an entertainment complex, and they had a video camera that I trained myself to use. I then did documentaries for UNICEF and other UN agencies. Because of my work with UNICEF, and the fact that I grew up within a culture that cares about children, when the civil war in Sierra Leone started in 1991 I became concerned about reports that rebels were using children as soldiers. I persuaded UNICEF to allow me and some MEDIAC (Media Alliance for Children) members to go to the provinces and find out what was going on. I was the first person down there with a video camera and that was how I became passionate about my country's war.

By 1993–4 a war was going on in Kosovo, a white war being featured in Western media 24/7, and the African wars at the time – Sierra Leone, Angola, Rwanda – were not making it onto the screens in the West. So I became really concerned that we Africans had to do something to get the West's attention and, trying not to play the usual African blame game, I asked myself some questions as to why the West should care about my continent and what we as Africans should do. I was fortunate to have spent some time in Britain in the mid-nineties where I worked twenty-two to twenty-four hours a day, six days a week, as a cleaner, doing odd jobs, moving from job to job, trying to make a living and buy good video equipment. So I went back to Sierra Leone to start a production company when the rebels invaded the city in January of 1999.

## LACK OF RESPECT

Two weeks after the invasion of Freetown, the BBC went there – they were the first Western media into the capital – and started looking for anyone who might have actually filmed the war (I was the only one who filmed the invasion because all the Western journalists had been frightened off and no one from government TV had filmed). A strange coincidence happened. I went to a chicken restaurant in the city and seated in the middle of the restaurant were the BBC crew with one of the so-called Nigerian 'peacekeepers'. I glanced at them but part of the problem in Africa is that we haven't learnt how to associate with people in the industry, especially the international journalists. If they are dealing with you without a recommendation then you are nobody; they don't even give you a glance. We Africans find it extremely difficult to just walk up to the international journalists and say, 'Oh, I am so-and-so.' I just didn't know how to break that ice. So I walked past them but as I did the Nigerian peacekeeper said to them, 'Hey, this guy was the one who was filming the atrocities during the attack.' They just said 'Hi' and continued eating their lunch. As I walked out of the restaurant, though, they dashed out and asked if I had filmed the war and what camera I used. When I told them I used a DV 9000 camera they seemed interested for the first time. They said, 'Can we see what you shot? Do you think that you have got good stuff?' I said, 'Well, it is up to you to judge.' Just to show that these people were not expecting anything they said, 'We are leaving tomorrow at one o'clock and will come and see your film at about midday, OK?' I just thought that they should at least have tried to see it that day or night.

Unfortunately, the first shot is a shot that we would not allow people to see – a bullet smashing somebody's head. Some of the BBC crew couldn't even bear to watch. One of them, the reporter Fergal Keane, then said, 'Please stop; this is great. We must get it but we don't have enough money to pay you.' I looked at the three guys in the room and I said, 'You don't understand. It is not about money. I didn't go out thinking I would make money. Yes, I want money because I have got to look after my family but I have seen how important and what a difference television journalism can make in Britain so take the footage – forget about money. Just make sure you tell the story properly.' They said, 'We promise you that we will pay you. We will submit your footage for an award.' Blah, blah, blah.

I found it disrespectful that nobody at the BBC sent me a copy of the news piece they did. When I came to Britain again and finally saw it I was really disappointed. I felt they misrepresented Moses, the little mute boy who got beaten up in the footage. They referred to him as a rebel. They had ignored what I told them about him being an innocent. Fergal had written articles about me and said good things about me so I don't know whether it was him, or his producers, or whomever, but someone got a lot wrong. I was very upset that they called Moses a rebel. That incident made me realise what had been the problem with the coverage of Africa: it lacked context. Most of what I had been questioning about the coverage of Africa was really confirmed there and then: the West didn't care about context. They told the story their own way. They don't show us respect; they don't trust us with our own stories; they just portray stereotypes. It is really frustrating. Sometimes you think, 'Why the hell would I want to continue taking risks when someone else goes into that cutting room and does what they want to do with your material?'

Somehow it kills the passion because, as a journalist, in most cases you represent innocent people who look up to you to tell their stories properly. They give all their respect and trust to you and then the story comes out differently or wrong. And some day, somehow they will see the stories and you lose the one thing that they have given you, all that they have: trust. Sometimes international journalists get into serious trouble because those who have been there before them have betrayed the locals. It is bound to affect the innocent journalists who arrive after them.

## Winning awards

I had been trying to give more of my footage of the invasion to the West but they wouldn't use it because it was too violent. But Fergal Keane recommended me to somebody and he made a recommendation to Nick Gowing, a presenter for BBC World, who submitted my footage for the Rory Peck Award in 1999 and that is how my career making documentaries all started. I thought, at the time, maybe it was just a token thing to be included in the awards night. It *never* crossed my mind that I would win any of the categories. To be honest, nobody cares about Africa so when I scooped two awards, one of which was the biggest award of the night, I had no speech. I stood up and I opened my heart to the men in suits: 'Take the award back. As far as I am concerned you should have been there. I would rather you go there and tell the story properly because I filmed my own people killing themselves. If we call it "one world" then let's do it properly, cover the world – equally, balanced coverage. Have your award back.'

To my great surprise my speech got a standing ovation. I still thought this was too much and I was confused. Ron McCullagh, who runs Insight News, came up to me and said, 'Great speech, man. Great pictures . . . We would love to work with you but please go and see everyone else first. If you feel that they are not offering you what you want then come and see me and my team.' I was keen to go with the BBC because everyone in Africa knows of the BBC but then they told me they wanted to use their own correspondent to tell the story to go with my footage in Freetown. I told them

I was not happy with what they had done originally with my footage.

Quite a few people did contact me after the awards night but Ron was one man who I realised cared about Africa. He had worked all over Africa and he was prepared to show the respect that is lacking towards Africa from the West. He was prepared to allow me to tell my story my way and that is exactly how we made the documentary *Cry Freetown* – the African story, told by an African, from the African perspective . . . maybe we had finally arrived.

Everything came too quickly. I hadn't had time to stand back and understand what was going on in my life. Two weeks later there was another awards ceremony in Barcelona and I made another speech. Afterwards, the president of CNN, Chris Cramer, came up to me and said, 'That was amazing. I want you to come to Atlanta and reproduce what you did here tonight. I have been trying to get my African editors to understand that we need to look for African voices. What you have done is exactly what I have been telling CNN but you can say it better.' I said, 'I don't think I have all that it takes and it is not just about coming to produce the message that you want. I want to tell this story and I want it to be seen. I want my editorial rights and the freedom. If you guarantee me that then I am ready to go with you people.' Also, Channel 4 said they would give me a chance to tell my own story. They all said, 'This is your story. You tell it how you know it happened,' and it was that respect that made my decision and marked the beginning of the relationship between myself, Insight News, Channel 4 and CNN. Apart from one story, all my stories have been produced by Insight News and all funded by Channel 4 and CNN. The last one, *Return to Freetown*, was fully funded by CNN.

Sorious Samura

## Telling the African story

We need to get people to see and understand that personal, human-interest story, the story about the human rights and social issues of the real heroes in Africa – the voiceless majority. But these stories that tell you about the social and political factors that helped dump us all into the mess in the first place are not told because most of the journalists who go there are only doing a job. Most of the stories force viewers to switch off because they are mainly negative stereotypes that lack context and are mostly shot by foreign journalists. But maybe it's not their fault. After all, African stories just won't make their shareholders happy and worse, we just don't have the celebrities to help them with their ratings. When wars are covered in developing countries the people are portrayed as helpless and hopeless. I will give you an example. The famine in Sudan was covered by the Western media as: 'These people are desperate; they are dying.' What most of those stories didn't show to the viewers who donated money for famine relief was that these people were not a hopeless bunch relying on aid. These people knew that they always had problems with famine so they used to go up to the anthills and do this thing called 'Amajong' where they sift the earth from the anthills and separate the grass seeds the ants have collected from nearby fields. This is wild rice and helps these people survive through times of hunger. It is a small thing but it shows that these people were doing something to help themselves; it gives a sense of hope. But in the stories told by the West, viewers and/or readers of media reports never saw the efforts that these people were making and so they would say, 'Why should we keep giving when they are doing nothing to help themselves?' To represent these people properly, you have to have somebody on the ground to tell the story from within looking out rather than from outside looking in.

Although over ninety per cent of Western journalists genuinely care and want to make a difference and probably don't intend to follow the stereotype, they come in quickly, never spend enough time to understand the situation, leave quickly and seldom follow up. They don't really look for or trust local fixers. The man on the ground is bound to know the body language of rebels or soldiers and can guide the foreign journalist safely. He is bound to know the real stories that need to be told, the grassroots people in the village. We African journalists are people who are talented but we don't have the logistics and the support in Africa so we have not been entrusted to tell the stories of our continent. Africa is the only continent where journalists can't tell their own story. The West will tell you, 'You have taken bribes. This story is not quite balanced,' and so on.

Some of my colleagues in Africa are accepting bribes but, for some, to tell these stories properly also means losing their own lives or the lives of their loved-ones. They have got to survive but it is no excuse. I have lived within that system and thank god there is not one single politician in Sierra Leone who could say about me 'We did "X" for him', but maybe I was lucky. So local fixers are part of what I have been advocating. If the Western media can train them and pay the local fixers, to avoid the temptation of bribes together with some real press freedom, I am convinced the world would see unbelievable, true and accurate stories from within Africa about the real heroes: all those ordinary people like Moses in *Cry Freetown*. These are the people whose story I would risk my life to tell. These stories of ordinary people are not being told.

Because my work has been rubber-stamped by the West I have got some kind of protection behind me now. It is not that

I am exceptionally different from the guys back home in Sierra Leone or that I am doing anything extraordinary. There are journalists in Africa who can do far better but they have not been fortunate to make that break and get the kind of support that I have. When I was arrested in Liberia\*, CNN, Channel 4, Jesse Jackson, Nelson Mandela and the Nigerian head of state, Lt Gen Olusegun Obasanjo, all played a big role in getting me and my three colleagues out. I know a few Sierra Leoneans who had the BBC standing up for them, too. In fact, when the Junta government threatened to kill a Sierra Leonean journalist, Victor Silver, the BBC helped get him and his family out and offered them protection. Lots of journalists are fleeing their countries and seeking asylum. People in the West don't understand what it even means to have to leave your home, what it takes away from you. I miss my parents, my relatives; I would like to go back someday for good.

You know, it's easy to criticise journalists in the developing world but perhaps it would only be fair to do that if media organisations here can help train these local guys and insure them, just like they're insuring their own people. These are the people who would have to live with the consequences once their material is broadcast. I am just one man. I can't quite make it happen but if we come together African leaders who are bent on breaking and disrespecting journalists would start understanding that the media needs to be freed and

---

\* **Author's note:** In mid-2000, Sorious Samura, British director David Barrie, British cameraman Timothy Lambon and South African cameraman Gugulakhe Radebe travelled to Liberia to film a documentary. Within weeks, they were arrested and indicted for spying for the British and US governments. In fact, they were trying to prove that the Liberian government was involved in the illegal Sierra Leonean diamond trade. Their lawyer claimed that they had been 'repeatedly threatened and told by their captors that their hearts would be cut out and their limbs cut off'. After intense international pressure, they we released.

respected. How much would it take to pay locals there? Just give them something that they can believe they are living for. Once people realise that there is that protection then we will start seeing some changes, a different kind of journalism in Africa: Africa by Africans. And if the West helps empower African journalists they will not only be empowering future generations but will also be paving the way for proper democracies and free speech in a very troubled continent.

But maybe they are scared that once they help empower African journalists and they, in turn, empower the youth of Africa, Africa will start seeing itself in a different light. I just don't know. I don't have the answers but what I would truly love to ask decision-makers in the Western media is this: what are you guys scared of? What is it that is holding you from forging a decent partnership with journalists from the developing world? I believe we both, Africans as well as Westerners, have a responsibility to see that the African stories are told, and told properly.

So that is the kind of noise in the wilderness that I have been making. At some point I have to go to Africa and look for Africans so that we can properly tell the African story. They are there and they can make those differences and then we in Africa will get the respect we deserve. For me it is like a mission. I know they say no story is worth dying for but at the end of the day that is what I am prepared to do. It is a responsibility.

## COVERING WAR

I don't go out looking for wars but sometimes I itch for a story on war. Sometimes I sit here in England and I look at the news and I see Africa, I see Israel, and I see an image and I want to know more. I can say that's a story I need to follow up. I should have been there. I would tell more about that innocent person. And I keep having that kind of buzz within me all the time, the blood boiling to go. I just identify with what is going on and it is as if this is the real me; this is where I belong. I want to engage and I want to make the viewers engage more. Of course, there are risks involved but that's part of the job.

I only had safety training after I joined Insight News. It was a blessing in disguise that I hadn't had this training before because if I had I don't think I would have ever shot the things I shot for *Cry Freetown*. Although there were times, like when I was in Uganda, that I just forgot about the training, just went with my personal, god-given instinct, nothing else. Sometimes the training goes out the window and I don't even know when it goes. All I rely on is my instincts and the instinct is usually right.

I have also always said God was up there looking after me when I was filming the invasion of Freetown because I should have been killed so many times, but part of what also helped me survive was the fact that I had spent time on the ground and I think God also wanted someone to tell the story. I knew the rebels, the soldiers and the language. I knew when they were influenced by drugs and how they react; what to say; when to look at them and when to put my head down; and when to get a stronger voice. I knew all these things about the people I was dealing with and that was why it was easy for me to come out with what I came out with. If I go now to certain war zones I think I'll know how to identify who is who.

For instance, everybody in the world can buy military fatigues now but it is difficult to get proper military boots. The guy who shot Kurt Schork and Miguel Gil Moreno was wearing these funny cheap trainers they have in Africa\*. All

---

\* **Author's note:** Kurt Schork from Reuters and Miguel Gil Moreno de Mora, an AP photographer, were travelling in two vehicles of the Sierra Leone army. They were ambushed by the combined rebels from the AFRC

of them, including the ECOMOG soldiers they were with, maintained that eye contact and didn't bother looking down at the shoes. They were fooled because they didn't notice the footwear. If they had have looked at the shoes they would have realised that the guy who stopped their car was not a government soldier; he was a rebel. Also I would not readily drive in a government soldier's vehicle going into war zones. You are safer with the rebels – strange but true. Nine times out of ten, disciplined government soldiers will try to arrest people rather than just kill them. Rebels don't care. It is this attention to small details that keeps you alive in war zones.

## Understanding the madness

I don't think that any amount of explanation would be able to make me understand why men commit the kind of atrocities that I have witnessed. Usually, most atrocities are against women but in Sierra Leone and Liberia – apart from the rapes of women – the killing and the maiming was particularly against men. Why? The rebels know that there is something about 'might being right' in Africa. The people with the might are the people you tend to fear and respect. So they go into a house and the first person they think they have to break is the man because once that happens it leaves the woman and children helpless. You would be surprised how quick families are willing to accept these rebel men as their protectors, their husbands, their fathers. Take what makes the man a man away from him and then you could quickly win over all those who are reliant on him.

Revolutionary United Front. Four soldiers were killed and two other Reuters employees, Mark Chisholm and Yannis Behrakis, were injured.

The rebel leaders also found out that if you teach children bad things it stays with them forever. Most of the kids that were used as soldiers by the rebels were about six or seven years old, the age where they are just learning, and if killing is what you teach them is right, that is what they understand. What added to that confusion was the rebels started drugging them, though not in the normal way. They had a concoction they would mix (cannabis, cocaine and local drugs) and inject it directly into the children's brains. Within seconds they were gone. If they were given a gun and told 'Go and kill', they would kill. It was only after an hour or two when the drugs had worn off that the children started realising what they had done but then the rebels would start praising them, treat them like chiefs, the heroes of the day and get people to sing and dance for them and give them women. The kids thought, 'Wow, I never got this from my parents when I was at home. Nobody treated me with respect.' Then the rebels would give the children four or five boys to control and look after in the same way and so on the violence went.

This war in my country broke homes, turned loved-ones against each other, neighbours against each other. This was a very peaceful country with strong community bonds. As a child I would sleep in my neighbour's house and my parents weren't even bothered. There was trust between people, between neighbours. I can identify some of the causes for the violence but I still can't understand where the bitterness that broke my society apart came from, where a child would rape his own mum and sometimes not even under the influence of alcohol or drugs. What really drove these guys to treat their fellow human beings the way they did is difficult to put a finger on but for me it showed the confusion, the madness that had come not just to Sierra Leone but to Africa. It was complete madness. It is very difficult to explain. We lost that innocence when the rebels came and I know my country; Sierra Leone will never be the same again.

Yet I have always said to people in the West, 'Who are you to judge another society if you have not lived in their shoes? You don't know how lucky you are.' Look what I had to go through to just get basic education. My parents could not afford to pay my school fees so I started selling things when I was seven or eight years old to pay my school fees and this is common for millions of African children. How many people here in the West go to school in the morning with just one handful of rice from their mum in their stomach all day. How many people here in England have lived that hard life? We need to stop and ask ourselves why these rebels and terrorists want to do what they are doing. I grew up in that system. I could have been a rebel because I wanted to be seen, to be heard and given a chance. Too many people in Sierra Leone were denied an education, a future. Some of the rebels are my schoolmates so all the reasons that made me do what I am doing now – frustration with the system, a desire to be heard and have a stake in the future – could have made me a rebel. Thank god there was somebody, my drama teacher, who helped me to find another way to vent my frustration.

## JOURNALISTIC RESPONSIBILITY – CROSSING THE LINE

Having people representing other people, telling their story, telling what's happening around the world, is crucial because it helps influence the decisions for or against them. We should therefore realise that we have a huge responsibility resting on our shoulders. I have been invited by the UN to be a witness in Sierra Leone's War Crimes Tribunal but I don't hold back when I explain why I won't. In Sierra Leone in 1997 when the renegade soldiers kicked out the elected president, Tejan Kabbah, they ruled for nine months. Within that time they forced journalists to record their atrocities because they were trying to put fear into the people they were ruling by showing these films. Then Kabbah was reinstated in 1998 and the government was looking for evidence against the rebels. What did they use? The videos. They also got some of the journalists to testify. One of them was my friend and I advised him not to go but he told me he had no choice. The journalists in Sierra Leone didn't understand that our job was to simply report the truth and remember that confidentiality has to be our watch word but they were scared, and they had every reason to be. Some of these rebels were tried and executed but in January 1999 the rebels attacked Freetown carrying lists of the journalists who had been forced to film and who had testified against their friends.

Our job is to report the stories as they happen and to make the important message interesting. I think it would be crossing the line to bear witness against war criminals. It is not a job for journalists. Also, to some extent, combatants are talking to us because they trust us but the moment we start testifying we betray that trust, that confidence they had in us. At the end of the day though it is not just about you, it is about other colleagues who follow you. They would definitely be walking into traps because no military general would be safe with journalists around, so they might decide to kill them. I pray to god that nobody makes that mistake.

## GRAPHIC IMAGES AND INFORMING THE PUBLIC

It looks to the West like the crimes in Sierra Leone weren't that horrific because the more brutal the crimes became the more the pictures were not being shown there. Why are we scared of seeing reality when Hollywood not only glamorises massacres but we also encourage our children to watch them? Yes, my footage on Sierra Leone was very graphic but it was reality. Perhaps we should have brought Hollywood directors to direct the killings; maybe that would have got broadcasters rushing to air it in prime time. I have no doubt that people should be allowed to see the pictures and decide for themselves. When I first came to Britain with this footage the media were like, 'No, it is too graphic,' and only about fifteen per cent was used.

But in Africa we don't have the opportunity of switching off. We have to watch this horror unfolding in front of our very eyes! You see the children in *Cry Freetown* sitting there watching these things happen. No one in Africa dares cover their eyes because they might be looking at a bullet. Guys with guns will turn around and say, 'Oh, don't you like us killing the rebels? You must be one of them; come here,' or 'Don't you like us killing the soldiers?' Or, 'You are supporting the peacekeepers.' So we don't have those opportunities to look away that people out here in the West had when they watched those tapes, and I don't have that opportunity now because I can still see what I saw in Freetown in 1999 happening all over Africa and I must keep looking – focused on our reality.

Why would I want to protect people from reality, from what is going on in their world? People deserve to be given the choice. The American people call their game show *Big Brother* reality TV but my people cross the Sahara Desert and the Mediterranean Sea dying in the process: this is reality, not what they portray in those shows. If they glamorise the violence in Hollywood and people go to see those movies then they should stop saying that the people don't want to see something because it is too violent. If they don't want to watch it on TV they can take the remote control and switch it off. And for god's sake let's also take you from point A to point B. That oil and those diamond rings come from these countries in Africa. Wouldn't it be right if the people in the West knew the human costs of getting the diamonds and the oil that they buy? If they just saw this for themselves. It would mean that they were given choices. That is the bottom line. The only way people can ask more questions or form informed opinions is if we in the media offer them choices.

We also know the responsibilities that come with all of this. There was a child-labour story in Bangladesh and because of the story the company sacked all the children. But the children were the breadwinners for their families and the families needed to get their children back to work. What happened was that the children were given a choice for the first time to make up their own minds. It was up to them. And the people who brought the products out here also had a choice to say, 'OK, now we understand that those families there won't be able to take their children off work but we will only buy the products made by those children if the employment practices of that company are changed.' That is the choice and that is why we should let people see these stories including the real human cost.

If people could see some of the pictures from Sierra Leone I think they would say, 'I will never wear a diamond ring.' People have said this to me. Ten to fifteen per cent of the oil America uses comes from Angola. For over three or four decades now the Angolan people have been killing themselves in a bloody factional war. America and the other Western nations also get some of their oil from this country. Don't the people, the tax-payers in these countries, deserve to know, to understand, that the oil comes from the blood of my people in Africa? Then they would at least have a choice to go with it or not, or make sure their government explains to them exactly what they are doing and what the cost of that oil is.

Why don't the Western governments want to inform the people? Why do they make decisions for them? The response to *Cry Freetown* in the West has shown me that people in the West do want to know more. Recently I had a room full of people asking questions and that is what we need to do: encourage people to ask more questions. That is what I am trying to do.

I try to understand who people are when they phone up and want to do an interview or use my material. I try to understand where they are coming from. Sometimes I give my material to people and Ron McCullagh says that is not how it is approached at Insight News. And I say, 'I am sorry, but I think that we all care and as long as we can establish a connection then money is not a driving force,' and he agrees with me. Maybe one will die a pauper; I don't care. As long as I can go home a happy man because I have contributed – I have made a difference. That is my dream – to leave our so-called One World at least a little better than when we met it. That is all I hope for.

# CHAPTER 18

# MAX STAHL

## Biography

MAX STAHL GREW UP IN CHILE and is the son of a former British Ambassador to El Salvador. He originally worked as an actor and presenter of the BBC children's program *Blue Peter*. He has worked as an investigative documentary filmmaker and freelance cameraman covering violence in Central America, the Middle East, Europe and the former Soviet Union. His work has been shown on national broadcasters around the world including Britain's Channels 3 and 4, the BBC, American PBS, National Geographic and Discovery. He is best known for his footage of the Dili massacre in Santa Cruz cemetery in 1991 (which helped end the Indonesian occupation of East Timor) and for his footage of escaping from the UN compound in Dili in 1999 to hide out with the East Timorese in the mountains.

Max has won or been nominated for numerous international awards for his work including the world's premier award for freelance cameramen, the Rory Peck Award, which he won in 2000 for his footage of escaping the compound in Dili, *East Timor Stories*. At the same awards he also won the Rory Peck Award for hard news. For his documentary, *Kosovo* (1998), which covered the fleeing of civilians from their homes due to ethnic cleansing, Max was commended in the Rory Peck Awards and received the New York Festival Bronze Award for coverage of an 'ongoing news story'. He has won one gold New York Film Festival Award, two silver and three bronze in 1982, 1998, 1999, 2000. He also won the Royal Television Society Award for Best Feature Documentary in 1993, the Amnesty International Press Award in 1992 for his documentary *In Cold Blood*, about the massacre in Dili and the Americas Grand Jury Prize US in 1984, to name just some of his awards.

Journalist Maggie O'Kane said of Max Stahl that he is one of the people who 'when the going gets dangerously tough in such places as Chechnya, East Timor and Kosovo he provides the only pictures we get of whatever contemporary hell they're still in. I've known four Max Stahls over the years, three of whom died.'

Max is single, has two children and lives in London.

\* \* \*

## Story

I can remember in 1999 when I left the UN compound in Dili in East Timor at night seeing all these ordinary people – women, children, babies, old people – with plastic bags and suitcases clambering up the rock face as they were being shot at. These hundreds of people were absolutely silent except for tiny whispers here and there. I remember what I thought was a little boy, but the Timorese tell me it was a little girl, who must have been maybe five or six years old and suddenly she fell and disappeared between two rocks. She must have hit her shins something horrendous and clambered out of this hole screaming silently. This little kid was so aware of the need to be silent. Imagine, she had done her shins in on a rock and was in total shock and she made almost no noise. That was one of those moments that you never forget.

I recently had a lady staying with me who was a child like that in East Timor in 1975 when her parents took her into the hills to escape the Indonesian attack. She saw my film *East Timor Stories* in Portugal and she said, 'You know that was just like me. I remember we couldn't speak. When we were hungry we couldn't speak and we couldn't cry because we might get killed and our parents were going to get killed if we did.'

This lady is a remarkable person. She has a little kid who is ten or eleven years old and she is on her own with him. She did some work here in London cleaning but got fired because she didn't go to work when her kid was sick. He was paralysed because he had some nervous problem so they fired her and kicked her out of her house and that is how she ended up staying with me. The house I am living in was a complete wreck; there were boxes everywhere and dirt and filth and nowhere to sleep but they had nowhere to go so they just slept on my sofa. Her son is one of the sweetest kids I have ever seen and he slept there with his mum. I saw him when she was ill, staying on that little sofa all day and all night and never complaining. He is the most radiant kid you could imagine.

I think the mother's experiences and the sweetness of her little boy are connected. I think she has this centred aspect about her because she knows ultimately, at some level or another, that life isn't about having this or having that; it is about being. And when you have your son, a sofa and a few boxes, you can survive.

## VALUES

A documentary or a piece of film is a relationship between the filmmaker and the subject. This relationship can be exploitative or it can be respectful, liberating or oppressive, and usually a bit of all these things. Respect for those I am filming certainly inspires my work. It makes me want to tell their story well and truthfully and I think that is common amongst many people who make stories and films. If you are a genuinely passionate reporter, somebody who really wants to see what is going on, then you want to observe other people, find out what is motivating them. I am fascinated by people: their courage, love, dedication to each other, as well as their hatred. There is also a certain respect for the dignity of people I won't let go of when I'm making films. I won't let go. That is fundamental. And dignity has to do with giving people value: valuing what they have, who they are, what they feel, and what they need.

Before I worked as an investigative documentary filmmaker, I was an actor and an aspiring writer who wanted to understand what makes people tick. To do that I think you need to look deep within people. I have a passionate interest in what goes on under the skin of people, especially when it comes to the choices they make. In an average situation people don't have to confront uncomfortable choices – hopefully. People say to me because of my line of work, 'Oh, you must be interested in nothing but death and destruction.' Actually, I am not. I am interested in ordinary people in ordinary circumstances but nobody is interested in showing ordinary people in ordinary situations on TV news or in documentaries so you can't make a living out of it and that's why I cover war. The thing that brought me to war was the drama of it. Not drama in a cheap, artificial sense, but in a profound sense. Showing the drama of war is a way of exposing the truth about people.

The notion of life and death obviously underlies many of the choices people make in war: who you are going to stick with or not stick with; why you stay; why you flee; why you stand up for something; why you don't; and, ultimately, why you take up a gun or why you don't. Why on earth are people prepared to die for things? You see many people rise to certain things and choose to do so not out of despair but out of conviction, which isn't to do with God or some abstract concept but has to do with certain things they are not prepared to let go of. Personal identity is one of those things. Now, in most cases, the victims are people who would have preferred not to have made any choices but in war everybody is forced to make a choice, even if that choice is simply to stay or to run.

I do think that as an independent filmmaker the ability to see ordinary people in extreme situations is a privilege because you witness some remarkable things. In my job, I have met certain people I hugely admire – many of them are now dead. The thing that links those people is not ideology; it is courage, courage where everything is mitigating against them. I am a great admirer of courageous people; I am encouraged by courage. Its most impressive manifestation for me is commonly in very ordinary situations, not necessarily at war. Just open your eyes. You can go to a hospital here in London and see courage that would make anybody feel humble.

One of the guys I have as a hero is a Timorese guerrilla leader, David Alex, who was tortured to death by the

Indonesian military in about 1997. Like most of the Fretilin guerrillas of East Timor, he had been fighting for twenty-odd years – a Trappist monk was living a life of luxury compared to this guy. His men were perfectly ordinary people, many of them young kids, yet on a day-to-day basis theirs was an extraordinary, focused and disciplined existence. The first time I met them they were living in a hole in the ground, a dried-up stream-bed. About 500 or 600 yards away thirty-odd Indonesian troops had been camped for weeks and there were about 3000 Indonesian soldiers within about a five- or ten-kilometre radius. There were only nine of them. This kind of courage of these men is important to me because I don't believe you can have values of any kind without courage. I don't think that it is possible to be honest or to have real love without courage; all these things melt away when fear wins in the battle. This is what makes me interested in extreme situations.

## A TOUGH BUSINESS

As a foreigner who doesn't know much coming into a new place, the first thing that you do is listen, isn't it? But when foreign correspondents turn up somewhere they usually have a very short amount of time to tell the story. Even with the best will in the world and the most extraordinary insights they couldn't actually have learnt very much. Imagine, in any family in the world a stranger comes in. How much does he know about what is really happening around the dinner table? Correspondents are in the position all the time of deciding what all the family relationships are like. Mainly what they tell is simply a regurgitation of what they have read on the plane; they have decided the story pretty much before they get there. So if you want to work well in a foreign country you have to have local fixers. They are absolutely vital and, in many cases, possibly in most cases, they are the authors of much, if not most, of what the journalists claim authorship of. The fixers are the people who suggest the story, who make it possible, who take people there. If there were some fairness in credits – which there certainly isn't – they ought to be credited.

I remember vividly the BBC correspondent in Albania during the Kosovo conflict literally did not leave the hotel in this shithole that was near the border except once in a while when he would be shipped up to the border to report. He was answering live questions to studio three times a day and he did not have a clue what was happening. I know for a fact in Afghanistan that many of the reporters were reading back to their audiences what they had been told by their offices back in London. The guy sitting on a hillside in Afghanistan didn't know what was going on. But there is nothing else you can do if you set up this requirement that news must be instant, that news is defined as something that happened a moment ago. There is a kind of illusion that if you get it now then you are getting the truth; nothing could be further from the truth. The people sitting in the editorial office back home do not have the time to assess anything. All they have time to do is keep up with the competition and all they can produce is instant banality. If you want to understand what has happened, you need to understand what goes on behind it, underneath it. For that you need time. In other words, the instant news machine is the enemy of truth and of real communications, but right now the instant is absolutely, oppressively, crushingly dominant.

One reason why documentaries have almost evaporated now is because the media think they know the story before they have ever heard it. By the time you have got something interesting to say they think that it is old hat. And of course, the fact that they never know the truth doesn't matter because the story has moved on. We are all in the business of trying to tell people something new and if you wait too long then the opportunity to tell them has passed. So if you want to get your story on air you should be aware of the agenda today. Typically, the person you interface with might be the editor of the newspaper or the TV channel but he or she will, in turn, be interfacing with a group of people who will have given the editor guidance as to whether they want this kind of story this week, this month, or at all. They would have been involved in what is essentially a marketing discussion. Press conferences and agendas set by politicians and spin doctors set the news and the editors play along with this and reporters have to conform because that is their job; they are part of the media circus.

So while I can recognise the black pit of despair that some people in the business feel, I have to tell you that my own particular black pit has more to do with my fellow journalists, with the editors or the people I am trying to sell to, or the lack of interest that I am finding, or the inability to finance my life or personal affairs, than it has to do with the people I am making films about. It is deeply depressing when you find that things of enormous value to you like courage, beauty, horror and injustice are not interesting to people who are, in theory, supposed to be interested in these things. I find the people that I am writing about or filming are much more normal, much more humane, than those other people in the news business back home.

So the choices that motivate your work and the issues you choose to cover should be informed by professional judgment as to what will be shown and what is of interest, but you are also going to have a motivating force as to why you want to do something and why you think it is important. It is these underlying values that you don't let go of. My main motivation is curiosity. A story that certainly has a very strong place in my own memory because of this is one that goes back to the first big film that I made in El Salvador in 1982–3. On this particular occasion I was in a refugee camp and I found a little kid who was probably six or seven years old who had survived a massacre. One of the things this kid came out with was that he had stayed hiding under the body of his mum for a whole day and a night because he felt safe (she had been shot on top of him). He didn't say she was dead but it became clear that she was. It really struck me that he remembered his mother lying on top of him as a comforting thing. I was absolutely determined to tell this story and I did. I got the pictures and I told the story and it went out as part of a big film I did.

There is a story now on Uzbekistan that I also think is important but Christ knows if I will ever get this story out. It's an incredible story about the rich American tobacco company, British American Tobacco (BAT) and these Uzbek peasants whose living standards have collapsed: they have now about five per cent of the income they had under the Soviet Union. The guys growing the tobacco used to get fifty or eighty per cent of the product value; now they get less than one per cent. The rest goes to factories, foreigners, local mafia types and local government people. The ordinary growers are in desperate straits and what we are led to believe, if you read BAT's publicity, is that this is a success story. Imagine if you lose in ten years ninety-seven per cent of your purchasing power!

The old Soviet system, in which these collective farms were like towns where the product financed everything including health care and education, had collapsed. So the workers are still being forced to grow tobacco, because the government has a contract with BAT, and BAT pays what it calls the 'market rate'. But because the co-op doesn't get the income they don't pay the workers so the workers work for no money. I found women there who, because tobacco-growing is so bad, were peeling onions and getting paid one-fifth of 1p an hour, which was better than what they were earning from tobacco which was absolutely nothing. That story needs to be told but what can you do as a filmmaker if the powers that make the decisions about what the public will see and not see decide it is of no interest?

Also you never get a good picture by taking one picture. A great photographer takes a hundred pictures and shows one. The biggest mistake I ever made was when I was doing a film in Guatemala for the *National Geographic* on the looting of the Mayan temples (I was with the looters). I had probably forty or fifty pictures of which maybe two or three were actually pretty good. Like an idiot, I thought I would show *National Geographic* my images and they could choose what they wanted. Big mistake. Editors, especially photo editors of a magazine like that, are incredibly snobbish and protective of the elitism that makes them rich. It's like: 'You can't come in off the street and tell me you have taken a good picture.' 'Why?' 'Because I don't know your name.' So what they are looking for when you show them these forty or fifty pictures are the bad pictures because they want to prove that you can't be good because they don't know your name. Being a photographer these days is really tough. There isn't a lot of demand for it and there is a huge amount of competition.

For me, the boring stuff about my job is just being able to stay financially viable. Psychologically and emotionally, the insecurity that you live with is chronic as a freelance filmmaker. I am an admirer of Robert Fisk in a lot of ways because he is one of the few correspondents who not only knows a lot but also is genuinely curious and wants to get under the skin of people. I respect that. Unlike many others, he believes that there are more important things than what the editor might want him to write about, or where his career is going to go. At some point, and probably at many points, he would have faced choices, faced pressure. You would have to suspect that he would have had to fight for the level of independence he has but he has been fabulously privileged to have a contract with *The Independent* and to be able to write about whatever he wants. I am deeply envious of him. I would be thrilled to have a contract with anybody at this time.

People like James Nachtwey also seem to me to be in seventh heaven because he can write his own ticket; at least it seems that way for me on the outside. Even if he goes somewhere on his own steam and takes pictures, he has got agencies and he can put his photographs out there. Video and film is not like that. God knows how many hundreds of hours of stuff I have that I think is absolutely fascinating that nobody has ever looked at or will ever look at.

## Dili massacre in Santa Cruz Cemetery, 1991

While the Indonesian military was still killing everyone in East Timor, a guy who had just been stabbed actually came to lie next to me and was holding up his T-shirt precisely because he wanted me to film him. The Timorese wanted it to be seen because at the moment of the massacre they knew instantly that this was absolutely crucial evidence of what the Indonesians were doing to them and they had to get it out. After the massacre I was arrested and taken away to a police station where the Indonesians interviewed me for most of the day and I also interviewed them for much of that time. Obviously there were times when it was frightening, but generally it was not especially frightening because once you get into the interview situation the Indonesians tend to be quite polite to foreigners. They didn't quite know how to handle me or what to do.

I had buried the footage of the massacre in the cemetery before I was arrested and I had one tape I had been using still in my camera. During the interview I had managed to go to the loo and view the tape so I knew what was on it and that, believe me, it was the most shocking tape of all. I decided that the Indonesians were bound to search me and if they found this tape they would not only confiscate it but would find that I had filmed stuff that was extremely damning to them. In that case they would probably arrest me and, at the very least, expel me from the country, which meant that I would never have the opportunity to dig up the stuff I had in the cemetery. So I destroyed the tape by recording over it while they were interviewing me. Ironically, they never did search me and so I destroyed the tape for nothing. I also had another twenty-five tapes in my room and they never searched it either.

Several weeks before the massacre some kids told me it was safe to sleep in the cemetery because the Indonesian soldiers were afraid to go there at night. So I thought about how much more they were going to be afraid on the night that they slaughtered all these people and that was why I had decided to bury the tape there. But I couldn't persuade anybody to join me to keep a lookout for Indonesian soldiers that night when I went back to retrieve the tape. I was a bit scared of going to the cemetery myself. It required some courage because it is one thing to rationalise that they were going to be afraid to be in a cemetery after killing so many people and another thing to go the cemetery at night by yourself when there was blood all over the place. That night I took a motorcycle back to the cemetery and dug up the tapes and a lot of people helped me get them out of the country.

## CALCULATING THE RISK

People who don't do this stuff, or even some of those who do, often think you have got these pictures because you happened to be in the right place at the right time. But think about how many times you have been at a wedding and got lousy pictures. Actually, to get good pictures is hard work. To be a really good conflict photographer you have to be an observer of everything and you get in the habit of observing everything to the point that you are not really a person. In a sense, you are not being; you are watching all the time, thinking, observing, and making a judgment in order to take that picture. You have to focus. That is the key. As a filmmaker, as a storyteller, you have to focus because if you don't focus you don't see what is going on. At the moment when other people are not focused you *have* to be because that is when people behave in an extraordinary way and you have got to pick that out.

So you are focusing, or you are trying to focus, whilst the people around you are kind of moaning and screaming and looking to you to rescue them because you are a foreigner. They are looking for something, anything, and you are it but you can't rescue them. When you are watching this stuff you have got to remind yourself of the fact that you got yourself into this shit for a reason. If you don't do the job, what are you there for? How can you justify getting killed if you don't even try to do the job? At one point during the killing in the Santa Cruz Cemetery, a soldier picked up his gun and pointed it right at my face. I was pointing the camera at his gun and he was pointing his gun at me – it is in the footage of the massacre. I said to myself, 'What are you doing getting killed when you only want a picture?' But you have got to get that damned picture. I started to back behind one of the gravestones but fortunately somebody fired a shot by his ear and he got distracted so he didn't pull the trigger. The key calculation you have to make is: is the risk worth it? Consciously and subconsciously you have to make a judgment.

## Engaging the audience

The great danger of war reporting is that it is like fireworks; explode a firework in somebody's face and you get their attention, but you don't give them anything, tell them anything, or let them share what is going on. If you simply grab their attention over and over again you are depriving and impoverishing the audience and prostituting the image. If you simply show a dead body or carnage and don't give the audience the means by which to engage with the human side of it – the reality that makes it a meaningful thing – then you have no right to show that image at all. When you are trying to get interest in a story that isn't on the news agenda, one of your few opportunities is the ability to connect with the people you are filming: make them human across the barriers of language and culture and so on. When the women and children in that chapel in the Dili massacre were praying they were saying their prayers in Portuguese. As the bullets were flying and the people were being stabbed, these prayers, which were of course desperate, were also in a sense an extraordinary testament to survival. And when these pictures of mine were shown in Portugal there was an enormous popular reaction amongst ordinary people; it made the women and children human.

So, as a filmmaker, or indeed as a writer, you are trying to connect the audience with the story you are telling by making a human connection because ultimately people are really not that different, whether they are poor or rich or speak this or that language or are this colour or that. And life is not cheap anywhere. Life is damned expensive wherever it is, including Rwanda. For the people who lose it and for their families it is everything. Nowhere have I seen greater care, greater respect, greater love for the dead than in theatres of conflict. People in the West often say, 'Oh, well they are used to it.' Bullshit! In the developing world people treat their dead with reverence. They grieve for the people they love who die, not less than the people in the West, but more. More than the rich people do.

## Killing and atrocities

I have no idea when the particular story I have been working on for two years will be shown but I would argue that anybody who would give me a chance wouldn't regret it because it is a hell of a story. It is focused on the massacre in Suai (East Timor), which I heard about while in the mountains of East Timor in 1999. I got there before the UN did and found the remains of the massacre victims. I went back a year later, investigated what really happened, found some of the survivors, and traced the evidence, step by step. Then I went to West Timor and found the killers happily ensconced in some refugee camps along the border, living under the protection of the Indonesian army.

I focused on one particular group of killers who carried out a massacre in this particular little village. Some of the survivors from the village have now returned but the guy who is the head of the village, and was number-one on the death list of this particular group, is still too afraid to live in his village because a couple of the guys from the military group are back there. The UN has said they are not militia people but everybody knows that they are and they told me they were. They even took me to where they carried out the killings and showed me how they did them.

The UN claimed that it would make justice in East Timor; that it would build peace. But what is the business of making peace? Who actually benefits and is there any justice? If so, for whom? The UN is desperately keen to bring people together. That is what is supposed to happen, right? But what does this reconciliation mean? It means, in this particular case, that the guy who was already a victim is not able to live in his own home because he is still afraid. Now, in one sense, what could the UN do about that? Put these blokes who killed the villagers in jail for how long?

As a filmmaker, as a storyteller, I am usually very reluctant to judge people, to come out and say, 'You are bad and you are good.' Of course, my films will imply that in many respects, but I am very reluctant to do that directly for selfish reasons: I am curious and I don't want to lose my contacts. And, in a way, I am happy to have a drink with the guy who did the murders. I have done it lots of times. I have known quite a few serious killers including some people who have done things that you would hardly credit. I understand the guy and I actually do get on with him. Most of the time these people are pathetic. Murderers are pathetic, weak people.

Some of the characters in the militias in East Timor were pretty sick also – psychopaths. I knew a girl who was captured in the hills and became one of the militia. She was raped by a policeman in a hotel in Dili and she was injected with something – probably speed. Christ knows why they injected her with the stuff because once she had been raped she couldn't go home. So she was thrown into one of the militia compounds and told, 'Here, you can have this gun and you can go off and kill now.'

I don't know exactly why those people, or anyone, commit atrocities but I think they mostly do it for incredibly trivial reasons. They do it out of greed and they do it out of fear – that is the biggest thing – and the two are linked. The people in the militias were deliberately screwed up and drugged but they were also afraid because Indonesian soldiers were controlling them. I saw these soldiers; many people saw them. Whenever the militia did a proper operation – as they called it – there were Indonesian soldiers organising them. So in the situation of the militias in East Timor you put all those factors together and people will do anything. The authorities have to get the people who were the authors of this violence in East Timor, not just the people who pulled the trigger.

## Assessing my career

I don't know if I have done well. I have written articles, made movies, done news and documentaries but I think that doing such a variety of things is a bad idea. Career-wise you want to be only one thing so everybody knows what you are. If you want to make an incredibly good living out of taking pictures you have got to have one or two out of the three or four sinecures in the entire world and you have got to be incredibly focused and determined. I regret career choices I made because today I would like to have a job, decent income and career structure. I would like to feel at the age of fifty or sixty that I am able to earn a lot of money and sit around in conferences telling other people what to do. It would be nice to have a pension. I would like not to concern myself with how the hell I would survive if I got injured, or be able to predict when I might be free to take my kids on holiday.

I meet people who are well paid, have careers, pensions, and insurances, who are jealous of me and I genuinely cannot understand it. I suppose what they feel is that they have clipped their wings in some sense and they imagine that I haven't. Well, of course I have barely even got any wings! These people are incredibly well off. No way would they give it all away and trade places with me. Not a chance. In some sense I am not a part of normal life. I remember when I was in El Salvador in the eighties and there was violence and mountains of bodies in the streets and someone called me from home and said, 'Look, your flat burnt and you have lost everything.' It didn't mean anything to me. Not a thing. It was just a flat. Who really cares? I am this kind of vagabond person and my lifestyle has some great pluses but it also has quite a lot of minuses. I suppose because of a pure ornery nature I have made my own choices and normally they lead nowhere, but on a few occasions it has been the reason why I have been able to do things that can have a big impact.

Certainly, if I look back on the relative successes that I have had, they have come as a result of my *not* being employed by somebody who would tell me what to do. On those occasions I followed my instincts, not what would have been a safer bet if I were interested in my career. In 1991 I would not have been in the cemetery in Dili had I been employed nor would I have been in the mountains in 1999, because the people who were employed were told to go home when the Indonesian military's scorched-earth campaign started. I could say the same thing about the stories I did in Kosovo, Albania, Chechnya and so on. I have done stuff that fascinated me because of something a bit deeper than just interest.

We can't all engage physically, emotionally and otherwise with everything that is happening around the world every day but, for the average reader or viewer to understand what is happening in our world, what we need are committed individuals who are willing to spend the time and the emotional and imaginative energy to engage in different issues and bring them to the world's attention. I do believe that in those circumstances amazing things could follow. I am not saying that the world is going to be turned around or even that things are always better – I am not a romantic – but change can and does happen. I don't believe that we should all necessarily feel despair yet. There is some hope and I have seen evidence of that. Certainly I think my Timor stories are full of hope. The way you convey hope is not to say, 'This is going to work,' because who the hell are you to say that? You don't know if it is going to work or not. Most of the time you probably think that it is very unlikely to work out. The hope you offer is in the eyes of the people you film. Hope is in the children and even in the soldiers, in the fact that they are human. Hope is in the humanity of the story that you are telling. You are there to record humanity and the fact that you are there at all and able to film the story is a kind of hope.

# CHAPTER 19

# PENNY TWEEDIE

## Biography

BORN IN ENGLAND, PENNY TWEEDIE has worked as a freelance photojournalist in over seventy countries for magazines, publishers, charities and non-government organisations including Oxfam and Save the Children Fund. She also photographs for industry and business as well as doing portraiture (including John Lennon and Yoko Ono, Germaine Greer, Groucho Marx and Colonel Gaddafi).

In 1975 she came to Australia on assignment for the BBC. Fascinated by Aboriginal culture, Penny stayed in Australia for a number of years, living with Aborigines and documenting their culture in Arnhem Land while forging strong relations with those whose life she shared. In 1999 she won Australia's most prestigious journalism award, the Walkley Award, for her images from the book *Aboriginal Australians: Spirit of Arnhem Land* (New Holland/Struik, 2001). She has produced two other books: *This, My Country: A View of*

*Arnhem Land* (Collins, 1985) and *Indigenous Australia: Standing Strong* (Simon & Schuster Australia, 2001).

She is single, has one child, and divides her time between Australia and England.

\* \* \*

## Story

I had been in Bangladesh for six weeks covering the war of Bengal's Independence from Pakistan for the *Sunday Times*. On 4 December 1971 India officially came into the war on the side of Bangladesh and by 18 December Pakistan was defeated and had retreated back to East Pakistan. The next day I heard that there had been a terrible massacre at the brickyard in Dhaka. During the war, the Pakistanis had rounded up Bangladeshi intellectuals, bureaucrats and teachers and kept them prisoner. When Pakistan began to lose the war they started disposing of their prisoners. Many were taken to the river where they were shot and their bodies dumped in the water; many others were taken to the brickworks where they were shot and pushed into the clay pits. The brickyard was horrific: piles of bodies, people whose hands were tied behind their backs some with visible bullet holes through their chests.

The Pakistan forces had also systematically raped many women because in a Muslim country a raped woman is an outcast. The Pakistanis undertook these horrific crimes in a last desperate effort to undermine Bengali society.

While I was at the brickworks, one of the locals alerted me that there was about to be a victory rally in Dhaka's football stadium. I joined the thousands of people pouring in – the figure was later estimated at 45,000 – and on the podium was the flamboyant Baqui Siddiqui in his black

*Bearing Witness*

Mukti Bahini* uniform working up his audience over their victory and Independence. It was a Mukti Bahini 'We've won the war' celebration. Other journalists and photographers arrived and I took pictures of the crowd and the speakers but after a while, as I couldn't understand a word of what was being said, I went exploring. Behind the podium I came across five young men roped together, sitting on the ground guarded by Mukti Bahini soldiers with guns. As I approached, one of the boys tried to speak and was kicked by a guard. I turned to the guard and asked, 'What's going on here? Why are these boys tied up?' The guards ignored me. Then one of the captives spoke in English: 'Help us. You must help us!' He was immediately punched with a rifle butt and kicked again by one of the guards.

Seconds later, the guards hauled the young men to their feet and dragged and pushed them forward into the stadium where something very odd was happening. Everybody was standing up singing; men were crying. I didn't know what was going on so I just shot pictures. Then the Mukti Bahini gathered around the five young captives and started to butt them with their rifles, punching and kicking them.

I stayed close to them, photographing and not knowing what the hell was happening. The guy at my feet, who was inches away – my feet are actually in the last pictures I took – was imploring me to help him. All of the other photographers crowded around (about ten of us). Then Siddiqui came over and I saw one of the Mukti Bahini soldiers take out his bayonet. 'Oh my god,' I thought. 'They are going to torture these guys!' yet no one was trying to stop us photographing. Siddiqui was only a few yards away so I tried to shout to him,

---

* **Author's note:** The Mukti Bahini were Bangladeshis trained and funded by the Indians to fight the Pakistanis. Baqui Siddiqui was their leader.

'What's happening?' Mark Riboud, an experienced photographer with the photo agency Magnum, was very close to me and he also tried to speak to Siddiqui. Richard Linley from ITN joined in and tried as well but we failed to get any answer.

Instinctively I thought that if they were about to start torturing these prisoners with bayonets and they weren't pushing us photographers away, then this could be deliberately being done for the media. Mark and Richard felt the same and we turned to the other photographers and tried to persuade them to back off, to stop photographing. Then we walked away, hoping they would follow. Most of them stayed. We waited at the stadium entrance, horrified by what seemed to be happening and Richard Linley worrying about his duty to be filming.

Later, Siddiqui and his crowd of cronies came flying past in their open-topped trucks. The victory rally was over. I noticed that one of the 'captive' boys was cowering in the back of one of the trucks so we went back to see what had happened to the others. On the ground were their bodies, bayoneted to death. Nobody ever explained who they were, or what crimes they were supposed to have committed. Siddiqui must have wanted the media to record this, and so I felt we were complicit in their deaths. I couldn't stop thinking about it.

I don't regret not photographing it. My reaction was instinctive and I stuck with my instinct, a gut reaction, but I got a lot of flak from some of the other journalists and photographers. When we got back to the hotel everyone was talking about the killing and I was besieged by media people asking me if they could have my pictures to use. When I told them I hadn't photographed it I remember being verbally torn apart. 'Well, what the —— do you think that you are doing here if you are such a wimp that you can't take it?' sneered one newsman. The next day I got a telex from the *Sunday Times* saying, 'Thank you for your great pictures, stop, war over and so is your contract.' I was shattered. I thought I was being punished for not taking those pictures but I learnt later that the dismissal was just a coincidence that had nothing to do with me not taking pictures of the bayoneting.

Bangladesh was a hard one because I had gone there as a freelancer to cover the victims of conflict, picking up assignments for NGOs, then had been assigned to cover the last weeks of the war for the *Sunday Times*. Their dismissal was a mega blow, because the story was not over (they were too far away to realise that!) so I stayed on as a freelancer to cover the terrible repercussions against the Biharis and suspected collaborators. I was in Bangladesh/India on this story for two-and-a-half months in all. It really stretched my stamina and commitment; I had never seen, witnessed or experienced such appalling human suffering before. The *Sunday Times* dismissal knocked me sideways! And getting back to the UK was hard: no one to unburden to because life had moved on . . . tough. I guess I should have gone to meditation classes and taken up yoga as I got quite seriously depressed for a few weeks. But one learns something from every situation whether good or bad and I learnt an awful lot from that experience. Sometimes I have to remind myself about that.

About three months later, Horst Faas and Michel Laurent won the Pulitzer Prize for their pictures of the bayoneting. By this time everyone in the media knew about the incident and there was much controversy. The BBC invited me and the *Express* photographer who'd stayed and photographed the bayoneting to discuss on TV our different points of view. I'd never been on TV nor spoken publicly before so I was very nervous, but it did allow me to argue my point and defend my reasons, and was ultimately cathartic.

## STARTING OUT AS A PHOTOGRAPHER

By the time I was sixteen I knew that I wanted to be a photographer. I had seen some of Henri Cartier-Bresson's and Robert Capa's work and realised that a photograph could sometimes convey more than words. I studied photography at the Guildford School of Art and, having acquired some skills, my ambition was to be a photojournalist: to work for one of the newspapers in Fleet Street. But being a young woman in a male world was a serious disadvantage. I got a staff job on *Go Magazine*, a precursor to the Sunday supplements, which gave me a chance to learn photojournalism on the job, travelling to Czechoslovakia, Lebanon, Jordan, Finland, Saudi Arabia and many places in Europe, and after two years I went freelance with great ambitions. But the only photography work I could get was for women's magazines and advertising. So I started doing stories on spec, not hard news but feature stories that I felt were being overlooked, such as stories on the homeless, teenage pregnancy, alcoholics. I then hawked the photographs up and down Fleet Street to the newspapers every evening and sometimes they were accepted and published.

In the wonderful razzy-jazzy time of the mid-sixties people didn't want to acknowledge that there was a serious homelessness problem in liberated Britain but my pictures hit a nerve. Suddenly I was working for the newly set-up charity Shelter and my pictures were all over the underground and in the papers. Occasionally, the *Mirror* or the *Express* bought one and, very occasionally, I got commissions. I started doing a few stories for *Paris Match* and when a staff job became available at the *Express*. Frank Spooner, the picture editor, encouraged me to go for it. I applied but the National Union of Journalists (NUJ) representative refused to employ a woman. A meeting was convened in St Bride's Church and the NUJ chapel father explained to the assembled company that they couldn't employ a woman photographer because she would have to do the night shift and she might be the only one on the desk when there was a train crash. The implication was that a woman wouldn't be able to cover a train crash because she might fall apart, so I didn't get the job. That was like a red rag to a bull. I continued doing assignments but I began to initiate more stories myself.

That was how I came to be in Bangladesh in 1971. Terrible atrocities were being committed and refugees were pouring into India telling of women being systematically raped, intellectuals being beaten to death and, inevitably, children starving. I decided to wing it but I didn't have an agent and wasn't part of an agency – one has to have an outlet for your pictures otherwise they will sink without trace. The *Sunday Times* agreed to pay for the shipment of my film direct to them so although they did not give me an assignment or fee, if my pictures were good they would be used and I would get page rates. With this initial guarantee I went to India and ultimately into Bangladesh. I fed the *Sunday Times* pictures every few days and, as the war hotted up, they took me on as their photographer.

## GETTING THE JOB DONE

No one ever instructed me on 'rules of journalistic conduct' and the magazines that commissioned my photography never mentioned the subject! I just had to use my own integrity. Obviously you have to be tenacious to get anywhere but, most importantly, sensitive to people and their situations. As a photographer, I am very conscious that the photograph has to tell it all but without pushing people around. So that means patience, involvement, putting yourself in their position, and being creative, even if you only have a matter of minutes to think about all this *and* take the photograph. But these are all personal decisions for the individual photographer.

You also have to take risks if you want to succeed. For example, on 4 December 1971, Mrs Gandhi, the Prime Minister of India, declared war on Pakistan and, as the world's press began arriving in Calcutta in droves, she imposed a press curfew. Yet for three weeks previously several of us had been working in and out of Bangladesh regularly, so we disobeyed the curfew, and headed back to Bangladesh.

We left our hotel at three o'clock in the morning and drove to the Bengali border to return to Bangladesh and head for Kulna, where we had been two days before. We had seen the terrible plight of refugees – roadsides littered with the bodies of those trying to escape the atrocities committed by the retreating Pakistan army. When we got to the border point beside the river the Indian police refused to let us pass, despite the fact we had military passes, so we drove down the river a few miles and took a boat. We passed bloated civilian bodies floating by. On the other side we hired three pedal rickshaws and started cycling. It was about seven o'clock in the morning with the mist rising over the paddy fields, the sun slanting gently through the trees and the doves cooing overhead – so seemingly peaceful; an unlikely war zone – but after a few miles a loud hailer shattered the illusion. Furious Indian police on pedal rickshaws were chasing after us! 'Come back! Stop!' It was surreal.

Back in India we thought we would be able to negotiate

our release with our official military press passes, but we failed. We were accused of spying and were marched into Bongaon jail. Here I was with the best opportunity to prove myself as a photojournalist when bingo, I am in jail, impotent! The fact that I was jailed along with the *Sunday Times* correspondent, the *Telegraph* correspondent and the *Observer* correspondent – all male – wouldn't matter one iota to the *Sunday Times*. I just imagined them dismissing me with 'Trust a woman to get herself arrested!'

The next day we were informed that we would be transferred to Calcutta jail. So we schemed about how to attract attention. We wrote our names and 'Please contact the British High Commission' inside our cigarette packets and it was decided that I should carry all our empty cigarette packets inside my shirt and, once in the crowded streets of Calcutta, drop them out at pedestrian crossings where people would be bound to pick them up. The journey was a nightmare. The men were in chains and one prisoner was dying of cholera at our feet – everything was pouring out of him, including his life. It was utterly horrendous but his death caused a distraction and I managed to post a few packets out of the cage before the guards caught me.

In Calcutta jail we made a huge fuss and demanded contact with the British High Commissioner, the hotel, our colleagues, anybody. This was refused and I was separated from the men who were dispatched to the men's wing and I was led off alone to the women's wing. The women's jail was vast: huge cages each containing about thirty women and it was quite evident that a couple of them were raving lunatics. I was terrified. I refused to budge and eventually they had to put me into a solitary cell. They dragged out an old woman, leaving her shit behind on the bare concrete floor, and threw me in with an army blanket. Stunned, my 'career' shattered, labelled a spy – it was all a terrible mistake but who would believe that? I was a prisoner in a foreign jail.

Fortunately, survival instincts kicked in. (1) In a solitary cell with no bucket and seriously dodgy swill called curry I must at all costs avoid getting dysentery! (2) I must attract attention, to make sure someone knew I was there. So I made a big fuss, went on a hunger strike, and demanded to see a doctor because I knew that a doctor would speak English. It worked. When she arrived I begged and implored her to contact the British High Commission. And after that I got my own survival rations – a mug of tea, an orange, a hard-boiled egg and a chapatti twice a day. Edible. But no contact from outside. Mysteriously, on the fifth day the jailer arrived and led me back to reception and there were the others – we were freed. And the next day we were back in Bangladesh. With alien cameras kindly lent by colleagues because my gear had been impounded (it was later returned), I went straight back to work. From there I followed the war to its conclusion in Dhaka and the execution in the stadium.

## MAKING THE IMAGE AND THE CONNECTION

I'm not really sure what makes people respond to the images they see. I know that when I am working with people who are the victims of famine, floods or displacement they are often women, children, the elderly and the frail and I relate to them. My body and soul are there with them. I don't feel that I am a voyeur. I am right there sitting in the dirt listening to their stories and photographing what is going on and I try to convey some of that pain and suffering through my work. I work very closely with people, following my gut reaction. Sometimes body language is our only form of communication. Some situations have been very difficult, some have been very upsetting, but I just focus on the story that needs to be told. The point, as I see it, about doing tragic stories, whether they involve conflict, famine, AIDS, refugees, or whatever, is to capture the essence of the situation in the photograph so it moves someone else to act, protest, give, understand.

I recently did a story on the palliative care of HIV/AIDS patients in Uganda. Because I had covered this before I knew I was going to witness hideous suffering and situations that were going to be very distressing, so I prepared myself for the worst. I was particularly anxious that my presence as a photographer visiting individuals dying in these painful circumstances in their intimate places – a shack, a hovel – and seeing them at their very lowest ebb would be intrusive. But the Ugandan carers and nurses I worked with who assisted the HIV/AIDS victims were an inspiration: they were joyous, caring and very positive. The AIDS victims were delighted to see them, not only because they brought pain relief but also because the patients could see that someone cared. Initially I was worried about being an imposition but to my astonishment they actually welcomed me and my camera. The carers explained that because everybody was now familiar with television my presence was welcomed as acknowledging and honouring them. It was the most humbling experience of my life. Here are these people dying who were actually thanking us for coming along to take their picture and tell their story. I just hoped that my pictures could do them justice.

I still believe that a photograph can stop you in your tracks. I am not saying that moving images don't have the same power but the best still images can live on long after they are taken. Take the girl burnt by napalm running down the road in Vietnam by Nick Ut. Everybody who ever saw that picture was affected. The image has been imprinted on our brains. I think I see the world as a series of still images. When I am photographing a person I don't see anything else: I am thinking and breathing through the camera's eyepiece, totally locked in there and focused on their every blink and twitch; it's working with their body language that tells the story.

Some people think the camera acts as a protection for the photographer. Not for me. In fact, I think it's just the opposite because you stick out and that can make you vulnerable to those oddballs who want to exploit you, rob you, rape you, strip you – all of which I've had to contend with. Being a photographer in certain countries is very difficult because you can become a target for their anti-Western aggression.

# Fear

Only once did I really think I was about to die. In 1973 I stuck my neck out to do the Palestinian story in Israel. I started off down in Gaza, then war broke out and I ended up in the Golan Heights covering the Yom Kippur War for the *Observer*. On this particular day, the Israelis were advancing to take Damascus, so another photographer, an Israeli minder and myself took off in that direction. We were up on the Golan Heights when I got these weird vibes. Instinct was telling me something – my 'situation thermometer' I call it. (Over the years I've begun to realise that I have a very instinctive feeling for the 'temperature' of a situation – dodgy, dangerous, hostile. These instincts have been spot-on and have saved me from problems many times.) We were driving through an eerie, empty landscape, across a vast deserted highland – obviously this was no-man's land – and my vibes were saying, 'No, no, let's turn back.' Then suddenly we spotted a Syrian tank, one that had been requisitioned by the Israelis. It was a hundred yards off the road and had come off its tracks. We jumped out and started going towards it when the tank commander yelled at us, 'This is a minefield; walk in the tank tracks!' Stepping carefully in the tracks we reached the tank just as the commander spotted fighter planes skimming the ground at 100 feet coming straight for us. The soldier shoved me underneath the tank and suddenly we were a sitting target in the middle of a minefield.

The Migs attacked. Above us the guys in the tank were hammering away with their anti-aircraft guns as I was watching the ground bursting with shells all around us. Then they were gone. In shock, I was about to crawl out, when around they came again. That second time, as they approached I thought, 'They can't fail to hit us . . . this is it . . . finale . . . I can't escape this, so at least I will record it.' So, as the ground was torn up around us, I just shot away with my camera thinking, 'That's it.' Miraculously they missed us and I'd wasted half a film on a blur of dust and smoke!

## COPING WITH THE JOB

Until a couple of years ago I smoked – nicotine, that is – but I've given up that particular friend. Friendship helps; some colleagues say sex is the answer, but I don't think that there is any real escape from the job that we do. I do get depressed sometimes but fortunately a relentless positive streak helps me out of this. Even when things go wrong I try to find a positive in every negative situation. Obviously talking also helps, but because I have always been freelance, often working on my own, I have never been part of the pack of photographers and journalists who can let off steam together. You need to talk and even joke about things get them out of your system. You can't expect people at home to know what you're on about, what you have been through, what you have seen. This is the hardest thing.

Relationships were always hard to sustain because I was often away. I wasn't wife material and didn't want marriage. Most of my relationships were with colleagues in the same business until I met this crazy Australian whose world was very different from mine. I believed we would complement each other and make a really strong partnership because we were so different. He was a charmer, a personality, a lateral thinker, and I was committed and tenacious. I knew that our relationship would be difficult but I thought, 'I can wear that. I'm strong, I'll be strong for both of us.' So we had a child, my wonderful son Ben. Unfortunately the relationship with his father didn't work out and when Ben was three we split.

In terms of regret, my only real regret is a professional one, that being freelance and without an agent pushing for me I haven't been able to do all the assignments I would like to have done. But the positive of that is that I haven't become blasé, jaded, desensitised. Each job is a challenge and I thrive on that challenge. And I am much more confident than when I was thirty and I am still lean and hungry for good projects and assignments.

## THE ABORIGINES AND EAST TIMOR

In 1975 I went to Australia on an assignment for the BBC, who I did a lot of work for at that time, to do the stills for a film on the explorers Burke and Wills directed by Tony Snowden. Within hours of arriving in Oz I was 'on set' in Alice Springs and there was a tea break. Rather than join the crew, I joined a group of the Aboriginal cast sitting in a dry creek bed in gorgeous late afternoon light. One of the older men, whose name was 'Nosepeg', started drawing beautiful patterns in the sand with his fingers. As I picked up my camera to look at this he said, 'Hey you, this one important Yippirringa dreaming – you photograph this. You tell those white fellas about our dreaming; those white fellas not understanding.' Over the next month he kept taking me aside to show me things: 'See that rock? That rock so-and-so. That where such-and-such happened.' He'd point out special markings and paintings one could barely detect. 'You photograph this; show those white fellas; they not understanding this special country for us; this our history, our dreaming.'

The Aborigines had an anthropologist 'minder' with them and over the next few weeks I pestered him for information about their culture and customs. I went to libraries and bookshops to look for further information and although I found several important anthropological tomes there was nothing for the ordinary reader. There were no photographic books, no leaflets, no cards, and yet here we were in the centre of Aboriginal Australia and there was no contemporary information about the world's oldest living culture. I was astonished. Then, one evening, a group of us, including some of the Aborigines, went to the nearest café in Alice Springs for supper but as we walked in we were stopped. The Aborigines were barred. We explained that we were all working together on the Burke and Wills film but the café staff was adamant that the Aboriginal people were not allowed in. I soon discovered this was the norm: at the hotels and bars the Aborigines had to drink outside. This was 1975!

During the next six weeks the more I learnt the more I wanted to tell their story and do a photographic book on the Aborigines and their surviving culture and traditions. It was arrogant of me to think I could do it but nobody else appeared to be doing so. I felt empowered by the Aboriginal people I'd met beseeching me to tell their story. After further research

*Penny Tweedie*

I decided that, rather than work in the desert, I should go to Arnhem Land where the culture was still thriving and intact. First I flew back to England and shut up shop, got rid of my studio and flew to Darwin, imagining that I might be away for a year. But – 'catch 22' – you were not permitted into Arnhem Land without an invitation from the Aborigines; and how did you get an invitation if you couldn't get there to meet them? Tenacity or perhaps madness prevailed, but it took two years before I was actually invited by the Aboriginal artist David Malangi and his family to start working with them in Arnhem Land.

While I was stuck in Darwin trying to make the Aboriginal connections, working with local groups and elders, the situation in East Timor suddenly erupted (the 1975 invasion of East Timor by Indonesia). I dropped everything and took off for Dili with six other journalists – I went on spec, several newspapers ran my pictures and then *Newsweek* commissioned me to work with their correspondent Lauren Jenkins. Lauren and I travelled with José Ramos Horta for many days through the western part of East Timor where Indonesian infiltrators were burning crops and attacking farmers and their families. The locals were arming themselves with machetes and spears and beseeching Fretilin, the local Timorese militia who were fighting the Indonesian military, to help them. On arriving in Balibo, the last town before the border, we found it utterly deserted: only Fretilin were camped there, many of whom were just young boys. The town had bad vibes – my 'situation thermometer' again.

That evening they took Lauren and me to a house in Batugade, a district that borders Indonesia. The house was Fretilin's ammunition dump with just enough room for us to sleep on the floor beside the ammo. They had no trenches and no protection. We were sitting ducks so we didn't exactly sleep! Before dawn, we joined five Fretilin on their patrol, creeping through the bush to the river (which was the border between East Timor and Indonesian West Timor) where in the soft dawn light I photographed the Indonesian soldiers washing and brushing their teeth. As we returned to the ammunition dump, Fretilin pointed out where the Indonesians had been during that night, not more than 200 yards away from where we had slept. It was too close for comfort. Bad vibes. Nothing was actually happening; innocent young soldiers were waiting for something to happen. We left.

On the way back to Dili we stopped when we saw another vehicle approaching. It was a team of New Zealand journalists who were heading for Balibo. I remember warning them that I felt it was a very dangerous place; even though nothing was happening it felt as if something was about to happen. A week later it did and tragically five TV cameraman and journalists who were working for Channel Nine and Channel Seven were caught by the Indonesians and shot dead.

## Working in Arnhem Land

Ben was eighteen months old when I finally got my invitation and permit to work in Arnhem Land. Several friends considered me very irresponsible – 'You can't take him with all those poisonous snakes, spiders, insects, crocodiles.' Little did they know what an amazing and life-changing adventure it would be for Ben and me. Although the people in Arnhem Land were used to the white teachers, missionaries and the occasional anthropologist, they'd never had a white baby camped with them. So everyone wanted to look after Ben and show us their way of life.

In those first couple of months I was sort of on probation, only allowed to work with Malangi and his extended family.

After a month I organised a simple slide show in order to show the community the photographs I was taking of them. More than a hundred people turned up; they evidently liked what they saw because suddenly many artists and elders were asking me to come and work with them too, 'to show those Balanda [white] people about us Yolngu people – about our culture and our country'.

Initially they were surprised that I wanted to photograph everything but they soon became enthusiastic, laughing amongst themselves about what they should show me next: how to catch goanna; how to find the rare orchid vital to artists from which they squeeze the juice to mix with the ochres so that the paint sticks to the bark; or how to gather and squeeze green ants to make cough medicine; and later allowing me to become an 'honorary male' in order to record the boys' initiation ceremony . . . It all happened and the project grew from a magazine piece for the *National Geographic* to my first Aboriginal book, *This My Country* – the title suggested by David Malangi.

During the next decade I was based back in the UK working on all sorts of stories for NGOs and for UK and international magazines including cover stories for the *Sunday Times* on health, on Beirut, Libya, and frequently Africa for NGO stories. In 1995, by which time Ben had left school and was travelling himself, I returned to Australia to do another Aboriginal book, *Spirit of Arnhem Land*. The year 2000 was to be the Year of Aboriginal Reconciliation so I undertook my third Aboriginal book, *Standing Strong*, to celebrate successful indigenous Australians in all areas of endeavour, from athletes to architects, doctors to designers, policemen to pilots – successful people of whom most white Australians were unaware.

Reconciliation has not been forthcoming under Prime

Minister John Howard and the struggle of indigenous Australians continues. I feel very privileged that the Aboriginal people accepted me and trusted me to record their life and customs. The time I've spent with them has been a real commitment, totally engrossing and truly enlightening.

Once again, as in the case of the bayoneting in Bangladesh, I was accused by some people of not being objective. I chose to take the Aboriginal point of view because I could see that there was a vacuum. It was obvious that their story wasn't being told fairly and I ultimately committed myself to trying to tell it. But the word 'objective' is a hard one because I do get deeply involved in my subject ... whether victims of HIV/AIDS in Uganda, genocide in Rwanda, landmine amputees in Cambodia, whatever; I am not deliberately taking sides but I am trying, through my photographs, to tell their story, to bring it to people's attention.

## DIFFICULTIES OF WORKING AS A PHOTOJOURNALIST

In the eighties I did some big cover stories for the *Sunday Times* running many pages, picture-led, but today serious stories are swamped by celebrities and lifestyle. Making a living in photojournalism nowadays is tough: less photo-led stories are published and the fees have gone down; for example, the *Sunday Times* is paying less per day than in 1986! Some people think I must be mad to continue ... they may be right, but I still believe in what I am trying to do and it can be truly rewarding on many levels. Sometimes colleagues suggest I should teach photography, but I see that as a diversion. It's hard enough getting editors to commission feature stories and I fear that teaching would become demanding and if it then began to take care of the bills one could lose one's incentive. I am still hungry to be a photographer so I haven't fallen into that trap – not yet.

Last year I had an assignment in Cambodia for one of the NGOs where I was working with landmine victims who were being trained to become landmine clearers. It was a great project, really positive for them both financially and psychologically, and was good for the country. But no magazine was interested because the world's attention was on Iraq. Occasionally I have been challenged: 'Don't you feel guilty being paid to photograph other people's suffering?' That is one way of looking at it but, on the other hand, if these stories aren't told then people wouldn't know about them. In many cases this awareness raises interest and raises money to help the charities that work with people who are victims of their environment.

For example, the *Telegraph* published the Ugandan HIV/AIDS story and within six weeks the readers had donated more than seventy thousand pounds for Hospice Uganda to help the AIDS victims. That's rewarding. Helping people to open their wallets – yes, I am guilty as charged! In 2002 I was in Rwanda working with orphans of the genocide and I can't believe that anyone could not be affected by their horrendous and tragic stories. It was the most emotionally disturbing story I have ever done, but the frustration was trying to get it published. Eventually, one single picture was used nine months later in the *Sunday Times* to accompany Ann McFerran's piece which also had a positive response. This is what makes it all worthwhile.

I certainly do not consider myself a war photographer. I've never gone anywhere to specifically cover war. But photographing the victims of conflict or injustice – whether in Ireland, Israel, Uganda or Sudan – has led me into some dodgy and dangerous situations, and by extension into war. With Vietnam, for instance, I had no interest whatsoever in photographing soldiers doing their thing, but I did a story that was being overlooked – the terrible abandonment of all the GI babies who were starving and dying of normal but untreated diseases in pathetic compounds: the 'unwanted children'. This story certainly raised awareness, charitable help and, I'm told, lots of adoptions. So I didn't go looking for war and later, when my son Ben was a baby, I was definitely not looking for dangerous assignments – adventure, yes; new stories, yes; let's face it, anywhere can be dangerous!

People who have 'real' jobs making 'real' money sometimes ask, 'Why do you keep doing this? You could do something else.' But this is my life, my passion; this is what makes me tick. My work has led me into so many adventures and I've been privileged to work with so many different and amazing people. I've learnt so much and it's never, ever been boring. I thrive on the challenge to convey their stories through my photographs. This is what I do; it's my life!

# BEARING WITNESS TO WAR

### The myths of war

War is not, as our politicians and military would have us believe, always a justifiable and moral enterprise. It is not a brave and noble endeavour. Bombs are not surgical, precise, clean or smart. War is, in the words of Prussian general Carl von Clausewitz, 'the continuation of politics by other means'. War is about power, destruction, pain, death and loss. It is the most extreme form of politics, and it signals political failure.

Because the reality of war is so dissimilar to the myths perpetrated by our militaries and politicians, those who wish to use it as a political tool would not be able to do so without a willingness, even eagerness, within society to embrace it. Many of us still cling to the myths of war because they are seen as filling a spiritual void by providing a patriotic and unifying ideal. In other words, like the generals and the politicians, society has an interest in sustaining the ennobling myths of war, for to do otherwise – to confront the reality of war, the duplicity of our leaders, or our own gullibility and accountability to those we sent to war and waged war against – threatens our comfortable definition of who we are. If war is not noble, if we are not necessarily the just (good) and our foes not always the unjust (evil), then who are we?

For many of our young men and women we have sent to war, the possibility that the pain and loss they witnessed, suffered or inflicted on others was not bravery or was not for a noble cause renders war as senseless carnage – a breathtakingly debilitating revelation for those whose sense of self has been built upon such ideals. What does it mean if you come to believe that you and your enemy were merely cannon fodder for the politicians in their political and economic games?

The Vietnam veterans were a group who spoke *en masse* against the dehumanising, brutalising effect of war. Coming back from war during a time when centuries-old social barriers were being torn down, many of them, unlike their predecessors, refused to hide and suffer in silence. In return, many of us shunned them and our rejection of them – or our patriotic fervour over acts they were ashamed of – only served to increase their guilt and trauma. In their honesty and refusal to uphold the noble myth of war, they became living testimony to the reality most of us do not wish to confront: war is neither heroic nor noble.

In a much-lauded statement, General Douglas MacArthur noted that a soldier who dies for his country 'is the noblest development of mankind'. The philosopher Immanuel Kant came closer to the truth when he wrote, 'War is an evil inasmuch as it produces more wicked men than it takes away.' Although there are undeniable acts of bravery and compassion in war – as conveyed by those in this book who have witnessed war up close – the death of a young person on the battlefield cannot be considered development, noble or otherwise: it is a tragedy. It is not something to be lauded; it is something to be lamented. When no one needs to lay down his or her life in the face of aggression *then* we will see the noblest development of humankind. In its baseness, war signals the ultimate failure of our politicians and the ultimate testimony to the failures and inadequacies of humankind – it is an unpopular message for such an arrogant species.

It becomes the task of those who cover war to cut through these lies for us because, as noted by the consummate politician and former war correspondent Winston Churchill, 'In wartime, truth is so precious that she should always be attended by a bodyguard of lies.'

## Patriotism and fear

To be a dissenter within your own community, whether you are a journalist or an ordinary citizen, takes courage because what is lined up against you is nothing less than the ideal of patriotism.

It is not enough for governments to attempt to hide the realities of war; they must create a reason for war. In this process they resort to two powerfully emotive tools of persuasion: patriotism and fear. In times of national crisis, calls to patriotism are also a government's way of uniting the nation behind its policies (its politics) and a powerful means of silencing dissent. If the government's use of fear and patriotism is successful then the media and the voting public's ability to think critically and their willingness to publicly articulate their concerns or openly debate their options are undermined. By closing down society in this way, the government ensures the nation's attention is turned outward against the threat of the 'other' and away from what might possibly be the greater threat at home – the undermining of democracy. In deceptively simplistic terms the government attempts to control debate by arguing that either 'you are for us or against us'. Within this paradigm, neutrality becomes unacceptable.

Yet in a democracy it is not unpatriotic for the media and the public to speak out against something they believe to be profoundly wrong: it is unpatriotic not to. Overt patriotism becomes the ultimate unpatriotic act.

## CENSORSHIP

Just as we censor the veteran's unpalatable truths, we also censor these war correspondents' and photojournalists' images (written or visual), or they are censored for us. Within this book there are myriad examples of censorship, either intentional or unintentional, practised by those who are the first to document human tragedy. There are also unseen levels of censorship practised by the photo agencies, the wire services, editors and our governments.

In 2003, Nabeel al-Jurani's picture of the little girl with her feet shredded (see picture section) was used by media outlets around the world but in Western countries her damaged feet were cropped out. The reason, explained Michael Bowers, picture editor at the *Sydney Morning Herald*, was that the public complain when confronted by such graphic imagery.\* How much did we see of war when all we saw was a pretty little girl with blood on her face rather than the reality: a pretty little girl with blood on her face without feet?

\* **Author's note:** Under the auspices of Bowers, who as a photographer covered conflict, the *Sydney Morning Herald* set up a web site (with appropriate warnings) where people were able to see the more graphic imagery that more accurately depicted the reality of war.

When speaking of his arresting image of an incinerated Iraqi man on the road to Basra photographer Kenneth Jarecke dismissed it as 'not a great image: just a snapshot of something I saw'. Yet this 'snapshot' became famous because, as Jarecke says, 'Although he is horrifically burned, the humanity of this person: his struggle to live, to survive, is apparent.' It was also one of only a few images made of the estimated 20,000 to 100,000 victims of that supposedly 'clean' war. This photo was nearly lost to the world because an AP photo editor in New York made the decision that it was not suitable for public viewing.

In 1989, photographer Deborah Copaken Kogan, believing her photos of the horrors of the Romanian orphanages after the fall of Ceaucescu to be the first documentation of the appalling tragedy, offered them for publication. Her agency, however, refused to distribute them because what they had wanted – and had been expecting from Kogan – were colour photographs of people voting in the Romanian election. It became a seminal moment in this photojournalist's career.

'It suddenly occurred to me that what I'd been sent out to shoot, what photojournalists in general were sent out to shoot, were pictures the photo editors had already planned out in their heads and placed on the page.' Being told by her agency that the orphanage photos could wait, Kogan realised that, 'No, the orphans couldn't wait. I suddenly understood the importance of my job: it was not about me; about getting a scoop; even about being the best photojournalist I could possibly be, it was about trying to use photography to somehow elicit change. It was about bearing witness and subsuming the self for the sake of others in need. So I gave the story to a better known photographer because I knew his photos would get published.'

No matter how talented a photographer may be, he or she cannot do what photo editor Peter Howe claims they *can* do: 'communicate...what it feels like to be a soldier pinned down by sniper fire, a civilian left homeless, or a child left parentless'. Photographers and their product can never superimpose the experience of the individual in the image onto the consciousness of the viewer. At best they show us a nanosecond in time and elicit a response from within our own emotional repertoire. Albeit powerful, the still image is a limited form of communication and so is, as David Rieff notes, the written word: 'As a journalist, you live with the fact that we all know so much more than we know how to say. It is not because we are being censored (although sometimes this happens) or, worse still, censoring ourselves (whether consciously or unconsciously) but I just think that we are trying to do something that is too much, that is overwhelming.'

While photographers and journalists must work within the limitations of their medium, it is also impossible for them to always understand the range or impact of their work. Roy Gutman spoke of his frustration and sense of responsibility when his initial article warning of the reappearance of concentration camps in Europe failed to create outrage. 'The reaction to my ringing of the alarm bell ... was zero. Well, that really gave me the feeling of a tremendous burden. That was about as much pressure as I have ever felt on my shoulders in my life.' Max Stahl, Sorious Samura and Chris Morris have also spoken of their frustration and pain at their inability to elicit a response to their ringing of that bell.

There are times – and they may be far too few – when their work can have an immediate impact, such as Penny Tweedie's and David Brill's work for NGOs in Africa, Glenn Middleton's footage of the Congolese 'prophet', Robert Fisk's reporting of the Qana massacre, and Marie Colvin's reporting from the compound in Dili in 1999. Or, as Susan Meiselas noted, the full impact of their work may take decades to be felt.

At the same time, the work of these professionals, especially that of the photographers which is essentially released into the free flow of information, may be misrepresented or misused. Ron Haviv's photos taken at the beginning of his career in Panama were possibly misused by his country's president; Eddie Adams believes his photo of the execution in Saigon was misrepresented; and Glenn Middleton described how, during the apartheid era in South Africa, the censorship of his work made it almost unrecognisable.

Government and military censorship, however, are not restricted to undemocratic or authoritarian regimes. In every war, Western governments have attempted to control our vision (and version) of war by attempting to control the media and its message. In the Falklands War, only two journalists were given official accreditation by the Thatcher government, and during the US invasion of Grenada the press was kept away from the fighting by a US gunboat. How the US military attempted to control the media during the invasion of Iraq was in direct response to their experiences in the wars of the second half of the last century or, more specifically, those of the 1990s.

In the 1991 Gulf War, most of the world's journalists were essentially kept from the front through a media-pool system where they were fed – and, in turn, many obligingly regurgitated – the US military's version of its 'high-tech' war of precision bombing and 'smart weapons'. While there were a few like Peter Arnett and Robert Fisk reporting from behind enemy lines, or Chris Morris with the British and US troops, essentially that war was a debacle for the media and for free and open press. Because Western militaries were not present until the end of the Balkan wars, people like Ron Haviv, Chris

Morris, David Rieff and Roy Gutman had greater freedom to report on humanitarian crises involving concentration camps, mass deportation, systematic rape and the failures of Western governments, reports that eventually forced the reluctant West, in the form of NATO, to intervene. The attack on Afghanistan in 1999 by the allied forces was essentially confined to an air war and to specialist operations from which the media were excluded. As a result, without military control or the military to report on, the press once again focused on the civilian casualties and 'friendly' fire incidents – exactly what the military does not want highlighted in a war. As noted by a Pentagon official to Jeffrey A. Smith in his book *War and Press Freedom*, there would never again be any war if we let people see graphic imagery of war and civilian casualties.

When they planned the invasion of Iraq, the allies knew it would be the most intensely covered war in the history of humankind. Their goal, therefore, was to control the media to minimise the coverage of civilian casualties while giving an appearance of openness and accessibility. Toward this end, they had a two-pronged approach – Central Command in Qatar, with its multi-million-dollar Hollywood production stage, would provide an overview of the war to the media while journalists 'embedded' within military units would provide the images the media demanded. There were, however, a number of problems with this plan.

The information given by Central Command was controlled, often incorrect or misleading, and, at times, propaganda. The savvy media quickly became disillusioned and frustrated. Embedding also had serious problems for balanced war reportage. The embedded journalist was rarely briefed by the military so that while they could provide the visuals, they were rarely able to provide more than banalities such as 'we travelled forty miles today'. Most importantly (as was the military's intention), often the journalist or photographer bonded with the soldiers he or she travelled with. While the most puritanical reporters needed to question their own objectivity, in the most extreme cases journalists found themselves becoming participants in the war. Because the 'embed' had little else to report, much of their coverage of the Iraqi invasion focused on their own experiences and the hardships and fears of the American soldier at the expense of the people who were suffering and dying in greater numbers: the Iraqi people. As the military had anticipated, the 'embeds' and the soldiers became the story of the war. How could it have been otherwise?

There was, however, a third form of reportage possible from Iraq. What came to be known as the 'unilaterals' (those not reliant upon the military) focused on the war from the Iraqi side and, by association, Iraqi civilian casualties. Prior to the invasion, these correspondents and photographers were warned by the Pentagon that they may be military targets. The allied governments also warned their 'unilaterals' and their media organisations that for their own safety they should leave Iraq – many capitulated, others did not. The majority of journalists who were killed during the Iraqi invasion were from within the ranks of the 'unilaterals' and were killed by so-called 'friendly' fire.

Since the invasion, it is becoming increasingly dangerous to travel into Baghdad: planes landing at Baghdad airport are targeted by stinger missiles and the road from the Jordanian border is patrolled by 'Ali Babas' – bandits in high-powered Mercedes who regularly relieve travellers of their money, their cameras or their life. Within Baghdad, recently a number of the well-funded media networks such as BBC and CNN have purchased a block of the city and cordoned it off with security. Yet from the words of those correspondents and photographers in this book and from the number of correspondents who continue to report from Baghdad or have returned after the invasion, including Goldenberg, Fisk, Haviv and Colvin, one can only conclude that they will continue to find their own way to war and to report it from the streets, as they have always done.

When control of the movement of journalists and their reporting fails, governments have resorted to direct pressure on media outlets. From the beginning of the invasion of Iraq, the US government forbade media coverage of the return of American war dead, while in 1991 in Iraq footage of the slaughter of fleeing Iraqi soldiers and conscripts on 'the road to Basra' was pulled from US television under government pressure. Not all media, however, need such pressure. The toppling of Saddam's statue in Baghdad (conveniently located in front of the international media's temporary home in the Palestine Hotel) was essentially a US military stage-managed event for the hotel's occupants and their audiences, with the military providing the inspiration and the means of toppling the statue. How many of our media outlets chose to report the event as a spontaneous outpouring of Iraqi joy momentarily exposed for what it was by the appearance of an overly enthusiastic US soldier draping an American flag over the statue's head? And in late 2003, *Time* magazine handed Washington and the Pentagon a priceless public-relations windfall when, on the suggestion of Donald Rumsfeld, it named the US soldier '*Time* Person of the Year' (although the accompanying article did refer to them as 'the bright, sharp instrument of a blunt policy'). At the lowest end of the war-reportage scale was unashamedly biased coverage of the Iraqi invasion by Fox cable TV.

Patriotism and the propensity for some within the Fourth

Estate to uncritically align with government policy means that such institutions fail in their assigned tasks to inform and to act as the guardians of democracy and defenders of the public interest. Essentially, what the public is fed from these mouthpieces of proprietorial interests or government policy (not always dissimilar) is little more than propaganda. Within a month of President Bush officially declaring an end to hostilities, London, Canberra and Washington were proposing legislation to relax media ownership laws that would allow certain media owners, the most loyal supporters of the war, the possibility of even greater control over what the citizens of the West saw, heard and thought.

The Federation of American Scientists has documented nearly 200 military incursions since 1945 in which the US was the aggressor. The self-proclaimed war president's 'greatest force for good in history' is today the most powerful and belligerent state in the history of humankind. How many of its own citizens know, or indeed, want to know about what historian Charles A. Beard describes as his nation's 'perpetual war for perpetual peace'? As Chris Morris says, 'We [Americans] had been taught since September 11 that they [the "terrorists"] hate us because we love freedom. I would say they hate us because we think like that.' It is not always clear where responsibility for this ignorance lies: with the media, the government, the citizens, or a combination of the above.

In the 1960s Marshall McLuhan termed the phrase 'the global village', arguing that advances in communications would bring humanity together to the point where people related to and cared for their fellow humans. Despite advances in communications that McLuhan could not have dreamt possible, David Rieff, like many others, believes that it is still not normal to care 'about people 5000 or 300 miles away' or 'the death of a stranger'. To care for a stranger, it is argued, takes a leap of moral imagination that is impossible for most of us. Other correspondents and photographers attempt to bridge that divide by appealing to our shared humanity. For David Brill it is through 'photographing hands, faces, eyes and mannerisms'.

Coming so close to another's tragedy may not always be comfortable. In the words of Marie Colvin: 'To make anyone in the outside world care about yet another famine in Ethiopia you have to talk to the most dangerously ill people and that is awful. I just steel myself a bit and I know that what I write, and the picture I have of this family whose baby is clearly going to die within hours, can have some effect.' To get through these situations, the journalist or photographer has to believe that their work may make a difference. Sometimes, though, as Monica Attard and Peter Charley have said, they do feel like voyeurs.

In one sense, the general public's caring or inability to care becomes irrelevant. The salient point is not necessarily that they are moved or not moved to care about the pain of the 'other' but that they are, at least, able to observe that pain and in that act of observing – of bearing witness – recognise that which is morally unacceptable, that which should not be, and in that recognition are moved to take action. If we can't bear to look at the photo of the little girl with her shredded feet, how can we bear to let that happen to her or any innocent child? As Susan Sontag argues in her book *Regarding the Pain of Others*, 'after a certain age [no one] has the right to this kind of innocence, of superficiality, to this degree of ignorance, or amnesia'.

Perhaps there is some validity to the photo editors' argument that it is we, the viewing public, who define what we see because we don't like being disturbed by the reality of war and exposed to the suffering of others. Perhaps there is also some validity in the argument that many of us have become desensitised by overexposure so that we find it hard to emotionally identify to the point where we are incapable of caring about the pain of others. Perhaps many of us have never really looked, never really seen.

The best journalists and photographers of human tragedy, when allowed to do their job well, attempt to create a bridge between our world and theirs, inviting, even compelling us to join them in bearing witness to a reality which, for most of us, exists beyond the boundaries of our comprehension. One of the most powerful tools in the testimony to war is the still image. In its relentlessness, its refusal to move frame, the eye is unrelieved and we, like the subject of the image, are caught in that intense, often too-full moment.

The use of graphic imagery is complex, with endless discussions in the West weaving around the issues of sensibilities, morality, compassion, rights, and what is and what is not art. Yet these debates are ethnocentric with their focus on the distress of the Western viewer rather than that of the subject. The argument for censorship of these photos, which says that such imagery is 'war pornography', 'not in good taste' or 'far too disturbing', confuses the cause with the consequence: it is war that is pornographic and not in good taste; the images simply depict these truths. What may be profoundly obscene and immoral to the victims of our aggression are not the images of their suffering but our refusal to acknowledge them – the seeming expression of our collective indifference to their pain. As we turn away from their humanity we turn away from our own.

It is not always possible for us to know who or what drives censorship, how we are being censored, by whom, and indeed, what our own role is in that censoring process. But while photos and accounts of human suffering are withheld from us, or while we refuse to acknowledge them, some of the most powerful images of the human condition will remain lost, as will the truth of war.

## LOVE AND ATROCITY

There are two powerful emotions in life from which every other emotion emanates: fear and love. In war, fear and death are magnified but so too are its counter-forces, love and life. It is these forces that give rise to extraordinary acts of bravery and kindness that help the individual emotionally survive the horror of war. Expressions of love and life that are the natural counters to death and fear are also reached for instinctively to sustain the photographers and journalists who immerse themselves in human tragedy.

In the midst of war, John Gaps' poem *The Unjust* reaches out for memories of gentleness, forgiveness and love, as does Chris Morris when he instinctively focuses on someone he loves in order to defeat his fear when faced with a dangerous situation in the field. Glenn Middleton deliberately takes a day to jettison the darkness of war and reacquaint himself with the loving father and husband that he is before returning home to his family. The ashes of Kurt Schork (who inspired love in so many he worked with and whose memory was evoked by many within this book) are buried next to his mother in Washington as well as in the Lion's Cemetery in Sarajevo – beside the grave of a young couple whose love, in the midst of the carnage that was Bosnia, he said changed his life.

Many of those who cover war deliberately seek the company of people deeply in love as a counter to the horror of war while strangers become casual lovers and intense friendships are formed. While such intimacy may be a response to thoughts of mortality or the adrenaline and raw excitement of war, it is also a response to loneliness and fear: an affirmation of life in the midst of death. In the absence of the emotionally charged experience of war, and without the need for an antidote to its negativity, often the relationships formed by the journalists in extreme situations dissipate. While the memory of what was shared survives, the need for intimacy or friendship may not.

In a final and poignant testament to the centrality of love as a counter to death, the last words often spoken by a young man dying in combat are for his mother. Quite simply, the energy of love, whether it is found in a photograph, the calling of a name, a memory, the retelling of a story, or the company of lovers, is life affirming.

Anyone who spends too much time immersed in the darker forces of life may find at some point that they are overcome with feelings of helplessness and inadequacy so that darkness is all that they see. For many in the profession, Rwanda, Goma, Grozny and Sarajevo were just such experiences. At the same time, because a physical place can retain a dark memory, there are areas around the globe where, in the words of Peter Charley, the 'atmosphere has been bruised by the madness'. Anyone who has been to the torture chambers of Tuol Sleng in Cambodia, the killing fields of Rwanda or the concentration camps of the Second World War, will tell you they are just such places, but there are many others. Those who have never been touched by these levels of darkness can only be grateful and, like Sorious Samura and Peter Charley, can only be left to wonder how those who have discovered this darkness within themselves can live with their memories.

While few of those interviewed in the book felt they could adequately explain atrocities – or even adequately describe them – Lt Col Dave Grossman's study, *On Killing*, documented the diffusion of responsibility and accountability possible within a group. Combine this with the phenomenon of group-killing hysteria and the fact that war gives opportunity and even acceptance to the individual with a 'taste' for violence, and you have created a fertile ground for atrocities. While such concepts explain the conditions that make an atrocity possible they do not explain the *why*.

In the words of Voltaire, 'Those who can make you believe absurdities can make you commit atrocities.' Indeed, it is the promotion of fear and hate of the enemy or the dehumanising of the enemy, together with the sanctioning of violence that creates the belief system that makes the behaviour possible. That is, it creates the moral distance that makes the atrocities probable. But such behaviour goes beyond the fact that the enemy has been dehumanised; it goes to the dehumanising of the perpetrator through their own fear, hate, anger, frustration and confusion – staples on which the violence of war feeds. When the perpetrator of violence dehumanises his enemy he has dehumanised himself – the atrocity lies only a hair's breadth away.

Like soldiers, little in the journalist's life will compare with the emotionally charged danger, excitement, intensity and raw power of war. Some will feel enriched by the strong bonds of camaraderie formed, but others, like the soldiers who prosecute the wars, will be disillusioned and damaged when they experience this darker side of war. 'One of the most difficult realisations of war,' explains journalist Chris Hedges in his book *War Is A Force That Gives Us Meaning*, 'is how deeply we betray ourselves, how far we are from the image of gallantry and courage we desire . . . In combat the abstract words of glory, honour, courage, often become obscene and empty.'

Baudelaire's 'wind of the wings of madness' must be a concern to anyone who continually documents atrocities and human tragedy. Some, like Robert Fisk, have been able to avoid its dark shadow; others in this book have been deeply affected. While Feinstein's study on post-traumatic stress disorder could find no difference between the degree of PTSD suffered by men or women, he did find that within the profession stills photographers suffered the greatest occurrence of the syndrome (twenty-nine per cent). It seems that, like soldiers, the closer one comes to human suffering (or in the case of the soldier, the closer one comes to killing), the more traumatised one is likely to be.

## THE HIDDEN COSTS OF WAR

The industrialisation of killing in the last century created the bloodiest and most destructive period of human history with around 150 million people losing their lives because of war. Prior to 1914, only ten per cent of war's victims were civilians; during the last century, seventy-five per cent were civilians (three-quarters of which were women and children); and today, despite advances in military technology that boasts smart bombs and precision targeting, it has been estimated that around ninety percent of the victims of war are civilians. Increasingly, it seems, war is about the death of innocents. Yet obscene approximates of death counts – give or take ten or twenty million – cannot come even close to giving us an understanding of the true costs to a people, a country, a world ravaged by war. Our politicians would have us measure the cost of war in outcomes, expenditure, infrastructure and body counts (ours, not theirs) and yet the hidden and pervasive costs that are never figured into the balance sheet of war – and never will be – are the ones that linger long after the guns have ceased.

Approximately 58,000 American soldiers lost their lives in

Vietnam but since that war ended around three times that number have committed suicide. On any given night in America the Department of Veteran Affairs estimates that around 300,000 homeless people – at least one in every four who seek shelter under a bridge, in an abandoned building or a cardboard box – are former soldiers. In other words, the soldier, like the journalist or photographer, may survive war physically but they, their families and the wider community may carry the burden for generations. Three million Vietnamese died in the war for their 'liberation' while their babies continue to be born without eyes, or limbs or brains because of our weapons of war. Cluster bombs and depleted uranium (DU) ordinance continue to kill long after the soldiers and their delivery systems have gone home; disease and famine often follow war, and the mutilation and rape of women and children are tools of war.

In war, children become soldiers, amputees, refugees and orphans. After the Rwandan genocide, 60,000 households were headed by children with seventy-five percent of those taking responsibility being young girls. Twelve million children worldwide are refugees because of war and over 200,000 children are soldiers. Every three hours a landmine blows up an Afghani child. Since the end of WWII, all wars waged by the most powerful military forces in the world have been against poorly armed and trained troops from the poor world. With global military spending annually exceeding one trillion dollars – $1,000,000,000,000 – every one of those dollars represents a windfall to those who deal in death and a loss to those who deal in the future.

While the hidden costs of war – its 'collateral damage' – are not what our political leaders would have us ponder after the soldiers have been sent back to the barracks, that is what those who cover war have increasingly focused on. Many of those interviewed continue to return to what once were war zones to tell us about the children in Rwanda post-genocide; American GI babies in Vietnam; civilians in Iraq struggling to reclaim their lives; the amputees of Sierra Leone and the rehabilitation of their child soldiers; the consequences of rape on women and society; the plight of refugees and the failures of the West – both political and humanitarian. How many people will find a way to live with their pain and loss from war; how many will pass it on to those they love; and how many will choose to nurture the collective memories of hate and violence through the generations? There is no mathematical equation capable of giving us a tidy cost/benefit analysis of war, and war has no political master. Each death and every act of destruction in war continues to create an ever-extending circle of pain and loss far beyond our ability to measure or even comprehend.

## A SENSE OF HISTORY

Yet if we are to truly understand the reasons for war and all its ramifications, those who document it need to place war within the wider political and historical framework. There is, as Marie Colvin states, 'a place for journalists who have seen what has been happening and know the story to do analysis'.

In an interview with the *Los Angeles Times* seasoned war photographer James Nachtwey said that although he had covered wars in the Middle East since 1981 he had always considered them to be separate wars. Then on September 11, as he photographed the destruction of the twin towers in his own city, he said, 'this idea crystallised that I had been working on the same story all this time'. As Robert Fisk points out, wars and violence have never manifested within an historical or political vacuum. There is a clear line of cause and consequence leading directly from the First World War, through the Second World War, the wars he and Nachtwey covered in the Middle East, 9/11, Afghanistan and Iraq to re-emerge . . . where?

It was no accident that the suicide bombers of 9/11 targeted the World Trade Center (economic power), the Pentagon (military power), and the White House (political power). They were targeting the power of the behemoth they believed had been destroying their societies for a good part of the last century. After twenty years of war and with ninety per cent of Afghani children believing they will die in violence, is it any wonder that the Taliban emerged from within such a traumatised society? And is it surprising that the Palestinian people, who have no military means of defence and who have been attacked and humiliated for decades in their own homes by one of the most powerful military machines in the world, are today taking the war to the streets of Israel? And what will eventually emerge from an Iraqi society traumatised and brutalised by what was for so long the West's dictator, the West's sanctions and the wars the dictator and the West dragged them into? Why are we naïvely professing shock as they turn upon us, today's self-congratulatory 'liberators'?

Our terrorism is good and their terrorism is bad. These 'ours' and 'theirs' are fluid and interchangeable depending on how far back in history we wish to go and on what side of the riverbank we are standing. Saddam's terrorism was good when he was 'our' strongman killing the Iranians and gassing the Kurds in Halabja. The Mujaheddin's terrorism was good when they were 'our' freedom fighters battling the Soviet Union. Saudi Arabia (where most of the 9/11 suicide bombers came from) and the military dictatorship in Pakistan (whose scientists have sold nuclear technology to the so-called 'rogue states') remain our good friends today, as once were Noriega,

Suharto, Somoza, Pinochet and a plethora of other dictators. Too often our political leaders' short-sighted machinations have given rise to that which eventually becomes our nemesis. There comes a time, argues Monica Attard, when 'as a journalist... you should actually show your colours, take a stand and say, "This is wrong, this is not right."' Not all within the profession agree.

Photographers and journalists remain the first to bear witness to the human tragedies of war, disease and famine. In their imperfect human way, and within their imperfect craft, they hold a mirror to humanity that reflects forms of behaviour and indifference that can be both challenging and discomfiting. Yet we continue to censor out the painful and the unpleasant because it makes us uncomfortable or we feel that we have too much to lose if the myths of war are shattered. As a species, we have too much to lose if these myths are not shattered.

War is not a brave and noble endeavour: it is a political tool that unleashes a fearful and damaging darkness within the souls of many. War is not an inevitable natural human phenomenon; it is a game of Russian roulette that leaves permanent scars on the psyches of the victims, the survivors, the perpetrators, their families and the witnesses alike. And war has no tidy end-sum game; no one can predict the costs of war or clearly define where one war stops and another starts. War is the ultimate atrocity and all of us its victims.

'War cannot be humanised,' said Albert Einstein, 'It can only be abolished.' If there is any possibility of ever abolishing war, or of at least ensuring that it is used as a political tool of last resort, we must know what it is that we are choosing. We cannot turn away from war; we need to confront it, to acknowledge it and to know it. The best correspondents and photojournalists disabuse us of our ignorance and our claims that, 'We didn't know; we weren't told.' The worst simply feed such claims.

Like the people in this book, each of us makes choices about where our responsibility in bearing witness begins and ends and, like them, we too must live with those choices.

# AFTERWORD

How will the coming generations look back on the last hundred years? Will it be with disgust at our brutality or will they be too busy dealing with their own horrors: a full harvest from the seeds we sow today? Obviously I don't have the answers to these questions. I often don't know what should be done and I certainly don't have an antidote to war – at least not unless humankind metamorphoses into a different species. And while I can theoretically explain atrocities, as a human being I simply do not understand them. The older I become it seems the less I know – there are fewer absolutes.

I have, however, been able to observe a dangerous malaise within our society today. We don't need war to destroy our societies; apathy and cynicism are doing the job very well. As people become increasingly concerned about international events and as the fear that today's political leaders are intent on instilling within our nations takes hold, the understandable reaction for many in the West has been to withdraw further into our private, relatively predictable and comparatively safe worlds. In the face of what appears to be a plethora of global catastrophes it has become too painful to watch when we feel utterly powerless to influence not only the course of world events but even our own governments' actions. Yet by adopting the mantra of, 'I alone cannot influence the government, end the famine, stop the war, change the world,' we do nothing and we are already defeated. Our prediction has become its own self-fulfilling prophecy and as the cycle of frustration, anguish and withdrawal begins again, so too does the violence that feeds it.

Perhaps it is the enormity of the task that we see before us, the seeking of perfection that defeats us: the perfect relationship, the perfect government, the perfect world. We are imperfect beings; there can be no perfections in human relationships so that the seeking of perfection ensures its own defeat. What is possible, however, is *better*: a better relationship, a better government, a better world.

Although it may be difficult to envisage an end to war as a form of political behaviour, there was a time when people could not foresee an end to slavery, the emancipation of women, the vote for blacks or the end of apartheid, but these things came to pass. Not because some magnanimous government or world body decreed them to be so, but because ordinary citizens said it should be so. We need not be Nelson Mandela, Aung San Suu Kyi, Martin Luther King Jnr, or Gandhi, for none of those people effected change alone; behind each stood millions of likeminded individuals with their own acts of moral courage. Our strength lies in the recognition of this – our shared humanity – rather than in the separation imposed by the constructs of state, religion and ethnicity.

Journalists and photographers like those in this book who

bear witness on our behalf; the individuals who write letters, articles, boycott products, strike, stand in demonstrations and picket lines; and those who refuse to be lied to or silenced in the face of an injustice, do so because there is something they believe in so passionately that they will not – cannot – let it go. These individuals, with their myriad small acts of outrage, are the real catalysts for social change.

The Nobel Prize-winning writer Gunter Grass wrote, 'I don't speak out because I am a writer. My profession is a writer, but I speak out because I am a citizen. I think the Weimar Republic collapsed and the Nazis took over in 1933 because there were not enough citizens. That's the lesson I have learned. Citizens cannot leave politics just to politicians.'

There are not enough citizens today. There are not enough voices at a time when our democracies need a strong defence. A fundamental of that defence is informed, robust debate to provide the necessary checks and balances on the halls of power. Through our actions and inaction – even inaction has moral and political consequences – we make statements every day about who we are, what we stand for, and what sort of world we wish to live in. Our silence, our indifference, and our apathy become the slow poisons we feed our beloved democracy daily. How ironic, and ultimately how tragic, that we send our young people to defend democracy and our way of life to the death – is that not why we go to war? – while at home we allow democracy to wither through inattention.

Historian Will Durant, who argued that in the history of humankind there have only been twenty-nine years free of war, compares history to a rural scene. In his analogy the river is often filled with blood from humankind's violence, including war, while on the riverbanks the majority of people go about their daily lives peacefully. Our general pessimism about humankind arises from the fact that historians favour the drama in the river, while essentially ignoring the story being played out on its banks. By dwelling on the darker side of human nature, wars have become the warped definers of history despite the fact that on any given day more people on Earth are living peacefully than are involved in waging war.

And so we can choose to give in to our sense of hopelessness and remain, as BBC correspondent Fergal Keane describes, authors of 'a guilty silence', or we can join those in this book to bear witness in what war correspondent Martha Gellhorn terms 'wakeful conscience'. Bearing witness not just to the darkness within humanity but, as those in this book have done, to the gentleness, kindness, and compassion that is being played out on the river banks every day.

# ACKNOWLEDGMENTS

This book would not exist without the support, encouragement and input of many individuals so that what you hold in your hands today is the sum of their giving. It has been, in every sense, a collaborative effort.

The first group of individuals who need mentioning is obviously the press. While as an industry the press has failed us and, indeed, itself more times than I care to recall, there have also been myriad examples of courage, honesty, tenacity and hard work. With the latter in mind I wish to express my gratitude to those who consented to interviews, who were generous with their information, who patiently tried to dispel my sorry ignorance, and who helped me make contact with individuals and find answers to my endless questions. In this regard I would like to thank Nabeel al-Jurani, Iain Finlay, Muzamil Jaleel, Kenneth Jarecke, Deborah Copaken Kogan, Teun Voeten and Asmaa Waguih, together with the staff at the agencies of Reuters, Associated Press, Contact, Corbis and VII.

My apologies to those I have not mentioned by name. I also wish to thank war photographer John Gaps III for permission to use 'The Unjust' in the book and Monique Rhodes for her haunting song 'Bearing Witness'.

For those who gave me sustenance and shelter in my travels to research this book I wish to thank Dr Duncan Clarke, Dr Tony Moll, Sue Price, Chris Kernes, Pennie and Andrew Elfick, Annie and David Jeffrey (who introduced me to their world which continues to repel and seduce me), and Dr Anthony Gorman (who always offers a bed).

I am more than grateful to the patience and commitment of Ankya Clarke who designed the cover of the book and to the hardworking staff at Random House Australia who worked behind the scenes to move the book forward. I also wish to recognise and thank those at Random who saw value in this work. In this regard I must first thank Jessica Dettmann who, as a new recruit, did what every sensible person should do: took her mother's advice. I thank Jo Butler, my infinitely patient and hardworking editor who saw so clearly what I could not and who graciously refined the manuscript with her endless questions and 'Post-it' notes. Finally, I am indebted to Meredith Curnow, my publisher, who enthusiastically supported this project and whose honesty, vision, tenacity and good humour were essential to its fruition.

I offer to George W. Bush, Tony Blair and John Howard, Nabeel al-Jurani's photo of the little girl in Basra (see picture section). If she was either Jenna Bush or Kathryn Blair or Melanie Howard and not some nameless person's daughter, would we still have had a war and would you still be able to claim you have no regrets? I also offer to you the words of Abraham Lincoln: Nearly all men can stand adversity, but if you want to test a man's character, give him power.

This book is for those who are dear to me and who have for

so long graciously accepted my frequent mental, emotional and physical absences without demands. I can only thank you again and continue to give to you what I hope is the best of me.

Finally, this book (although not the argument in the chapter 'Bearing Witness to War') belongs to the people whose words lie within its covers. For your generosity of spirit, for your patience and trust and for your dedication to bearing witness, I am humbled. And for all those in the industry who practise their craft with a passion and a fine eye I offer my deepest gratitude and respect.

The first note I made when considering writing this book was of the inadequacy of written language. Words can never be the emotion or the event: they can only ever be representations of those things – symbols on a page interpreted by the reader, or words uttered, for the most part, inadequately. Others within this book have also spoken of the inadequacy of their own form of communication. 'You can only make pictures of things that are there before you,' said Susan Meiselas. 'You can't always make images of loss and of all that you feel.'

Thus, having come full circle, I am struck forcefully again by the inadequacy of my chosen medium and my own greater sense of inadequacy within that. What can I possibly write about war that has not already been said and, indeed, said far more eloquently and persuasively? And what can the people in this book tell you about war that has not already been told? Yet I comfort myself with the fact that we each do our own small acts of witnessing and that must be enough. In the end I offer to all of us – the victims of war – the words of one far wiser and more courageous than most, Dr Martin Luther King Jnr:

> Our lives begin to end the day we become silent about things that matter.

## Picture Credits

**Cover**
© Juda Ngwenya / Reuters / Picture Media

**Picture section**
Page 1: © Eddie Adams / AAP
Page 2: © Kevin Carter / Corbis / Australian Picture Library
Page 3: (top) © Penny Tweedie / Penny Tweedie Photography
    (bottom) © Susan Meiselas / Magnum Photos
Page 4: (top) © Greg Marinovich / AAP
    (bottom) © Ron Haviv / VII
Page 5: (top and bottom) © Ron Haviv / VII
Page 6: (top) © Christopher Morris / VII
    (bottom) © James Nachtwey / VII
Page 7: (top) © Glenn Middleton
    (bottom) © Ahmed Jadallah / Reuters
Page 8: © Nabeel al-Jurani / AAP

## Cover photo

The cover photo was taken by Juda Ngwenya in Thokoza township, South Africa, during a gun battle between Inkatha supporters and the National Peacekeeping Force on 18 April 1994, eleven days before South Africa's first democratic election.

In the foreground is wounded photographer Greg Marinovich being assisted by photographer James Nachtwey. In the background (right) Joao Silva takes a photo of photographer Gary Bernard and a peacekeeping officer as they carry fatally wounded Ken Oosterbroek, chief photographer for Johannesburg newspaper *The Star*. Juda Ngwenya, who is now chief photographer with Reuters in South Africa, was also shot at the time. It is understood that these photographers were all shot by UN peacekeepers.

At the time this event occurred, photographer Kevin Carter (who made the image of the little starving girl in Sudan being stalked by a vulture) had just finished a radio interview discussing his Pulitzer Prize and was in his car travelling to join his friends working in Thokoza when he heard on the radio of the death of his best friend, Oosterbroek. All the photographers in this image were friends, with Carter, Marinovich, Silva and Oosterbroek known in South Africa as 'the bang-bang club' because of their work in the townships.

Three months after this photo was taken, Kevin Carter committed suicide. Part of his suicide note read: 'The pain of life overrides the joy to the point that joy does not exist.' Gary Bernard also committed suicide four years later.